An Ethic of Queer Sex: Principles and Improvisations

An Ethic of Queer Sex:
Principles and Improvisations

Theodore W. Jennings

Exploration Press
Chicago, Illinois

Exploration Press
Chicago Theological Seminary
1407 E. 60th Street
Chicago, Illinois 60637

ISBN: 978-0913552-72-8

Library of Congress Control Number: 2013946859

Contents

Contents

"Desire is the origin of friendship."

- Socrates

To my Friend,
John Noble

Preface

This book has its origin in the development of what was initially a "gay studies" program or emphasis at Chicago Theological Seminary (CTS) that began in 1991. CTS was the first mainline seminary anywhere that consciously committed itself to a continuing emphasis on the academic study of same-sex sexuality and the issues that an affirmation of that sexuality entails. While such an emphasis was related to the presence of "out" lesbian and gay students at CTS, it was also based in the recognition that issues related to same-sex relationships and practices were central to some of the most difficult challenges facing the churches. Since the late 1960s denominations have been increasingly divided by opposing positions regarding what was then called "homosexuality." Forty years later, these same issues continue to threaten to divide many denominations. It was and is therefore crucial that these issues be addressed in graduate theological education so as to prepare leaders for effective ministry in church and society.

Of course these issues are not only issues for the church, they are also issues that are the subject of intense debate within our society. In the national elections of 1992 through 2004 the Republican party mobilized its base through scare talk of the "gay agenda," and a fierce opposition to what was called gay marriage in the name of "family values." While the usefulness of this tactic has diminished somewhat as citizens become more open to lesbian and gay rights, it is still an important factor in many local and regional political mobilizations. This mobilization of an evangelical (and Catholic) religious base, however, served a much different agenda: the promotion of war policies that asserted "America's" right and responsibility to unquestioned rule of the planet, the promotion of rapacious forms of neo-liberal capitalism that gave free rein to institutionalized greed on a planetary scale, the dismantling of all government checks on international financial institutions in the name of the free market, the wholesale selling off of public goods and responsibilities to the private sector (water and prisons, paramilitary subcontractors, even Social Security) and of course a radical redistribution of wealth from the majority of the population to a tiny fraction of the unimaginably wealthy.

The point is that the politicizing of sex, especially focused on abortion and homosexuality, served (and still serves) the interest of a politics of unbridled avarice, arrogance and global violence. It was especially useful in mobilizing the poor and working class to support their own domination. This wider context makes the work we do with respect to developing a different perspective on sexuality so crucial for a theological education that prepares persons to be agents of transformation of church and society toward greater justice and mercy.

In the mid-1990s, when CTS developed its current statement of commitments the struggle against homophobia was identified, along with struggles against sexism, racism, classism, anti-Judaism, and other forms of oppression as core values of this institution's vision of being an international force for justice and mercy. It is important that these commitments not be separated from one another but rather reinforce one another.

To return to the evolution of our emphasis on combating homophobia. As I indicated, we began with the development of a programmatic emphasis open to all students at CTS and the wider group of seminaries in the Chicago area. At first this meant simply that I devoted at least one seminar a year to different ways of approaching these issues: Homosexuality and the Church, Homosexuality and Hermeneutics, Homosexuality: Theory and Ethics. In the course of time, as new faculty came to CTS, others took up this work as well, and we further developed these perspectives in the context of additional seminars.

One of the new seminars that I developed in 2001 was a seminar on "Frontier Questions in Gay Sexual Ethics." This seminar focused principally on gay male issues as addressed in the literature to that point. The seminar went well but because of other work, including work on books related to the Bible and same-sex love, I did not offer it again in the next few years.

However, when we were approached by Arcus Foundation with the idea of developing resources on Queer sexual ethics that would "widen the conversation" about sexual ethics, the Steering Committee of the LGBTQ Center (which now guided our efforts in teaching and research to combat homophobia) agreed to pursue a project that would include an expansion and update of the work already begun in the former seminar.

In the grant proposal written by Scott Haldeman we agreed to examine the materials already available from denominational bodies and groups within such denominations in order to prepare the ground for considering issues that were not addressed or were not addressed affirmatively in those documents.

In the Fall 2009, student research assistants worked with me to develop new bibliographies for the materials to be revised and tried out in the new seminar on Queer Sexual Ethics. New documents were written and some older topics scrapped (pornography, for example). Documents that had been prepared for the previous seminar were revised to take into account the new situation.

The result was a set of documents that originated as lecture notes for a seminar on gay ethics, then as resources to be discussed by the seminar on "New Horizons in Queer Sexual Ethics." The enthusiasm of the many students in that seminar provided a decisive impetus toward going forward with this project and the notes of class discussion (provided by Alison Baker) were invaluable in thinking through subsequent revisions.

Most of these documents were then discussed by the Advisory Board of the Center at meetings in April and August of 2010. As a result of these discussions and based on a number of invaluable suggestions made in those meetings, these documents have been revised to form the current body of material. These revisions have not attempted to leave the pedagogical context behind, but to broaden it so as to make available to a wider public the materials that students as well as advisors have found to be useful.

The material in this project is divided into four main parts, and each of these divided into chapters, which in turn are divided into briefer segments to make the material user-friendly for those who wish to use the material as the basis for group discussion or for personal reflection. Several chapters also include brief first person (but anonymous) narratives provided by persons who have explored one or more of the horizons that are under discussion, since ethical reflection sometimes proceeds more constructively when real people's lived experience is included in the material to be discussed.

While for purposes of publication the material is ordered in a certain sequence, which is explained shortly, an attempt has been made to make the chapters relatively independent of one another so that persons may select certain topics while postponing others.

The first set of chapters provides a set of orientations to the work as a whole. The sequence argues, in turn, for the necessity of discussing sexual styles often repressed from public discourse, the helpfulness of incorporating the work of so-called secular theorists in developing a general ethic perspective on sex, and the need to rethink one's approach to specifically Christian sources and perspectives that inform discussion of sexual ethics.

The second set of chapters explores issues related to debates about marriage and includes an argument for same-sex marriage as a way of positively transforming heterosexual marriage, a discussion of the limits and unintended consequences of a focus upon marriage rights, and an exploration of patterns of relationship like open marriage and polyamory that reshape the marriage paradigm toward greater flexibility and inclusiveness.

The third set of chapters explores issues related to prostitution. This discussion merits special attention because of the ways in which it brings together many of the issues that are discussed elsewhere in this study, the amount of research and reflection that has been developed around these issues, and the opportunity for exploring biblical materials that are more abundant for this expression of sexuality than for many of the other issues discussed in this book. This will also include the much controverted issues related to what is called sex tourism and sex trafficking.

The final set of chapters explores horizons that are often simply ignored or even directly marginalized in religious and secular discussions of sexual ethics. These include discussions of sexual styles that value multiple partners without long-term commitment (promiscuity), the ways in which persons may seek relatively anonymous sexual encounters (public sex), the exploration of fantasy through BDSM, and issues related to cross-generational sexual relations (pederasty).

The concluding excursus brings together these reflections on aspects of queer sexuality in order to show concretely how ethical reflection happens as we seek to improvise forms of sexual life that aim at embodying justice and generosity.

Acknowledgments

This work could not have been undertaken without the support of the Arcus Foundation for the work of the The LGBTQ Religious Studies Center at Chicago Theological Seminary. However, this support by no means entails the endorsement of that foundation of the positions propounded in this study. In fact, I rather suspect that the Foundation will be less than fully comfortable both with the choice of issues that are explored here and the approach taken in relation to several of them. However, that does not diminish the reality that resources from the Foundation supported research by students and gatherings of outside advisors that enriched the conversation and would not otherwise have been possible. I, along with the Center and CTS more generally, acknowledge the support of the Arcus Foundation with gratitude.

The Arcus grant supported the work of many students who labored long and hard to support the development of the seminar and the documents that serve as the basis of the text below. The supervision of student research was undertaken by Kunitoshi Sakai. He also provided crucial resources for the work of the seminar, including the recruitment of sex workers to speak of their lives and work with the students. The extensive notes on all class sessions and meetings of the advisory board were provided by Allison Baker. Many other students were engaged in the production of extensive annotated bibliographies that served as the basis of research; others drafted executive summaries and discussion questions for the chapters.

The project has benefitted from the volunteer advisory board, which included academics from other institutions, church and secular grassroots organizational activists, and church leaders. I benefitted especially from my discussions with Julianne Buenting, who agreed to work with me on the considerable revision of the chapter on BDSM (or, bondage/domination, sadism/masochism).

Finally I must express my gratitude to the faculty and staff at Chicago Theological Seminary who serve on the Steering Committee of the LGBTQ Religious Studies Center, especially to Benjamin Reynolds, who is the operational director, and to Scott Haldeman and Ken Stone, who have been especially active in the support of this project.

None of those named here should be supposed to endorse the views expressed in these pages. Their contributions have been invaluable and they have contributed significantly to the thinking that goes into these reflections, making it more adequate than it would otherwise have been. The limitations of this work are due to my own inability or unwillingness to embrace all the suggestions and cautions that they have offered.

Part One

New Horizons in Queer Sexual Ethics

Chapter One

Presuppositions

For more than half a century, there has been a good deal of discussion about the acceptance of same-sex love as an appropriate expression of sexuality, both in public political discourse and within a number of religious traditions. While the struggle for the recognition of same-sex love has by no means concluded, either in political or religious discourse, considerable progress has been made. Most democratic societies no longer criminalize sexual acts associated with same-sex love. In many democratic societies, most recently in the U.S., hate crimes against gay and lesbian people are punishable by law. Many societies now accept unions between persons of the same sex as having equal standing before the law as heterosexual partnerships, although here as in other areas, like acceptance of gay and lesbian persons in the military, the U.S. still lags behind other democratic societies. Among the mainline Protestant churches there has been some positive momentum toward full acceptance of both ordination of gay and lesbian clergy and the celebration of same-sex unions.

While much work still needs to be done in relation to political and ecclesial acceptance, the basic theological, biblical, and ethical work that supports full inclusion of gay and lesbian people has been largely accomplished. However, there is a danger that the movement toward full inclusion may come at the price of a continued marginalization of sexual minorities and sexual practices that have an important place within the lives and the experience of queer people. The purpose of the essays that are developed here is to extend the conversation toward a more inclusive appreciation of marginalized sexual practices and groups that have a significant place within (but also outside) the LGBTQ community. The hope is that by pursuing these issues, a contribution will be made to a more just and holistic sexual ethic that overcomes the erotophobia that is at the base of the homophobia that often governs discussions of sexuality in religion and in politics.

In this introductory chapter it will be helpful to flesh out a few of the basic assumptions and perspectives that govern the work as a whole and to indicate the context within which this discussion has emerged.

On Not Defending Same-Sex Practices

The debates in church and society have often been about the appropriateness of same-sex sexual expression. This issue has been much discussed in the literature and there is a growing consensus that same-sex love is consistent with basic ethical values. Many years ago homosexuality was removed from the list of psychological disorders that is the basic guide for psychologists, psychiatrists, and clinical social workers. More recently the legal climate has significantly changed with the Supreme Court's *Lawrence v. Texas* decision whereby U.S. law finally began to catch up with that of other democracies in decriminalizing "sodomy."[1] The religious discussion has also made significant advances since my essay "Homosexuality and Christian Faith" was published in 1977.[2] On other fronts, the U.S. military policy put in place in 1993 popularly known as "don't ask, don't tell" (DADT) was repealed by congressional action and executive order in 2011, allowing LGBTQ persons to serve openly. And the movement towards marriage equality, both globally and in the United States, is gaining momentum even as many states have added constitutional provisions declaring marriage as limited to "one man and one woman." For the purposes of this text, I both acknowledge and bracket these debates, proceeding instead not to justify same-sex love but to explore an ethic of sex that presumes the legitimacy of same-sex practices and moves on from there.

I propose that if any arrangement of sexual relations is in need of justification today on an ethical basis it is not "homosexuality" but "heterosexuality" that requires such a justification.

The standard justifications for heterosexual relations are that humanity is dependent upon them for a) the reproduction of the species, b) the rearing of children, c) the "containment" of an unruly sexuality, and d) the transmission of social values. These justifications of cross-sex relations will not withstand scrutiny.

It is unclear, for example, that the production of progeny is exactly an urgent question with the human population approaching 8 billion. If anything, reproductive sexuality is in need of careful delimitation: hence the emphasis on population control and family planning.

---

1. *Lawrence v. Texas*, 539 U.S. 558 (2003).

2. This essay was originally published as "Homosexuality and Christian Faith: A Theological Reflection" in *The Christian Century* (February 16, 1977), 137; it has also appeared in *Homosexuality and the Christian Faith: A Symposium*, ed. Harold L. Twiss (Valley Forge: Judson Press, 1978) and is available online at http://www.religion-online.org/.

The supposition that the modern family structure of institutionalized heterosexuality is appropriate for raising children is one that can hardly be justified, given the extraordinary levels of child sexual abuse that occur within the home. With an incidence of at least 6 percent for male children and at least 19 percent for female children, it appears endemic, rather than incidental.[3]

The notion that heterosexual relations provide a container for sexuality supposes the sexuality requires such a container, and the cross-sex relations provide one. The latter supposition (that institutionalization of heterosexuality is an effective container of sexuality) represents the triumph of hope over experience. It also conduces to marital rape. That is, the policing of the boundaries between legitimate (institutionalized) and non-legitimate (adultery, promiscuity) has served to render invisible the coercive character of sexual relations within marriage. Thus only in the last couple of decades has it become plausible to speak of marital rape.

But this whole apparatus relies upon the notion that the proper way to deal with a strong sexual impulse is to lock it up, rather than provide it with any of a number of non-abusive outlets. This is one of the issues that will be broached in our discussion of promiscuity and prostitution.

Above all, we must ask which social values are reproduced through so-called traditional marriage and family values. The institutionalization of cross-sex relations has been the incubator of patriarchy and of extreme violence against women. Heterosexual marriage appears to be the principal carrier of the domination of women and children. This was already recognized with considerable acuity by John Stuart Mill in his 1869 essay "On the Subjection of Women."[4]

It is no accident that the Jesus tradition as transmitted through the Gospels regards marriage and family with deep suspicion.[5] One of the most remarkable things about people who think that they know what the Bible says is how shocked they are to discover that Jesus is actually anti-family (and that most of the New Testament, including Paul, is no better).

In any case, same-sex sexuality is at least unencumbered by the structural involvement in patriarchy and is not directly implicated in the violence against

---

3. Christine Courtois, *Healing the Incest Wound: Adult Survivors in Therapy* (New York: W.W. Norton & Co., 1996); for higher estimates, see Dan B. Alleuder, *The Wounded Heart: Hope for Victims of Childhood Sexual Abuse*, new ed. (Colorado Springs: NavPress, 2008).

4. John Stuart Mill, *On the Subjection of Women* (London: Hesperus, 2008).

5. See Theodore Jennings, *The Man Jesus Loved: Homoerotic Narratives from the New Testament* (Cleveland: Pilgrim Press, 2003), 171-232.

women and children so characteristic of heterosexuality. Of course, it does not exist in complete isolation from systems of patriarchy and what Pierre Bourdieu rightly describes as masculine domination.[6] Thus much gay male discourse exhibits unmistakable traits of misogyny.

The ancient Western world was quite familiar with debates on the relative merits of same-sex vs. cross-sex relationships. These debates focused on men and their advantages and often entailed a certain degree of misogyny. While the issues I have pointed to have some points of contact with some of those earlier debates, which I discuss at length in *Plato or Paul?*,[7] I believe my arguments are more closely related to feminist concerns as well as to the Jesus tradition. For the question is not, as it was in antiquity, whether young males or females are better sexual partners for males but rather whether we can learn something important about human sexuality generally by starting from forms of sexuality somewhat less determined by structures of the male ownership of women.

Beyond Assimilation by Amputation

Even when the church is not debating about same-sex sexual expression as such, the theological and ethical debates about "homosexuality" are dominated by questions of marriage and holy unions between persons of the same gender. This issue is one that is high on the public agenda as well, along with debates about gays in the military or, in the church, the ordination of "practicing homosexuals." These are all interesting issues. But by turning to what I have called boundary or frontier issues in gay ethics, I intend to bring into question the normalizing and assimilationist rhetorics of the gay rights movement, both in society at large and in the church. Generally church-related discussions that favor the inclusion of same-sex oriented persons into the community somehow manage to almost entirely exclude questions of sexual behavior.

The questions to which we will attend include the following: promiscuity, prostitution, pederasty, pornography, public (anonymous) sex, BDSM, etc. The basic approach to these issues will be to ask: Why should this be a problem?

These are the very practices that normalizing strategies wish to repress from consciousness and from discourse. This is true in the general culture with the ascendancy of gay-rights rhetoric that maintains that LGBTQ people are just like everyone else, indeed are into marriage, conspicuous consumption, patriotic

---

6. Pierre Bourdieu, *Masculine Domination* (Stanford: Stanford University Press, 2001).

7. Theodore Jennings, *Plato or Paul?: The Origins of Western Homophobia* (Cleveland: Pilgrim Press, 2009).

military service, etc. While this may be the case for some LGBTQ people, it is nonetheless the case that assimilation at the price of disowning significant sectors of LGBTQ experience entails a strategy of assimilation by amputation.

This is historically the way in which "liberation movements" become enforcers of the same sort of oppressive status quos they have tried to escape. As a liberation theologian, I believe it is profoundly unethical (and ultimately counter-productive) to purchase "my" liberation at the cost of another's oppression, or my acceptance at the cost of another's marginalization. It is the way in which previously marginalized groups become the enforcers of other people's marginalization. Think of the Irish or Italians in Boston or Chicago fighting a long and difficult battle for respect, only to become enforcers of discrimination against African Americans. Or of African American civil rights movements winning victories in relation to racial discrimination and segregation but reinforcing sexist and homophobic dynamics. Or of the labor movement's historic struggle in the 1920s and '30s leading to racism and red-baiting in the '50s and '60s.

It is this history that raises the possibility of a pyrrhic victory for the LGBTQ rights movement. Indeed, there is good reason to suppose that the largest and most visible groups that lead the movement are deeply involved in the marginalization and even oppression of more radical sexual minorities as a consequence of an assimilationist strategy (see the exclusion of the North American Man-Boy Love Association, for example, from many public demonstrations in favor of gay rights). The strategy of assimilation by amputation may be rationalized in the world of compromise that is legislative politics. It should not be the way of those who follow the Crucified One. However, many progressive church organizations also follow this strategy of bringing into the fold those who can fit in the box called "respectability" while still excluding those who do not, cannot, or will not.

I contend that to avoid assimilation by amputation we must focus on to "boundary" or "frontier" questions. This is because many of the practices to which we will have reference are excluded from consideration by a good deal of the rhetoric of the LGBTQ rights movement. Thus prostitutes, pederasts, and those who engage in anonymous or adventurous sex are often simply ignored in favor of an emphasis on the appearance of monogamous, and therefore respectable, sexual practices. This, in spite of the fact that when there is an attempt to reconstitute a "gay history," there is considerable reliance on, for example, the pederastic traditions of Greece or the existence of "molly houses" in early modern London.

Much contemporary gay rights rhetoric, aided and abetted by the concerns that arise from the HIV/AIDS epidemic, has contributed to the focus upon same-generational, same-sex romantic and monogamous relationships. Given the veil of privacy that is customarily drawn over marital sex, this results in something like a de-sexualization of same-sex sexual practices. It has recently been primarily my contention that this de-sexualizing serves to marginalize other sexualities.

Because contemporary political activism of LGBTQ groups in the U.S. is directed to "marriage equality" and to the repeal of DADT in the military there is a huge temptation to simply refuse to acknowledge sexual patterns and practices that do not imitate hetero-normative and monogamous patterns.

Queering Sexual Ethics

Many may wonder why the perspective here is designated "queer" rather than homosexual or gay. Accordingly, a few over-brief remarks about how the terminology has changed and what difference this change makes in the consideration of sexuality and sexual ethics may be helpful.

As noted above, the early seminars on same-sex sexuality and theology at Chicago Theological Seminary used the word "homosexuality" in the titles consistently. When the seminar that was to serve as the impetus for the current study was first offered in 2000, it was called "Frontier Questions in Gay Sexual Ethics." By that time those of us teaching in this area had already moved from thinking of the work as a program in gay studies to a program in gay and lesbian studies. This soon was overtaken by thinking of what we were doing as Queer Studies and, in 2005, we founded an LGBTQ Center, with an emphasis on "queer." What lies behind these changes?

Homosexuality, as a term, was invented in the late nineteenth century. It replaced earlier terms like "sodomy" that stigmatized and criminalized same-sex relations. Homosexuality was originally a term of medical and psychological origin that classed persons of same-sex orientation as "inverts" (rather than "perverts") who were congenitally disposed to attraction to the same sex, rather than the opposite sex, for sexual pleasure and for relationships inclusive of sexual satisfaction. (It was also regularly associated with the notion of males who were psychologically female, and of women who were psychologically male).[8]

When, nearly a hundred years later, the overt struggle for the decriminalization and social acceptance of same-sex love was coming into the open, this term was favored in order to make the case that persons had a irreversible orientation toward same-sex relationships that should make them a class of

---

8. John P. Cecco and Michael G. Shively, *Bisexual and Homosexual Identities: Critical Theoretical Issues* (New York: Routledge, 1984), 47.

persons with civil rights, and, therefore, analogous to movements pressing for women's rights and (in the U.S.) civil rights for persons of color.

In the meantime, another nomenclature was taking hold in the newly emergent cultures or subcultures in the cites where persons attracted to the same sex began to live and develop institutions and styles. That term was "gay." In part, this name change referred to a particular culture then emerging and to a certain militancy. The term "gay" also connoted a growing recognition of the sheer diversity of persons who identified with that culture. For example the notion of homosexuality identified with effeminacy was replaced by a variety of styles that included "macho" males and "fem" females within that culture.

For a time, "gay" served as a generic term that included, as a small and often unacknowledged minority, women who identified as being attracted to members of the same sex.

Eventually it became clear that the word "gay" was used primarily to talk about men, and that women were marginalized or silenced within that culture. Indeed, gay male culture in the early 1960s was often misogynistic, and women were often harassed in, or excluded from, gay male institutions like bars. Gay male misogyny was quite blatant (and has not yet disappeared). Meanwhile, the women involved also became heavily involved in the struggles of feminism, and in that context found their own voices. Progressive movements in church and society increasingly spoke not of "gay" but of "lesbian and gay." In part, this led to an acknowledgment that lesbians were not simply female versions of gay men. They had, for example, quite different sexual histories and practices, as well as distinctive forms of relationality and other notable differences. The fluidity of female sexual orientation (many were wives and mothers for example) undermined the self-evidence of the irreversible, exclusive sexual orientation claimed by dominant voices within the gay movement. The supposed pattern of favoring long-term, rather stable relationships contrasted with patterns of recreational and anonymous sexuality that characterized some of the most visible sectors of gay male subculture. Yet, in the aftermath of the AIDS epidemic when gay males often found that the only persons who would care for them or advocate for them were lesbians, the most virulent forms of misogyny (often directed against lesbians) no longer seemed appropriate, and alliances were formed.[9]

The inclusion of lesbian perspectives means far more than a simple expansion in the terms "homosexual" or "gay" to include persons who are just like gay men, but of a different sex: Lesbian experience and engagement is

---

9. John D'Emilio, *Sexual Politics, Sexual Communities: The Making of a Homosexual Minority in the U.S. 1940-1970* (Chicago: University of Chicago Press, 1983).

significantly different from that of gay men. In the first place, women who identify as lesbians are still women who suffer most directly at the hands of a still-virulent patriarchy. As a consequence, lesbians are generally engaged in the struggle against patriarchy, a struggle that gay men may simply be oblivious to. Lesbian activism is by necessity often first and foremost a struggle against misogyny and patriarchy, and then secondarily a struggle against homophobia. While these struggles are certainly related, it is the experience of lesbians that brings this relationship into open expression.

Alliances between gays and lesbians then serve to bring into question a rather one-sided emphasis on sexual orientation or preference as the site of struggle, and thus to open up wider questions of gender justice, and indeed of justice generally. This also means that attempts to construct a single narrative of "gay" or "homosexual" experience is greatly complicated by the inclusion of additional and quite different voices. Sometimes this has taken the form of raising important questions about male and gay male privileging of penetrative sex as the only way of thinking about sexual expression. Sometimes this has taken the form of introducing stories of the fluidity of sexual attraction that had otherwise been drowned out in the dominant gay male discourse. It is in this connection, for example, that the question of bisexuality emerges.

The introduction of bisexuality into the mix was the beginning of the recognition that multiple sexualities might also be a part of the movement. This was much contested, since the very idea of bisexuality cast into doubt the rhetoric of irreversible and exclusive sexual orientation. In other words, for bisexuals, same-sex attraction might be a choice rather than a fate. Further, many who identified as gay or lesbian were suspicious of bisexuals as those who were really gay but not brave enough to say so or those who were passing through bisexuality on the way to finally "coming out" or those who liked to toy with gay and lesbian hearts but then retreat back in to heterosexual privilege. No wonder there was great controversy about including bisexuals in the movement. The ambivalence is clear in the way terms began to shift from gay and lesbian to les-bi-gay to GLB or LGB.

All this begs the question: Is bisexuality a sexual identity alongside heterosexuality and homosexuality? To be sure, there are some who seek to create such an identity, together with the formation of magazines, chat rooms, and other forums in which to nurture it. This is perhaps a result of the ways in which bisexuality can be marginalized in both straight and gay circles. (Lesbians tend to be far more open to bisexuality than gay males.) The sense of not belonging in either gay or straight culture may produce the sense of the need to establish an identity alongside, and in tension with, these other more-recognized sexual orientation identities.

However, there is another way to go. In his book *A History of Bisexuality*, Steven Angelides notes that bisexuality was actually much discussed in the 1970s[10] before basically disappearing from view. In that earlier discussion, there were essentially two approaches: one was to regard bisexuality as the basic default of human experience, which subsequently divided into heterosexuality and homosexuality. This was the view of Freud, who had noted that bisexuality belongs to an earlier stage of human development. Others looked at historical and anthropological evidence to suggest that what might be termed bisexuality appears in historically earlier and in contemporary "primitive" societies. Angelides notes that in these views, bisexuality has its primary location in the past. Of course much of the apologetics for same-sex love made use of these antecedents to argue for its acceptance. But contemporary bisexuality was viewed with considerable suspicion, because bisexuals could be viewed as either those who did not share the same experiences of exclusion as gay and lesbian people (that is, they could enjoy heterosexual privilege) or as those who had not yet bitten the bullet to become fully "homosexual" or "gay."

Accordingly, there was a tendency to come to regard authentic bisexuality as a vision of the future—after the dismantling of homophobia, then people could actualize all their sexual potentialities. As Angelides notes, what all this meant is that bisexuality comes to be that which has no present tense.

There is another point made by Angelides (along with Marjorie Garber in her related work): Bisexuality may be understood as that which is neither heterosexuality nor homosexuality without actually being a third. For it also both homosexuality and heterosexuality. It is the third then not as a stable position but as the "excluded middle," as that which destabilizes the presumed identities labeled hetero- and homo-. As such, bisexuality names a fluid and even mercurial or protean sexuality; one that is unpredictable with respect to object choice—where it is sometimes supposed there are only two possibilities: male or female.

So what Garber and Angelides are arguing, then, is that if one's sexual life is constituted by an openness to desire for sexual encounter with male or female, then one is certainly not, in the current way of understanding things, "homosexual." For we suppose that homosexual means not sexually attracted, to or sexually involved with, members of the "opposite sex." But one is also not heterosexual, for we suppose that being heterosexual means not being sexually involved with (or attracted to?) members of the same sex. Yet if being

---

10. Steven Angelides, *A History of Bisexuality* (Chicago: University of Chicago Press, 2001). A similar point is also made by Marjorie Garber in *Bisexuality and the Eroticism of Everyday Life* (New York: Routledge, 2000).

homosexual means being sexually attracted to members of the same sex, and a bisexual person is, then that person is homosexual, except that she or he is also attracted to (and involved with) members of the opposite sex and so heterosexual.

As I have previously suggested, a certain fluidity in sexual object choice may be more often encountered in the autobiographical accounts of lesbians than of those who identify themselves as gay males. Again there may be an actual difference in experience here, or else a difference in the hegemonic discourses that produce fluidity in one case and "identity" in the other.

The destabilization of the binary of straight or gay had already begun with the articulation of the voices of lesbians and, as we have seen, is further advanced by the inclusion of bisexuality. The picture is further complicated and enriched by the addition of "transgender." This is complicating and enriching in at least two ways. Considering those who are transgender (the "T" in LGBTQ) draws attention in a different way to the underlying supposition of much discourse around sexual ethics that there are really only two stable sexes and gender identities. Transgendering points to the instability of the distinction between male and female in a variety of interesting and helpful ways. Sex is apparently not a simple biological given; a not-insignificant number of infants receive a sort of sex assignment via surgical intervention that seeks to eliminate possible confusion present in the biological endowment of the infant. The existence of this practice testifies both to the indeterminacy of sex/gender in many cases, as well as to the steps that are taken to reduce this indeterminacy as much as possible, often without even notifying the parents of the child (the growing child is almost never informed that this has transpired). There is increasing awareness of the existence of persons (by no means rare) who are positioned along something more like a spectrum of female to male.

"Transgender" is also something of a catchall term, since it also includes persons who may be attracted to adopting the apparel of another "sex" (transvestism) or the mannerisms associated with "the opposite sex." Thus transvestite performers may be included here, as well as those who adopt these practices beyond the public gaze. In the Philippines, it is generally the case that to be considered "gay" this level of transgendering is presupposed. And this corresponds to certain institutions such as the "molly houses" of eighteenth- and nineteenth-century England.

Transgendering may also include something far more than a recreational or even professional adoption of the clothes and manners associated with "the opposite sex." It may also include chemical and surgical interventions of a far more permanent kind. Some who were raised as males for example may elect to undergo procedures that provide them with breasts and to undergo hormone therapy to adopt many of the secondary physical features of women (relative hairlessness and so on). In many cases (transgender prostitutes in the U.S. or Latin America) this is the extent of the transformation undertaken. But for others it is important to also undertake a transformation of the genitalia as well. It is here that we speak of persons who are transsexual. Typically, in this case, people speak of finding their true sex/gender or of bringing their bodies into alignment with their true sexual identity. (I leave aside here the question of whether this entails an acceptance of a gender binarism that transgendering otherwise often brings into question.)

The inclusion of transgender (or trans) people in our reflections not only brings into question our assumptions about gender, but also about sexual orientation as an identity. What does heterosexuality mean in the case of a female-to-male (FtM) transsexual who has a female partner? Or a male-to-female (MtF) transsexual who has a male partner? What does homosexuality mean with a FtM transsexual who has a male partner? Or a MtF transsexual who has a female partner? This may be further complicated by including some of the other forms of transgendering that I have mentioned.

But there is another complication or enrichment that is also at work here. Whether one is called gay, lesbian, or bisexual is in significant degree determined by sexual object choice, preference, or orientation. But this is not so in any direct way with persons who identify themselves as transgender. Instead what is at stake is the transversing of gender and sex differentiation. As a consequence of the increasing visibility of trans-folk, movements for lesbian and gay rights have expanded their mission and now increasingly speak more generally of the rights of sexual minorities or of those with marginalized sexualities. Such inclusion has been marked by the addition of the "T" to LGBTQ.

The "Q" in LGBTQ stands for "Queer," but the word means more than a summary of the LGBT that precedes it. While the term queer is often intended to include the other terms with which it is associated, it is also intended to respond to a wider and more diverse set of identities, practices, and experiences than those former terms could embrace.

One of the areas where this has been quite crucial is in cross-cultural studies of sexual diversity. The modern West is the provenance for terms and categories like heterosexual/homosexual, or lesbian and gay. But persons in other cultures whose sexual practices and experiences bear a certain resemblance, for example, to what is sometimes meant by "gay" by no means recognize themselves in the standard Western narrative or depiction of what this means. The differences of culture are too great. This is how some self-appointed spokespersons in certain cultural contexts (such as the Middle east or sub-Saharan African, to name just two often-cited examples) can claim: "There is no homosexuality here!" On one level, the claim is ridiculous—if it is used to mean that there is no indigenous practice of same-sex love or sexual encounter. On another, it is plausible because the forms of life associated with Western gay male or lesbian culture in the U.S. are alien to those societies, including those who engage in practices that a western observer might classify as homosexual or gay.

Further, the adoption of the term "queer" also makes possible the inclusion of other sexual minorities or practices that are too easily overlooked if we use only the older terminologies. For example, in the subjects that we will be considering in the next several chapters, several of the sexualities might not be evident if we remain within the bounds of those older categories. We will be discussing "open marriage" and polyamory, for example. Both are ways of breaking out of the suppositions of heterosexual monogamy that governs much of our thinking about sexual ethics. While bisexuality may be an important way into this discussion, it is one that embraces or may embrace persons who think of themselves as "heterosexual" or as lesbian or gay as well. In a different way, while the gay male culture may have a certain stake in celebrating non-marital sexuality (sometimes called promiscuity), those who adopt this form of sexuality as primary may include more than gay males. Yet all such persons are certainly outside the mainstream of standard accounts of sexual "normalcy." BDSM is a topic we will discuss because of its importance for sectors of lesbian and gay community, but often times putatively straight practitioners are similarly marginalized as well.

In sum, the term "queer" does have a certain utility in expanding the horizons of inquiry with respect to marginalized sexualities. It also has the danger of becoming a sort of innocuous catchall that can efface the specificity of the subsumed sexualities. Thus the protest on the part of some that "I am not queer, I am gay" has a certain cogency as a protest against the possible loss of the particularities of a certain history of oppression and tradition of practices. As we go forward in these discussions it will be important to attend to both the opportunities and the limitations provided by the adoption of any particular terminology.

Chapter Two

Fundamentals of an Ethic of Sex

In this chapter, I indicate some of the general ethical perspectives that will inform our discussion. I begin with a perspective based on the work of Gayle Rubin that among human beings there is a wide variation of sexual practices and this diversity is benign. This provides an overall framework for the discussion of particular sexualities that will be discussed in subsequent chapters. To this I have added the reflections of Raja Halwani and Martha Nussbaum that develop notions of virtue and character ethics (derived ultimately from Aristotle) that are open to a consideration of significant variation in sexual practices. I will then look at the importance of a consideration of sexual practices within the general field of what may be termed the erotic. I conclude with reflections on the difference that may be made in a discussion of sexual practices by taking into account the practices of men who have sex with men.

Sexual Variation

The challenge for developing a theological ethic that is useful for consideration of "frontier issues" is to test principles against sexual diversity. In this way the principles can be refined and made more helpful. As a starting point for this process I think it useful to begin with Gayle Rubin's extraordinarily insightful essay "Thinking Sex."[11] In this essay, Rubin shows that the recent history of sex law may be understood as the result of a series of sex panics. It is important to note that it is very difficult to remove legislation once introduced. What is instructive is to see how this removal has succeeded. As an example, so far as I know, there has been no specific act in a state legislature that decriminalized "sodomy." It has happened in more than thirty states, but always by a method of indirection: court action or modernization of the penal code. The first state to modernize its code so as to decriminalize "sodomy" was Illinois in 1960. Other states followed by indirect means. Federal, and so

---

11. Gayle Rubin, "Thinking Sex: Notes for a Radical Theory of the Politics of Sexuality," in *Pleasure and Danger: Exploring Female Sexuality*, ed. Carole S. Vance (Boston: Routledge & K. Paul, 1984). Subsequent references to this text in this chapter will be given in-text.

national, decriminalization happened only in 2003 with the Supreme Court's ruling in *Lawrence v. Texas*.

While a certain strain of Christian erotophobia stands in the background of the sex panics that Rubin highlights, they seem to operate even or especially in a post-Christendom situation. While it is crucial to contest erotophobia within Christianity, as I suggest in the next chapter, it is nonetheless the case that other forces are powerfully at play. The language of psychology, for example, was used to enforce virtually the same Victorian sexual ethic that it replaced. Homosexuality supposedly represented immaturity or the result of a dysfunctional family structure. Similarly the medicalization of sexual discourse in the HIV/AIDS panic curiously replicates anti-sodomy legislation: Only in the U.S. was oral sex criminalized; only in the U.S. was oral sex identified as "unsafe sex." Is this coincidental?

While Rubin identifies six conceptual issues—essentializing, sex negativity, misplaced scale, hierarchical valuation, a domino theory of sexual peril, and the lack of a concept of benign sexual variation (11)—the last is, I think, inclusive of the others and the most important. Is it possible for us to free ourselves of a notion of a normative sexuality in relation to which all else is, if not evil, at least "immature" or deficient? If we cannot do this, do we not still stigmatize some sexualities unfairly?

It is important to distinguish decriminalization from ethical or moral discourse. Rubin suggests decriminalization of all sex acts save those involving violence or coercion (19, 23), but that does not necessarily make all acts ethical. On the one hand, we may be worried that decriminalizing homosexuality does little to address mechanisms of social control that stigmatize homosexuality. On the other hand, we may think we should decriminalize prostitution without thinking that it ought to be free of stigma (that, by the way, is not my position). The fact that something is decriminalized does not answer the question of whether it is a good idea. (I think crack cocaine should not be illegal, but I would not recommend that anybody use it.) Nor does the fact that heterosexual marriage is legal begin to address important ethical issues about how it contributes to the domination of women or the violation of children. All this is to say that there are complex relations between law and ethics that we will have to explore in our discussions.

While there are many important issues that Rubin raises regarding ways of thinking about sexuality, I believe the most important is to attempt to arrive at a theory of benign sexual variation. This would mean not only that all forms of non-coercive sexuality be legally tolerated, but also that they would be seen as having value for society. What we will explore is the extent something like such a perspective may also be appropriate for a theologically informed sexual ethic.

Rubin herself identifies "sexual essentialism" as the most important obstacle to the project of "thinking (or re-thinking) sex." (9). To be sure, there has been a considerable body of literature devoted to showing how sexual desires, practices, and relationships are "constructed" through social institutions of control and supervision. For example, what is sometimes called heteronormativity is shaped by a variety of social instruments. Legal protections such as those related to taxation provide incentives. Similarly, informal institutions like family reunions, church weddings, anniversary celebrations, and so on serve constantly to underline the social and personal value of participation in standardized marriage and family values. In fact, when all this is taken into account, it is remarkable that there are some who resist the power of this "apparatus" (to use Foucault's term). Moreover there is considerable debate about whether there is such a thing as "homosexuality" that remains more or less constant across cultures and time. There is growing recognition that that social construction plays a fundamental role in shaping same-sex desire, practice and relationships as well.

Of perhaps greater importance for the construction of theological perspectives on sexuality generally, and queer sexuality particularly, is what she terms the "sex negativity" of the Western tradition (10). This will be the focus of some of the work of the next chapter.

As she notes, the question of misplaced scale is a corollary to sex negativity (11). It has to do with the ways in which activities with a sexual component are judged or punished far more harshly than similar acts with no sexual component. In the discussion of prostitution, we will see that instead of applying laws regarding workers protection, society develops a whole series of enforcement procedures that make sex work radically different than other types of wage labor. Perhaps even more remarkable is the panic regarding sexual predation of strangers on children that takes little or no account of the fact that the home is the most likely place for children to be sexually molested.

The hierarchical scale will also need to be addressed (11-12). For example, the differences in the legal status of porn actors and prostitutes shows a remarkable disparity. The supposition that certain sexual practices are appropriate to different levels of intimacy (identified by duration and commitment) will also be addressed in our reflections.

Of particular importance for our reflection is Rubin's proposal: "A democratic morality should judge sexual acts by the way partners treat one another, the level of mutual consideration, the presence or absence of coercion, and the quantity and quality of the pleasures they provide" (15).

Virtue and Character

Gayle Rubin's frankly libertarian approach to sexuality is, of course, not the only perspective that can be helpful in the development of an affirmative Queer ethic of sex. The proposal of Raja Halwani in *Virtuous Liaisons* to develop a sex-positive ethic on the basis of a virtue ethic with roots in Aristotelian moral reflection also provides an important perspective that will enter into our reflections on such topics as prostitution, pornography, and promiscuity. [12]

Halwani seeks to liberate Aristotelian virtue ethics from some of its limitations in Aristotle's own presentation. This means first liberating it from the male-centered notions of virtue—virtue being itself a term with reference to masculinity (vir = male or manly)—and its ethos of aristocratic bias as an ethic developed within a class-bound (aristocratic) and slave-holding social order. What he seeks then is to emphasize the idea of virtues: things like courage, temperance, justice, practical wisdom, and so on that go to make up the good life, a life that more fully realizes human capacity and increases human flourishing.

He further seeks to incorporate within the framework of virtue much of the perspective developed within what is called an ethic of care, which is concerned for the well-being of the other person. This counters the tendency of virtue ethics to focus inordinately on the agent's well-being without strong concern for the well-being of the other.

His basic question is therefore: "Can one be a decent, morally good human being, lead a flourishing life, and yet also be promiscuous, be in an open relationship, or be a sex worker?"[13] And he will argue "that not only can one be morally decent and yet be promiscuous, a sex worker, or in an open marriage, but also that there is nothing about these ... that raises the likelihood that one's virtuous character would be put at risk by adopting such ways of life."[14]

The significance of an ethic of care was introduced into ethical discussion by Carol Gilligan, who suggested that while male psychology may be more attracted to abstract notions of justice, female psychology is more rooted in relational contexts in which emotional knowledge plays a role along with various forms of reasoning.[15] Halwani investigates the position developed on this basis by Nel Noddings's *Caring: A Feminine Approach to Ethics and Moral Education*.[16]

---

12. Raja Halwani, *Virtuous Liaisons: Care, Love, Sex, and Virtue Ethics* (Chicago: Open Court, 2003).

13. Halwani, *Virtuous Liaisons*, 10-11.

14. Halwani, *Virtuous Liaisons*, 11.

15. Carol Gilligan, *In a Different Voice* (Cambridge: Harvard, 1982).

16. Nel Noddings, *Caring: A Feminine Approach to Ethics and Moral Education*

Some of the objections to an ethic of care raised by other feminist writers have to do with the way it can lead one to identify with an evil person in the name of care. Halwani then suggests that placing care within the framework of virtues, in which it is understood as a crucial but not the exclusive virtue, can respond to these objections.[17]

One further note that is of importance here is that Halwani, like Nussbaum, is skeptical of making romantic love the test of relationships. Indeed romantic love can in fact be at odds with virtue in a number of respects. Thus while romantic love may be a good, it must be tested against virtues, rather than being understood as a virtue itself, or as the sort of good without which one cannot live a morally decent life.

When it comes to sex, Halwani seeks to make the case "that there is nothing as such about a monogamous sexual way of life that enhances, or makes more probable, its agent's flourishing."[18] His procedure is to try to bring together reflections on virtue with what might be thought of as the limit cases of sex work, promiscuity, and open (that is, not strictly monogamous) relationships. He argues that the virtue traditionally associated with the area of sex, namely temperance, is not adequate by itself to define what is moral in these cases but that it must be supplemented by a consideration of other virtues (including care). This leads to an awkward identification of temperance as concern for something like a golden mean in satisfying an appetite (which Halwani designates T1) and, alternatively, as concern for not harming others, associated with care (designated T2, with the corresponding forms of intemperance identified as IT1 and IT2, respectively).[19]

Furthermore, Halwani lifts up the importance of attending to the experience of gay men as well as sex workers. The latter is important because of the pertinence of the question of sex work, the former because of the important light it sheds both on promiscuity and on sex work when considered as ways of life. We will return to Halwani's perspective when we discuss open relationships, prostitution, and promiscuity.

Eroticism and Sexual Practice

Because our focus in these reflections is on overcoming the marginalization of certain sexual practices and patterns, the focus will generally be upon what

---

(Berkeley: University of California Press, 1984).

17. Halwani, *Virtuous Liaisons*, 74.

18. Halwani, *Virtuous Liaisons*, 170.

19. Halwani, *Virtuous Liaisons*, 171ff.

might be termed sex acts rather than a more general eroticism. One of the many important contributions to contemporary thinking about the sexual from feminist and lesbian thinkers has been a recognition of the wide sphere of the erotic that serves not only as the context for, but in some cases as a substitute for, specific sexual practices. What this means is that the features of intimacy and sensuality exceed the limits of what is often thought of as sex acts.

It is possible for such a celebration of the erotic to lead back into a Platonizing sublimation of sexuality in favor of something like a non-sexual sensuality that leaves actual sexual practices in a sort of moral limbo or even denigrates these in favor of a more enlightened appreciation of the erotic. This is certainly not the perspective that is taken in these reflections.

However, the affirmation of the erotic generally and the suspicion directed against an over-preoccupation with specific sex acts is certainly crucial to understanding the contexts, patterns, and practices to which we will be devoting attention. This is true first because there is a certain ineradicable confusion about what constitutes a sex act in our culture.

We have the famous and entertaining example of President Clinton's plausible or implausible denial of having sex with Monica Lewinsky. Is non-penetrative sex actually sex? For many folk trying out their sexuality, considerable importance may be placed on the distinction between "going all the way" and other forms of quasi-sex (such as "heavy petting"). It is this discursive discrimination worthy of a country that gave Clinton's denials a certain peculiar plausibility. Is non-orgasmic S&M sex? Are non-orgasmic water sports (i.e., urination play) sex? Is mutual masturbation sex? Is phone sex or even cybersex really sex? That is, does sex require penetration? Does it require orgasm or orgasmic intention? Does it require physical proximity? These issues don't have to be fully resolved at this point, but they do show how we are often confused by our lack of specificity in terminology.

This anticipates a further reason for taking seriously the sphere of the erotic within which sexual or quasi-sexual practices may take place. Many of the forms of sexual expression we will be considering are not generally reducible to the specific sex acts that they encompass. Specific sexual acts make up a relatively small share of the time devoted to bathhouse cruising, for example. For some, the atmosphere of sexual freedom and possibility would be enough to make an evening in these surroundings worthwhile, even if they did not themselves engage in what they might think of as a specific sex act. Time with a prostitute or hustler may often include far more than a particular sex act. In many cases, the point may, instead, be sensual companionship. The term "escort services" is more than the cover for potential sexual acts; it also designates the companionship that is specifically desired for its own sake as well as the sexual encounter that may also occur within that framework. But the *possibility* of sex acts does serve as at least one, perhaps the primary, "reason for being" of these contexts.

Men Who Have Sex With Men

In several of the discussions that follow there will be an emphasis on the literature concerning men who have sex with men. This must be briefly explained.

In the first place the preponderance of the literature concerning Queer sexual ethics focuses upon the context of gay male practices and patterns. This is true whether the literature is written by men or women, heterosexual or gay/lesbian. In large part this has to with the greater visibility of the gay male culture in western societies as the focal point of discussion. This is especially true of issues such as pederasty or public sex. It is also due to the fact that it is more often male-to-male sexuality that is the object of criminal legislation, at least historically. Thus sodomy statutes typically were written with men rather than women in mind. In addition, much of the literature on marginal sexualities has been developed in recent years in response to the AIDS crisis, and this has typically focused on the behavior of men who have sex with other men. Only in the case of prostitution has there been a comparable focus on women who have sex with men.

Furthermore, in the disputes about sexuality that constituted what are sometimes called the "sex wars" in feminist discourse, there was considerable dispute about pornography and especially prostitution. These discussions naturally placed considerable stress upon the ways in which these sexual forms were to be seen as extensions of patriarchal institutions. What was often missing in these discussions in the 1970s and '80s was attention to the difference that might be made in the analysis if the experience of male sex workers were to be taken into account. It was often supposed that this was simply an extension of patriarchal perspectives into the domain of male-male sex, but closer attention to the practices and experiences of male prostitutes has brought that supposition into serious question. Thus in the discussion of sex work we will attend to the difference that a consideration of male sex work makes to the discussion.

There are other areas of our discussion where there is less salience to the perspective of men who have sex with men. As we will see, the institutions that cater to a desire for BDSM experiences seem to be similar whether the clubs in question cater to heterosexuals, to gay males or to lesbians.

In the past, the focus on male-to-male sex has often emphasized the experience of gay men. But in many cases, what is at stake are the practices of persons who do not define themselves as gay (or bisexual). In general, I have favored the nomenclature of "men who have sex with men" so as to avoid the question of a certain identity politics. How people view themselves or are

21

viewed by others is certainly an important issue. But if we are to take into account cross-cultural perspectives, it will not do to impose upon the evidence preconceived identity categories. Perhaps one could say therefore that in this sense the perspective adopted is "queer" rather than "gay."

This emphasis does not mean that we can ignore the contribution of lesbian perspectives on a radical or inclusive sex ethic. On the contrary, while discussion by lesbian activists has sometimes focused on gay male practices as a way of opening discussion into sexual possibilities (prostitution, promiscuity, BDSM), it has also increasingly added important insights from the experience of lesbians who engage in non-traditional sexual patterns and practices. This is an important—indeed, indispensable—contribution to discussions of sexual ethics.

What about Heterosexuals?

Are the perspectives discussed here of relevance only for LGBTQ people, or do they have importance for persons who identify themselves as straight or heterosexual?

In many cases the relevance of these discussions for "straight" people is pretty obvious. For example, the discussion of marriage, its transformation and troubles, clearly pertains to the experience of many folk who do not think of themselves as "queer." The divorce rate itself is testimony to the problems associated with traditional views (and practices) of marriage. When one adds to this the problematic character of the marital contract as a sort of property arrangement as well as the tragic history of spousal and child abuse so often associated with heterosexual marriage, there is more than ample reason for serious-minded heterosexual folk to consider alternative views of sexual partnership. In this they may be helped, as these chapters will argue, by a consideration of perspectives generated through some attention to queer experience and practice.

Something similar might be said about promiscuity and casual sex. No doubt there is quite a lot of this going on among heterosexuals. But a consideration of gay experience may help to dispel some of the ways this has been inscribed within patriarchal perspectives. In a different way, this may also be true of considerations of prostitution, as I have already indicated.

But if much of what is discussed here has bearing on heterosexual experience, why not take this as the starting point of discussion, especially since many who study this material may be more familiar with heterosexuality?

The reason is twofold. First, as I have indicated, there is the advantage that a queer perspective actually provides an important counterpoint to many of the assumptions involved in a discussion of heterosexual sexuality. But even more important is this: Heterosexuals tend to take up all the space in discussions of sexuality, and especially sexual ethics. It is past time for a fresh perspective, one that looks at sexuality from the margins and brings into question rather than takes for granted the heteronormativity of so much ethical and theological discussion. It is the very supposition that heterosexuality is normative that must be brought into question if we are to develop a truly inclusive sexual ethic.

Chapter Three

Theological Issues

The concern with "An Ethic of Queer Sex" has a number of theological bases. The suppression of sexuality from the discourse regarding gay rights and gay acceptance in the church has a root in the fear of sexuality, especially unregulated sexuality, that has been long a part of the Christian theological tradition. This erotophobia is, I believe, a fundamental distortion of basic theological principles. The regulation of sexuality distorts the notion of sin, impairs the affirmation of the body, and makes the affirmation of pleasure problematic. In order to undo some of this damage it will be necessary to emphasize again the relational character of ethics, the importance of improvisation around the central theme of justice and mercy, and the suggestion that sexual lifestyles be understood in relation to the category of vocation.

The Regulation of Sexuality in Early Christianity

It should be noted that a fear of sexuality was already a significant part of the Greco-Roman cultural tradition prior to its (partial) incorporation into Christian rhetoric and discourse. Aline Rouselle and Peter Brown make clear that prominent Roman discourses made suspicion of the body, and especially of sexuality, a prominent part of their world view.[20] Indeed, already with Plato and especially the Plato of the Laws, there is a strong suspicion that sexuality when expressed in any way undermines the project of self-mastery that enables one to be a "free man."[21] For Plato this is especially true of relations between males or of what was then called pederasty. It seems that Plato did not imagine that cross-sex relations (between a male and a female) could be a source of pleasure or that they could be a topic of much philosophical interest. Unfortunately, the views Plato expressed in this text came to have very

---

20. Aline Rouselle, *Porneia* (New York: Barnes & Noble, 1996); Peter Brown, *Body and Society: Men, Women, and Sexual Renunciation in Early Christianity* (New York: Columbia University Press, 1988).

21. Robert Gregg Bury, trans., *Plato's Laws* (Cambridge: Harvard University Press, 1984). For an extended treatment of Plato's views on same-sex love and its affects in Christianity see my *Plato or Paul?*

great influence on emergent forms of Christianity that came to dominate the Christian tradition.

In early Christian discourse, an even more marked fear of sexuality expressed itself in the views of the Encratites (the so-called "self-controlled"), who supposed that Christians should not engage in any sexual practices at all. A number of second-century Christian philosophers (among them Tatian and Athenagoras) took up this extreme view. It also appears to have been adopted by the Marcionites who promulgated universal celibacy for all Christians. This view, while it may seem extreme to us, actually appears to have enjoyed great popularity, especially in the second century. It seems to have been a development from the ideology of self-mastery that was gaining ground in Roman discourse of the period (although one may wonder about the possibility of rootage in certain ascetic traditions of India or the Zoroastrian traditions of Persia).

This extreme view was countered by the Alexandrians like Clement, who insisted that sexual expression between male and female was acceptable within the context of marriage, especially when was it aimed at procreation. Thus the argument that sex was aimed at procreation served to counter a totalized suspicion of sexuality. When Clement argues against the Encratites, he affirms conjugal relations more strongly than Plato. On the other hand, he can also become rather restrictive: Not only should sex be only for procreation, but it also should never happen during daylight hours or involve excessive pleasure. It would take several centuries before Clement's view, inherited from Plato and from certain stoic philosophers like Musonius Rufus, would become common currency in what became "Catholic" Christianity. This would happen above all with the development of the theory of natural law by Thomas Aquinas, a theory that subsequently provides the basis for Vatican teachings about matters related to sexuality today.

There appears to have been another, albeit suppressed, option in the early church that was more open to unregulated sexuality. This can be glimpsed through the cracks of a polemic against the Carpocratians, a sect that arose in the early second century.[22] Irenaeus in *Against Heresies* characterizes this group as advocating promiscuity and as claiming: "We are saved indeed by faith and love; but all other things, while in their nature indifferent, are reckoned by the opinion of men—some good, some evil, there being nothing really evil by nature."[23] In a subsequent section he writes: "Others again, following upon Basilides and Carpocrates, have introduced promiscuous intercourse and a

---

22. Morton Smith, *Clement of Alexandria and a Secret Gospel of Mark* (Cambridge: Harvard University Press, 1973), 266-278.

23. Irenaeus, *Against Heresies* (Whitefish: Kessinger Publishing, 2004), 66.

plurality of wives, and are indifferent about eating meats sacrificed to idols, maintaining that God does not greatly regard such matters."[24] We may be able to glimpse here the "road not taken"—at least not so far. What may be particularly striking is that the principles evoked by the Carpocratians seem rather familiar: Only faith(fulness) and love save humanity; God doesn't much care about meat offered to idols and so on. These views seem to have a decidedly Pauline provenance and their opening to a more permissive sexuality seems at least a plausible interpretation of these principles.

However, the desire of Christian apologists to argue that ordinary Christians exceeded the model of the philosophic person in popular philosophical discourse made Christianity susceptible to the allures of an erotophobic (and homophobic) popular philosophical discourse. This in fact turned out to be a remarkably successful strategy especially in the years of martyrdom when Christian courage in the face of death attracted many to a faith for which death had lost its "sting."

It was, however, with the Council of Elvira in 305 CE that Christianity began officially to attempt to regulate the sexual expression of its members.[25] Brown notes that thirty-four of eighty-one rulings deal with sex and marriage—and most concern the control of Christian women.[26] John Boswell notes that one ruling concerned the sexual seduction of minor boys.[27] Thus Christianity embarked upon the sexualization of sin and the ecclesial regulation of sexuality.

Sex and Sin

A theological rationale for this regulation appears for the first time with Augustine's struggles against the flesh in his own person and with the development of the motif of the interior war of desire. As Brown has indicated, one of the ways in which the focus on the control of the body came into being was in the attempt to develop a kind of Christian heroics that replaced the call of martyrdom.[28] But it is also the case that this serves as a way for the church to situate itself at the center of people's experience of themselves and their desires.

---

24. Irenaeus, *Against Heresies*, 71.

25. Samuel Laeuchli, *Power and Sexuality: The Emergence of Canon Law at the Synod of Elvira* (Philadelphia: Temple University Press, 1972).

26. Brown, *Body and Society*, 206.

27. John Boswell, *Christianity, Social Tolerance, and Homosexuality: Gay People in Western Europe from the Beginning of the Christian Era to the Fourteenth Century* (Chicago: University of Chicago Press, 1981), 179.

28. Brown, *Body and Society*, 193-197.

Indeed it must be suspected that one of the consequences of this sexualization of the human predicament is that the church makes itself necessary to laity in terms of the administration of forgiveness for commonplace "sins."

Ordinary Christians are made to discover in themselves a struggle with desire. This struggle is invented in order to be lost; for the loss may and must be made good through recourse to the offices of the church. This may even be intensified by aspects of the Reformation, which transferred views of body and sexuality from the monastic sphere (restricted to closed communities of exemplary persons) to the wider public. Thus worries about sexual temptation characteristic of attempts to maintain celibacy become concerns about straying sexual desire even among the married. This concern grows to include the not-yet-married through the emergence of what Rubin terms a sex panic about masturbation in the nineteenth century.[29]

A very interesting document in this regard, from the late eighteenth century shows how this panic arose and grew. John Wesley published a number of two- to four-page tracts for the people called Methodists on a range of subjects dealing with physical and moral health (for example, on drinking tea). Among these was a tract on "onanism" (or masturbation), so called because one of the sons of Judah, named Onan, refused to carry out his conjugal duties with Tamar after previous brother-husbands had died after having sex with her.[30] He "spilled his seed on the ground" rather than carry out his family duty to sire a son for his older brother. The tract published by Wesley, as was often the case, simply popularized the views of another writer, a medical professional who had raised alarming fears about the effects of masturbation. Wesley helped to promulgate these views and they later became a staple of Protestant and even Catholic sexual ethics. In the Vatican's response to the sexual revolution in 1970, there was some mention of homosexuality—but the bulk of the teaching had to do with masturbation! The point is that there is strong concern about the toxicity of any sexual practice, which then is used to inflame the sense of shame and guilt among the young, resulting in their need for repentance and vigilance and discipline.

The consequence is that sexuality is made to be the privileged site for the struggle against sin. This is in contrast even to the early monastic and anchorite movements in which the regulation of desire for food, sleep, and even conversation take up far more energy and provoke far more comment than sexual desire. What does seem to be the case is that the conflation of sex and

---

29. Rubin, "Thinking Sex," 3-4.

30. John Wesley and Samuel Auguste David Tissot, *Thoughts on the Sin of Onan* (London: Author, 1767).

sin is a disaster for the theological interpretation of sin; in biblical language, sin is most often associated with damage done to the other person, and especially with the practices of injustice that violate the vulnerable and marginalized. One of the ways this switch is perpetrated is through the translation of Greek words for justice as righteousness (or injustice as wickedness) in English. The deflection of attention from injustice as the biblical site for sin and thus from economic and political dimensions of injustice is a catastrophe for theology. Indeed, it is a catastrophe that has dire consequences for the cultural traditions that inherit this theological error.[31]

The result is that persons may focus upon "marriage and family values" as a substitute for practicing justice in those domains that destroy the lives of uncounted millions. Here may be the root of the odd alliance between religio-sex traditionalists of the religious right and the promotion of radical capitalism and imperial ideology in the U.S. political landscape. This produces the rather extraordinary emergence of the religious right with its concern with abortion and homosexuality on the one hand, and tax cuts for the super-rich and limitations on the power of unions on the other. Preoccupation with sex becomes a way of persuading people to adopt policies that are not only against their own economic and political interests, but that are obviously unjust in biblical terms as well.

Meanwhile, persons are made to feel the most extraordinary guilt for sexual misdeeds or even desires, even if they are not acted upon. Their experience of themselves at the level of their own bodies and desire becomes a sphere of shame and unwarranted conflict. This is an issue of pastoral theology that often surfaces in areas such as pre-marital counseling.

The Body

The damage done to the coherence of Christian doctrine extends far beyond distortions in the doctrine of sin. The affirmation of the body is at the very heart of Christian doctrine at every level. Christianity has always struggled against Gnosticism's denigration of the bodily reality of the story of salvation. Yet, since the late Middle Ages and increasingly in the modern era, Christianity has come to be associated with fear or suspicion of the body. This is deeply ironic.

The mission of Jesus was not concerned with saving disembodied souls. He was above all known as a healer of broken and damaged bodies. It was

---

31. Theodore Jennings, "Reconstructing the Doctrine of Sin," in *The Other Side of Sin*, ed. Andrew Sung Park and Susan Nelson (Albany: State University of New York Press, 2001), 109-122.

this that drew the crowds to him in Galilee. And in dispute with religious authorities, he maintained that feeding or healing bodies was more important than any sort of religious observance. Indeed, it was this commitment that stirred the wrath of the righteous against him, a wrath that would ultimately lead to his death.

When it became necessary to defend Christian faith against the suspicions of Greco-Roman philosophy, the starting point had to be the assertion at the beginning of the Gospel of John that the word became flesh. The "incarnation of the word" was the focal point of the development of Christian doctrine. This sometimes took the form of the bold assertion that Jesus was "born of a woman's body," something that seemed incompatible with contemporary views of divinity. (Controversies over the birth of Jesus tended to focus not on the virginity of the mother but on the problem of there being an actual mother at all.)

Against those who would later suggest that Jesus as the divine son only seemed or appeared to suffer and die, the early theologians insisted that his suffering and death were real. Indeed, their view was that it was precisely the bodily reality of suffering and death that made it plausible to suppose that salvation could come to the whole human being. With the bodily reality of death came also the bodily resurrection from the dead. It was the hope for the return of their own body to life that demonstrated for many that the God who created humanity was committed to the redemption of humanity.

And thus Christian hope anticipated not the immortality of the soul taught by Platonic philosophers, but the resurrection of the body, a body that no longer had death ahead of it as its fate, a body animated by unending liveliness. This was the consequence of maintaining that the God who created all creatures, including human beings, was the same God who would redeem them. Thus from the resurrection of the body came also the hope for the restoration of the whole of creation. The God who created the body would not abandon the body but would instead make it whole and vital.

The struggle against the denial of the body was never completely victorious, but it seems that in the early modern period a gnostic denial of the body nearly overwhelmed Christianity. God is made to be the enemy of the body that God created. Christ is made to be the enemy of the body that Christ has assumed in the incarnation. The hope of redemption is made contingent not on the resurrection of the body but on its being left behind in an immortality of the soul. All of this introduces fundamental incoherence into the very substance of faith.

One essential aspect of the development of a new sort of sexual ethic is the reaffirmation of the body against modern Christian (and secular) suspicion and fear, even hatred, of the body. This leads to a further question: Can this include a privileging of the body not only as the site of suffering and death, but also of pleasure?

The Question of Pleasure

There is no reason that the good news of God's love should render the celebration of pleasure problematic. The traditions transmitted through the Hebrew Bible give expression to a strong affirmation of human pleasure. The image of wholeness as represented by the promise or vision that "everyone shall sit beneath his vine and fig tree" represents a general affirmation of embodied life characteristic of biblical themes. Only in the rather extreme versions of Nazirite vows (abstinence from wine) do we see anything that comes close to the suspicion directed toward the pleasures of the body. To be sure, some priestly traditions discriminate between acceptable and unacceptable foods, but the basis of discrimination appears unrelated to the issue of bodily pleasure. While some elements of the Qumran traditions adopt semi-ascetic views, these seem to have little or no impact on the later development of Judaism.

The affirmation of the body and of pleasure continues in the traditions associated with Jesus. Throughout the Gospels. Jesus is presented as one who enjoys the companionship of the disreputable. In contrast to the practice of John the baptizer, Jesus ironically notes that he is known as a wine-bibber and a glutton; that is, as one who indulged freely in food and wine. Many of his teachings, especially in the Gospel of Luke, have the form of a sort of "party etiquette"—who to invite, where to sit, and so on—that betray no suspicion of bodily pleasure as such. In the Gospel of John his first public act is to attend a party and to change copious amounts of water into very fine wine so that the celebration could continue. Thus it is no accident that liberation theologians in Latin America depict the eschatological consummation as the messianic banquet, a fiesta without end. This certainly does not mean an "anything goes" ethos reigns either, however. The same tradition is strongly critical of material possessions of all kinds, of all forms of violation of the neighbor, and also of what might be termed marriage and family values.

Early Christianity did retain this memory of Jesus as one who relished pleasure. And from Paul to the Pastoral Letters, we have the insistence that food and wine is be received with gratitude rather than suspicion. In Romans, Paul does offer the possibility for persons to adopt an ascetic ethic for themselves but insists that this should not be imposed on anyone else. He identifies himself as one who thinks all things are good if received with gratitude. All this is consistent with the perspectives of ancient Israel as well.

Even in First Timothy, we have the condemnation of groups that seek to problematize the sphere of bodily pleasure. The teaching of "deceitful spirits and of demons" is characterized as follows: "They forbid marriage and demand abstinence from foods which God created to be received with thanksgiving by those who believe and know the truth. For everything created by God is good, and nothing is to be rejected, provided it is received with thanksgiving; for it is sanctified by God's word and by prayer" (4:1-5). This text already indicates the grounds for a celebration of bodily pleasure. The chief ground is the assertion that the world is created by God. This means that it is to be received with thanksgiving. Note that this text specifically gathers together the pleasures of sexual companionship and the companionship of the table.

But in the late second century, Christianity came under the spell of views derived from Stoics and others that pleasure was to be avoided— that pleasure destroyed the firmness of the character and made it, as they said then, effeminate. A near-contemporary of Paul, Musonius Rufus, insisted that pleasure was debilitating in all cases and that one should avoid pleasure in all aspects of life. This view comes to be appropriated first in Alexandrian Christianity, especially in Clement of Alexandria, and subsequently gains prestige through the examples of the desert ascetics whose self-discipline made them rivals of the martyrs in spiritual heroics.

A crucial condition for the development of a new and progressive sexual ethic is overcoming the radical suspicion of pleasure that has insinuated itself into Christianity. There will have to be a return to the affirmation of the goodness of creation so fundamental to Jewish and Christian scriptures (and to the Qur'an as well). Pleasures of the body should remind us of the good gift that is life itself, bodily life, and so should engender thanksgiving rather than fear.

Perhaps delighting in bodily life can sensitize us to the horror of the deprivation inflicted upon the bodies of others made not for suffering but for pleasure, play, and joy. Certainly the Jesus traditions combine a commitment to the well-being of others, including the health and wholeness of bodies, with an affirmation of the pleasures of companionship in food and wine.

The fear of pleasure traditionally has focused on the practices of masturbation. From the late eighteenth to the early twentieth century, from warts to insanity, the specter of the violence done through self-pleasure was invoked to frighten the impressionable. Of course, one is more likely to hurt oneself jogging than masturbating. But because sex is regarded as toxic, preposterous distortions of moral scale are introduced to make one fear pleasure. But what if our capacity for pleasure is tied to our capacity to rejoice in life and liveliness? What if it is not opposed, but essential, to being glad to be alive and so grateful to the One who gives us life?

This attitude of grateful reception is jeopardized not by indulgence but by a greedy refusal to share and to recognize the equal rights of others. Although it is possible to appropriate the language of self-mastery here, what is genuinely at stake is rather the question of "covetousness" that deprives the other of the pleasure one claims for oneself. We should note that this idea of respecting the rightful claims of the other person is made central in Paul's reflections of conjugal relations in 1 Corinthians 7.

But this will mean that the ethical question above all is the question of the other, as philosopher Emmanuel Levinas has taught us. This then leads to the question of relationality as the proper sphere of the ethical.

The Question of Relationality

The initial orientation toward the import of a doctrine of creation as underwriting a grateful and unsuspicious attitude toward bodily pleasure points to the potential significance of the creation narratives for an understanding of sexuality. And this is what I attempted to underscore many years ago in my essay "Theological Perspectives on Sexuality."[32] Several of the principles I articulated there still make sense to me:

1. Sexuality is not peripheral to our humanity.
2. Sexuality undermines an attempt to be human in isolation from the other person: "Our sexuality reminds us that we cannot remain alone … Our sexuality may serve to remind us not only that we stand in need of one another, that we owe our lives to the sexuality of our parents, but in reminding us of these things, to remind us also of the way our existence depends upon God's creative act."[33]
3. Finally, "a strong revulsion toward sexuality is connected with the will to be independent and absolute."[34] To this, however, I would now add that a revulsion toward sexuality may also be a consequence of the experience of sexual abuse, especially when this has been inflicted upon persons at an early age. As I noted in Chapters 1 and 2 of this text, this is an all too common experience for children in our society, and for those in other societies as well.

---

32. Theodore Jennings, "Theological Perspectives on Sexuality," *Journal of Pastoral Care* 33, no. 1 (March, 1979): 3-16.

33. Jennings, "Theological Perspectives," 4.

34. Jennings, "Theological Perspectives," 5.

But it is also the case that the perspective of co-humanity that I develop in the essay on sexuality lies very close to the rhetoric of heteronormativity. I make much of the polarity of male and female as indicating the partiality of our humanity and our need of one who is "other." However, in an earlier essay, "Homosexuality and Christian Faith," I maintained that:

> our humanity as co-humanity cannot be interpreted only in a sexual or genital way. If this is done, nothing remains of the symbolic and thus ethical significance of co-humanity....That significance is this—that human beings differ from one another; that it is this difference we constantly seek to abrogate....But the otherness of the other is God's gift to us, by which gift we are summoned out of our isolation and thus into the co-humanity of love.[35]

Thus, I maintained, homosexuality is not intrinsically inferior to heterosexuality.

There are concrete signifiers of otherness. One is gender. But there are other such signifiers: race, class, age, even gender practices, or sexual tastes. But what is of greatest importance is that to which the concrete signifier points: that the other as other is not the "same" as me, cannot be appropriated into the "same," nor subjugated into a totalizing project of the self. This is, I think, the importance of Levinas for a clarification of ethics, even if Levinas, in much of his work, leans toward something like heteronormativity.[36]

Notice that taking this position seriously opens the way for a positive valuation of age and race and class differences in sexual relations (without necessarily absolutizing these). We will return to these themes in the discussions of promiscuity and of pederasty.

In general, I also still subscribe to the view of the "systematic ambiguity" of sexuality discussed in both of my essays. I do not suppose that the only problem with sexuality is society's repression of it. I do not suppose, as Michael Bronski does, that eliminating sexual repression makes for the ushering in of the reign of justice and freedom.[37] In my view, eliminating repression is a necessary, but not sufficient, condition for moving toward greater justice and mercy.

I still embrace the idea that we should ask: "To what extent is [any] relationship predicated upon the reduction of the other to our own desire,

---

35. Theodore Jennings, "Homosexuality and Christian Faith," 138.

36. See in particular Emmanuel Levinas, *Totality and Infinity: An Essay on Exteriority*, trans. Alphonso Linguis (Pittsburgh: Dusquesne University Press, 1969).

37. Michael Bronski, *The Pleasure Principle* (New York: St. Martin's Press, 1998), 3 and 248.

and to what extent does it, however brokenly, embody the mutuality of co-humanity?"[38] Another idea that informs my current argument is that precisely to the extent that sexuality reminds us of our need for the other, to that extent it becomes a temptation to reduce the otherness of the other. Hence I still rather like the idea of temptation and vocation that I developed in the homosexuality essay. I will return to the question of vocation below.

I would, however, modify my rejection of the position of what I called "healthy-mindedness."[39] The danger of what I wrote then is that it may make sexuality too central to human selfhood and thereby may lead to an all or nothing approach: Either sex is extremely fraught with meaning or it is trivialized. Martin Stringer's essay "Expanding the Boundaries of Sex" rightly points to the way in which ideas of intimacy may be mobilized to denigrate sexual activity insofar as it aims at pleasure rather than monogamy.[40] Hence the importance of trying to advance toward an affirmation of bodily pleasures.

I am not, however, persuaded by Stringer's attempt to correlate a scale of sexual practices (from penetrative to general but non-specific eroticism) with a scale of intimacy in which penetrative sex would be appropriate for long-term, committed, and emotionally intimate relations, while other practices would be fine among friends and some presumably among relative strangers. For male-male sex, it is even possible to play with inverting this relationship (that is, casual encounters may begin with penetrative sex, but expressions of erotic familiarity may be reserved for longer term relationships). Instead it will become evident that the "acts" versus "intimacy" scales are importantly different and admit of various combinations. What is useful is the recognition that there are variations both in practices and in relational structures (duration, intimacy, and so on). Whether these are gradations of value is another matter about which I believe Gayle Rubin and her concept of benign diversity helps us to have a critical perspective.

On Improvisation

Another set of considerations for sexual ethics may be brought into focus by thinking about improvisation. In his letter to the Romans, Paul makes much of the distinction between a mechanical working of the law and the spirited activity of faithfulness. Sometimes he even uses the term "work"

---

38. Jennings, "Homosexuality and Christian Faith," 138.

39. Jennings, "Perspectives on Sexuality," 11.

40. Martin Stringer, "Expanding the Boundaries of Sex," *Theology and Sexuality* 7 (1997).

for both. But the distinction seems to have to do with what might be called responsible freedom.

In Paul's view, the law intends good and justice, but it becomes an instrument of death and violence. It may make us zealous repeaters, enforcers, even practitioners of legal codes, but in such a way as to lose sight of the whole point of law, which is to provide some expression of the divine claim and call of justice. So, instead of law, he proposes faithfulness and specifies that what that means is love. Love does not harm the neighbor (and so, for example, does not kill), but instead aims at the good, the well-being, of the other person.

But there is no legal code that can concretely enable us to do good to the other, to escape the violence of the law. Rather, love requires something like improvisation. This is in one way unpredictable, unprogrammable, and yet, in another, it is also reliable in that it genuinely seeks to benefit the other, each other, all others.

It may also be that taking seriously the possibility of a love ethic helps to break the impasse of prohibition, incitement, and transgression that had been so clearly identified in the psychoanalytic theory of Jacques Lacan.[41] Slavoj Žižek suggests that it is Paul's love ethic in Romans 13 that breaks the deadlock identified in Romans 7.[42]

Concretely what this means is that it may be the very legal prohibitions of both church and state that incite sexual violence and violation of the other. Thus the substitution of love, a regard for the other, for any legal prohibitions may well serve to greatly reduce the temptations to violate one another that seem to contaminate our experience of sexuality.

Justice and Mercy

Thus improvisation aims at justice and mercy. And this is the appropriate standard, I think, for sexual ethics as for any religious ethics. In what way can sexual practice bring into play both a celebration of pleasure and a concern for the other that enhances the dignity, the well-being, the life and liveliness of the other? (This includes the virtue perspective inclusive of an ethic of care that we have noted from Halwani).

Thinking in this way can help us to see what is good and bad in heterosexual marital relations, what is good and bad about living together

---

41. Jacques Lacan, *The Ethics of Psychoanalysis* (New York: W.W. Norton & Company, 1997).

42. Slavoj Žižek, *The Ticklish Subject: The Absent Centre of Political Ontology* (London: Verso, 2000).

outside marriage, what is good and bad about relationships with prostitutes or other sex workers, what is good and bad about anonymous sex in bathhouses or one night stands, or what is good and bad about the fantasy sex of BDSM. We can think about this not by finding a rule to be applied as a law to ourselves or to others but by thinking clearly about how creative improvisational ways of thinking can lead us towards acts that are oriented toward the coming of justice and mercy, toward even what Derrida calls the "democracy to come."

These are the kinds of questions that we will have to consider as we look at a variety of marginalized sexualities. It is my contention that Christian ethics in relation to sexuality can be largely reduced to questions of the appropriate respect for the other person. In that sense there may be no specific "sex ethic" for Christian theology.

An ethic of queer sex that explicitly affirms sexuality and that contests the marginalization of any particular sexual practices has an important role to play in the recovery of a theological ethics that is not complicit with the erotophobia that, I contend, is destructive of the intelligibility of faith, destructive of the lives and health of the faithful, and complicit in the acceptance of economic and political injustice on a massive scale.

It is not to be expected that all will come to the same conclusion about these difficult matters. When it is a question of improvisation, there will of necessity be remarkable variation in ways of deciding. Here, decision is not programmable or predictable. That is in the very nature of the case. Thus the importance of what Paul says about welcoming one another in spite of and within strongly divergent opinions and perspectives.[43]

Vocation

This welcome may be facilitated by use of the Pauline notion of vocation, which may be a more appropriate category for dealing with questions of sexual orientation or preference than the appeal to creation, which stabilizes sexual identity in an essentialist fashion. However, this means taking this category much further than I did in the essay on homosexuality. Within the domain of queer forms of life, we will need to learn to be welcoming of a variety of different sexual vocations. In this case, a vocation means something like the conjunction of certain aptitudes, orientations, and contexts with the calling toward the realization of justice and mercy within these specific conditions. Whether we speak of the vocation of the prostitute, the call toward polyamory or promiscuity, or the attractions of BDSM, we will be enabled to embrace

---

43. See, for instance, 1 Cor 12:12 - 13:13

forms of life that differ from our own, but also seek to heed the call toward greater love of neighbor as the essential way of actualizing the love of God.

Just so, while I will be promoting a view that seeks to provoke a different way of looking at queer sexual ethics, I have no reason to believe that my way of looking at these issues is the only acceptable one for Christian people, or for others. But I hope it will at least provoke the sort of discussion that will enable us to practice with one another and with others, the hospitality (and generosity) that is the foundation of all ethics and of all justice.

Part Two

Marriage and Beyond

Chapter Four

Why Christian Marriage Needs Same-Sex Unions

It is my contention that the debates about marriage need to be turned on their head: The question is not whether same-sex unions can be legitimate and so worthy of inclusion in the category of "marriage," but that, in fact, same-sex unions have much to teach us about Christian marriage in general. But that is a big claim and needs to be made in a series of steps. This chapter looks first at same-sex unions generally and second at biblical materials (both New Testament materials and Hebrew Bible texts, respectively). Some of what I say will seem to suggest that gay unions ought to be celebrated in the church, but I want to argue something a little stronger. The case I will be seeking to make is this: that same-sex unions are essential to the life of the community of faith, and that they have already helped to transform what we call marriage from a patriarchal institution that Jesus's ministry deeply opposes into one that is rather more humane. Whatever is good about marriage is dependent already on models of same-sex unions, and therefore, these unions are essential to the community of faith if we are to be able, honestly and evangelically, to celebrate heterosexual unions. Put another way: We can authentically celebrate heterosexual unions only if we also celebrate same-sex unions. And, speaking plainly, this means that the current policy of many denominations (including my own United Methodist Church) is in direct and open conflict with the Gospel witness to the mission and ministry of Jesus.

But before getting into that I should say a word about the debate itself. In the 1990s, there was a growing inclination on the part of progressive pastors to celebrate same-sex unions or holy covenants between persons of the same sex. This was one way that pastors were able to open an outreach to the gay and lesbian persons who often felt excluded from the church.

This outreach was an attempt to begin repairing the enormous damage done by the church to gay and lesbian people. Let me just mention a couple of indices of that damage: In our society, there is an alarming incidence of teen suicide. The sociological evidence is that suicide and attempted suicide among teens who are, or think they might be, gay makes up a disproportionate percentage of suicidal behavior. Teens get the message at home, in school, and in church that it would be better to be dead than gay, and, as a result, they seek to take their own lives. Another index is that of teenage homelessness: A very high percentage of kids on the streets of our cities is made up of teens who are, or think they might be, gay or lesbian. They find the streets of our cities safer than their own homes, their schools or their churches.

Those who survive "Christian" homophobia bear the wounds of that homophobia their entire lives. Most of the pastors who engaged in this outreach and welcome to people who had been so scarred by the church were straight and felt strongly that the mainline churches needed to engage in outreach to, and affirmation of, gay and lesbian people in their area. In response, there was backlash from more conservative elements within these denominations that succeeded in passing legislation prohibiting pastors from participating in such ceremonies of blessing and affirmation. As a consequence, a number of pastors in mainline denominations were the subject of disciplinary action. The case of Jimmy Creech in Nebraska and of Greg Dell in Chicago were covered in the national press. (Notably, the cases of women pastors received far less attention in the press.) Conservative groups made illegal (in terms of church law) one of the most effective ways that progressives in the churches had found for reaching out to gay and lesbian parishioners. It should also be noted that these pastors were not doing anything especially radical. They were simply giving congregational blessing to same-sex relationships that were already increasingly recognized by major corporations and by some civil jurisdictions.

More recently, the struggle has moved to the courts and legislatures. There was considerable flurry of activity after Hawaii came close to permitting same-sex marriages in 1996. The state of Vermont accepted same-sex civil unions in 2000, and then the Massachusetts Supreme Court ordered the state to permit same-sex marriages in 2003. We are currently caught up in the aftermath of that struggle, a struggle that is basically about the question of civil rights. It is essentially the question of whether the non-recognition of same-sex marriage deprives people of equal protection under the laws. In the 2004 presidential campaign, the fears of religious traditionalists were cynically inflamed and manipulated in order to produce a vote for tax cuts for the wealthy, benefit cuts for the most vulnerable, and a policy of unending war. This bait-and-switch tactic duped millions of Christians into supporting policies that are incompatible with the Gospel and with Christian tradition.

In the current discussion, then, a number of issues come together. One is the issue of what might be termed civil rights. Here it is a question of whether gay and lesbian people have the same rights before the law as their "straight" siblings. This question has been especially exacerbated by the experience of many during the height of the AIDS crisis who found that long-standing relationships simply had no standing when it came to things like hospital visitation rights or decisions with respect to medical care and funeral arrangements. It is this concrete experience that provides some of the emotional fuel for this debate. In a great many ways, the refusal of the rights that often go along with "marriage" in our society seems like an intolerable refusal of basic civil rights, like an irrational discrimination.

In addition to questions of legal rights or of rights and responsibilities before the law, there is also the question of the affirmation of relationships that is traditionally bestowed by marriage. If the first has to do with civil law, civil rights, and civil responsibilities, then the second has to do with respect, affirmation, and celebration; that is, with the symbolic or even religious celebration of the miracle of love.

To those of us steeped in the waters of the separation of church and state this intertwining of civil and ecclesial/symbolic concerns may strike us as odd. For the first half of Christian history it would have been; less so in the more recent past. For well over a thousand years, Christianity in the West had nothing whatever to do with marriage or civil union. Christianity simply did not involve itself with an institution that seemed only to perpetuate the structures of the world. Of course people could enter into relationships (preferably monogamous ones) if they liked. But they did so without the blessing of the Church. The Church generally supposed that virginity was the preferred and favored option.

Only in the second millennium did the leadership of the church begin to cave in to the demand of laypeople that their marriages be recognized, legitimated, and celebrated alongside the still more prestigious option of celibacy. We should recall that in the early church celibacy was undertaken far more often by laypeople than by clergy and that in fact only in the sixth century did celibacy become expected of clergy in the West (and seems to have been enforced only from the eleventh century). Further, celibacy never became the norm for clergy in the East. Celibacy and marriage were options available in some way to all, but only celibacy or virginity was symbolically honored.

There were no church weddings until the second millennium of Christian history. Not until the thirteenth century, in 1215, did the church declare marriage a sacrament that required the participation of clergy to officially bless the union of men and women. And only 300 years later, with the Reformation, did marriage begin to really become the preferred option, the symbolically sanctioned option. Though today many people think that Christianity is all about marriage and family values, marriage as a sacrament is something that is in fact utterly unimaginable for most of the history of Christianity.

All of this is simply to say that any official celebration of marriage in the Christian tradition, even for heterosexual couples, was a long time coming. For what is still most of church history the church did not officially participate in the celebration of cross-sex (or heterosexual, as we now say) unions.

Rather than going further into the question of precedents in the life and liturgy of the church, however, I want simply to point to what may be relevant to this discussion in the study that I have undertaken in *The Man Jesus Loved*. This book has been characterized as maintaining that Jesus "was gay" or as even saying that: "Jesus had a gay lover." There is no need to go into the many ways in which these assertions, while understandable, are nevertheless not accurate descriptions of the book. What I have suggested is that Jesus seems to be depicted in the Gospel of John as the lover of another man (the disciple Jesus loved), that this relation could be construed as homoerotic, and that the Gospel of John does not seem to preclude the sexual expression of this sort of relationship. Moreover, I maintain that the Gospels seem to depict Jesus as accepting of same-sex relationships, at least in the case of the centurion and his lad in Matthew 8. All of this may fairly raise the question about the affirmation of same-sex relationships as this relates to the questions of civil unions or even "marriage."

Further, a good deal of my argument in the book also shows that the traditions about Jesus that come to us from the Gospels indicate that Jesus was highly critical of the institutions of marriage and family. William Countryman's wonderful study *Dirt, Greed and Sex*[44] accurately anticipates much of what I have also found in studying the Gospels. Thus, to the extent that the question of gay marriage is cast as assimilating gay and lesbian folk into these same institutions, then it looks like the matter may not be quite so simple. As we shall see, it is this very complexity that may prove most illuminating as we seek to understand how the church can be faithful today.

Jesus and the Man He Loved

Let me first turn to a discussion of the relevance of the relationship between Jesus and the man he loved for any discussion of holy unions and especially same-sex covenants or unions. I will not repeat here the arguments concerning the erotic intimacy of the relationship between Jesus and the man he loved. Rather, I will underscore three aspects of this relationship that may be of particular interest for our discussion. They are the apparently public or non-closeted character of the relationship; the apparent permanence of the relationship that not even death can end; and finally, the way in which the relationship restructures Jesus's "family relationships" in much the same way that marriage is thought to do.

---

44. William Countryman, *Dirt, Greed, and Sex: Sexual Ethics in the New Testament and Their Implications for Today*, revised ed. (Minneapolis: Fortress Press, 2007).

A Public Relationship

In the Gospel of John, the relationship between Jesus and the man he loved is depicted as being witnessed, known about, and accepted, at least by the members of Jesus's inner circle. This is typically most dramatically clear in terms of Peter's relationship to the man Jesus loved.

The "man Jesus loved" is first identified as such in the scene of that dramatic night we now know as The Last Supper. Jesus makes an enigmatic reference to the one who will betray him. The disciples are confused. Peter turns to the one closest to Jesus, thinking that physical intimacy might also entail special insight into Jesus's words. But the one whom Jesus loved knows nothing more that any other disciple. Peter has been mistaken. The point is that the physical intimacy of Jesus and this one is simply assumed and leads to other assumptions about their relationship—even if those turn out to be false in the end. It seems the physical proximity of Jesus and his beloved is a natural part of the pattern of interaction among the disciples.

This is underscored in other episodes. For example, Mary Magdalene finds Peter and the beloved together after the death of Jesus and tells them that Jesus has been raised. They race together to the tomb. This further suggests that Peter takes the relationship between Jesus and the beloved for granted, and has turned to the beloved for consolation following Jesus's death.

In the last episode in which the beloved appears, Peter supposes that he is to take on responsibility for the man Jesus loved as part of his commission to "feed the sheep" that Jesus will be leaving behind. Now all of this suggests that the relationship between Jesus and the man he loved was not closeted but was recognized by Jesus's circle of friends and associates.

This is, of course, what many gay and lesbian couples seek when they speak about same-sex marriage, holy unions or covenants. They seek ways in which their love for one another can be recognized and affirmed by their friends. Thus what weddings often do is provide an occasion for such recognition and affirmation.

Beyond Death

The last episode in the Gospel of John to which I have just referred is also one in which the permanence of the relationship between Jesus and his beloved is also affirmed. The risen Jesus has appeared on the beach as several of the disciples are out fishing. He is recognized by the beloved and there is then a reunion at the beach. There follows a long dialogue between Jesus and Peter with the beloved disciple as a silent witness. The dialogue has to do with Peter's responsibilities for the community of faith. Peter asks about the beloved and

Jesus says that the beloved is Jesus's own concern; Peter need not concern himself with the beloved. That is, even after the death and resurrection of Jesus, the personal relationship between Jesus and his beloved continues.

Indeed if, as is certainly possible, the beloved is Lazarus, then the relationship between Jesus and the beloved survives the death of each of them. In weddings we often say, "till death do us part." But here in the case of Jesus and his beloved it is clear that death does not end their relationship. Love is stronger than death.

One of the things that is at stake, I think, in the discussion of gay and lesbian marriage is precisely the insistence that, despite popular stereotypes to the contrary, not all gay and lesbian relationships are fleeting or ephemeral. The insight that the miracle of committed companionship throughout life, in a world in which everything is transient and relationships are fragile, ought to be welcomed and celebrated is one that holds true regardless of the gender of the partners.

Here in the depiction of the relationship between Jesus and the man he loved, even death could not finally break the hold of that love. When we recall that much of the impetus for the recognition of gay relationships came precisely because of the problems encountered by lovers with the approach of death, we see how important is the suggestion that the relational ties between lovers persist even in the face of death. This is why spouses are regarded as having a special claim to accompany the dying in their final hours and to have responsibility to care for the dead. What was so painful for many in the midst of the AIDS crisis was the denial of this most basic feature of committed relationship.

Restructuring Family

It is the scene of Jesus's death that is perhaps the most dramatic portrayal of the relationship between Jesus and the man he loved. He is the only man present among the women who are witnesses to Jesus's final hours. In this too, the love between Jesus and this man stands out from the relationships between Jesus and the other male characters in the narrative.

But our attention is drawn to his presence there in order to introduce the only word of Jesus directed toward those who are witnesses to his death. To the beloved, he says: Behold your mother. To his mother according to the flesh, he says: Behold your son.

This is a startling scene. As I said in *The Man Jesus Loved*, if Jesus had said to Mary of Magdala: Behold your mother, and then to his mother: Behold your daughter, we would undoubtedly conclude that the Magdalene was the beloved, the betrothed, the "wife" of Jesus. It would sound for all the world as if Jesus was commending his beloved to his mother and his mother to his beloved. Henceforth, they are to care for one another as the one who was son to one and lover to the other dies. Isn't that indeed what happens or ought to happen in those relationships we call "in-laws"? Isn't it the case that the relationship between lovers means that the beloved becomes, as we say, "part of the family"?

But the one to whom Jesus first addresses himself is not Mary of Magdala, nor a woman at all. He addresses his (male) beloved, the man he loved. Because of Jesus's love for this man, he becomes son to Jesus's mother, and she becomes mother to her son's beloved.

One of the ways of distinguishing a relationship that is called "marriage" from a relationship that is simply that of lovers is that the marriage relationship is one that restructures the family of origin, that has implications for that family, that should be acknowledged by the family of origin, and that imposes new roles and responsibilities upon family members. It is precisely that which seems to take place in this scene at the cross.

Whatever may be the case with the various legal implications of civil unions, my sense is that when people talk about gay and lesbian marriage, one of the things they are talking about is precisely this sort of acknowledgement.

This quick review of some of the episodes in the Gospel of John concerning Jesus and the man he loved suggests that this narrative offers a certain authorization for the aspirations of many same-sex lovers to have their relationships celebrated and affirmed by family and friends within the community of faith. Certainly if Jesus's presence at the wedding feast at Cana of Galilee in this same Gospel could be taken as warrant for Christian celebration of cross-sex relationships, then it is hard to see why the much greater place given to the relationship between Jesus and the man he loved should not be taken to warrant the Christian celebration of same-sex relationships that exhibit features of permanent commitment and shared responsibility.

A Medieval Reader: Aelred of Rievaulx

In this discussion, I have not said that Jesus and his beloved were married, any more than I have maintained that they were "gay." What I have said is that the way the relationship was depicted in the Gospel of John lends itself to encourage those who seek to have their loving commitments recognized and celebrated by their friends and family and affirmed by the followers of Jesus in the community of Jesus. Whether this is called "marriage" or something else is another matter.

The magnificent Yale historian John Boswell addressed this question in his last book and brought forward considerable evidence to suggest that same-sex relationships of deep and passionate (and possibly sexually mediated or expressed) friendship were no less honored in early and medieval Europe.[45] The various liturgies that John Boswell translates and discusses in his book as models of the blessing of same-sex relationships by the church would be quite relevant to this discussion and to the transformation of our ecclesiastical practices.

Furthermore, Boswell, in his ground-breaking work *Christianity, Social Tolerance, and Homosexuality*,[46] discusses the texts of Aelred of Rievaulx, a twelfth-century theologian of love and friendship. Remarkably, not only did Aelred understand the relationship between Jesus and the beloved as something like a "marriage," but he also supposed that this kind of relationship should actually serve as a model for both same-sex relationships and for what we would call heterosexual marriage. Let's take these in turn.

The "Marriage" of Jesus and "Saint John"

Aelred was the foremost interpreter of love and friendship in his day. Books like *The Mirror of Charity* and *On Spiritual Friendship* became two of the most influential medieval reflections on the themes of love and friendship. In these reflections, he has occasion to turn to interpretations of the relationship between Jesus and John and to describe this relationship as a kind of marriage. Aelred writes of this relationship as exuding "the fragrant secrets of the heavenly bridal chamber."[47]

Now this is especially remarkable when we recall that marriage, what we call heterosexual marriage, was not yet recognized as a sacrament of the church. We are still nearly a century away from marriage being defined as a sacrament. Indeed there are still rather strong misgivings about marriage among the increasingly celibate clergy and adherents of monastic orders. And Aelred was the abbot of such an order.

Thus when Aelred describes this relationship as a kind of marriage he is not saying that it is "just as good as marriage." Actually the argument works the other way: Since this relationship is a kind of marriage, then maybe marriage is okay. Pointing to the relationship between Jesus and John as a kind of marriage will make it possible for the church to think about blessing heterosexual or

---

45. John Boswell, *Same-Sex Unions in Premodern Europe* (New York: Villard Books, 1994). Mark Jordan provides a sympathetic but critical reading of Boswell's interpretation of the liturgical evidence in Mark D. Jordan, *Blessing Same-Sex Unions* (Chicago: The University of Chicago Press, 2005).

46. John Boswell, *Christianity, Social Tolerance, and Homosexuality*.

47. Aelred of Rievaulx. *Mirror of Charity* III.39.110 (Kalamazoo: Cistercian Publications, 1990), 299.

cross-sex relationships. It is really perhaps because of the value of same-sex relationships that Christians like Aelred accept heterosexual marriages at all. This is obviously the reverse of the logic of what we experience today when churches routinely bless cross-sex relationships but forbid the celebration of same-sex relationships. We have indeed lost our way.

The Transformation of Marriage

For Aelred the model relationships were same-sex relationships. The models were David and Jonathan, Jesus and John. He could have mentioned Ruth and Naomi, but alas did not. What was it about same-sex relationships that made them an appropriate model for, and even a legitimation of, cross-sex marriage?

In Aelred's day, heterosexual marriage was definitely a mixed bag. In addition to the many ways leading voices in Christendom had become deeply suspicious of any form of sexuality, there was also the problem that many of these relationships were simply marriages of convenience. This would be true in the aristocratic circles in which Aelred had moved before leaving the secular world to devote himself to God. Marriage was also a relationship of subordination in which the male simply owned the rights to the female.

In contrast, same-sex friendship was a relationship of mutuality in which the partners were drawn to one another and committed themselves to one another as equals. This made it possible to suggest that these relationships could and should be the model for heterosexual marriage. Thus Aelred remarks on the relation between male and female: "How beautiful it is that the second human being was taken from the side of the first, so that nature might teach that human beings are equal and, as it were, collateral, and that there is in human affairs neither a superior nor an inferior, a characteristic of true friendship."[48]

If we were to pursue this into our own day we might say that the celebration of same-sex unions would be a very important way to make clear that marriage is not a property relationship but a partnership relationship.[49] That is, the affirmation of same-sex unions serves the important purpose of transforming heterosexual relationships, of abolishing the relationship of domination and possession. Put another way, if we want heterosexual relationships to be relationships of genuine commitment and lifelong partnerships between equals, then the best way to foster that is by blessing same-sex relationships.

---

48. Aelred of Rievaulx, *Spiritual Friendship* I. 57, 63.

49. For a fine discussion of the transformation of wedding ceremonies in Judaism from property to partnership covenants see Rachel Adler, *Engendering Judaism: An Inclusive Theology and Ethics* (Boston: Beacon, 1998), 169-208.

And one is, I think, entitled to wonder whether the fervent opposition to same-sex unions in some segments of traditional Christianity does not arise precisely from a fear that heterosexual marriage will not be able to continue precisely as a relationship of ownership or of masculine domination. I will return to these questions below.

Questions and Implications

In order to address some of these questions, it is necessary to turn to the other side of the issue that I indicated at the beginning. So far I have drawn out some of the potentially favorable implications of the study of the Gospels for the celebration of same-sex unions. But as I mentioned at the beginning, there are a number of ways in which these same Gospels call into question what we think of as marriage and family values, which also may be helpful in relation to our contemporary discussion.

No Marriage in Heaven

One of the many texts from the Gospels that may be cited to illuminate the relation between the Jesus tradition and what may be termed the institution of marriage is one that comes from Jesus's series of confrontations with the power brokers of first-century Judea in the last day of his life. A version of this confrontation occurs in all three Synoptic Gospels, with some significant variations. I will begin with Mark's version. Jesus has already disposed of the priests and elders with respect to the question of authority, showing them up for lacking the authority to even ask him about his own authorization for the march on Jerusalem and the blockade of the temple. He has similarly disposed of the Herodians and Pharisees who sought to trap him with a question about taxes, revealing them as bumbling collaborators in the politico-economic system of empire. Now it is the turn of the Sadducees: Those who find the meaning of life in the inheritance of property and the production of progeny from the bodies of women have no use or need for the strange hope for the resurrection from the dead. They believe they have an unanswerable dilemma for those who do hope for the resurrection of the dead, that is for a resurrection of the bodies of the dead. The dilemma comes from the custom of Levirate marriage in which the death of a brother without progeny entails that another brother will seek to produce progeny from the body of the woman who had belonged to his deceased brother.

We have a remarkable tale about this custom from Genesis in the story of Tamar, who had been passed from brother to brother among the sons of Judah without bearing progeny—grandchildren, and so a future, for Judah himself. She solves the problem by posing as a cultic sex-worker and thus bears not grandsons but sons for Judah, thereby becoming the rather shady ancestress of all Judeans.

The Sadducees concoct a rather more extreme version of this story by having the woman pass from hand to hand through seven brothers. They then pose the question: In the resurrection of the dead, to which of the brothers will she belong? Note that the question is a question about property, specifically about the woman as private property, about the woman as the means of assuring a future for the dead by bearing them children in her not just borrowed, but privately owned, body.

This is a remarkable story, for, as Claude Levi-Strauss demonstrated in his seminal text, *Elementary Structures of Kinship*, the entire social order rests upon the exchange of women who are the very beginning of all private property.[50] Men own women and trade them to one another for the purpose of producing progeny who will continue the name and the property of the father.

We perhaps have forgotten that the basis of marriage and family values is the expropriation of women as property for men who through women produce progeny, another kind of property, in order to produce and inherit still more property. The Sadducees simply ask therefore to whom the woman will belong.

Jesus's answer is rather devastating in its effect: In God's reign inaugurated by the resurrection, there will be no ownership of women. There will be no giving or taking in marriage; that is, women will not be traded among men as private property.

Now it is one of the staggering facts of biblical blindness that interpreters have suggested that what Jesus means is that there will be no more sex in the resurrection. But that is not what the text says. It abolishes marriage as the ownership by men of women and their bodies and of course also their sexuality. But this doesn't mean the end of sex, or more generally, of the erotic. It merely means that marriage can no longer be restricted to the institution of the ownership of women's bodies and the instrumentalizing of their bodies for the production of progeny.

We may get a clearer sense of this if we recall that Jesus in these Synoptic traditions has also said something positive, if not about marriage, then about the union of desire and delight that brings people together in ties of gratitude and loyalty. For he is recalled as citing with approval (Mark 10:6-8) the saying in Genesis 2 that male and female are drawn to one another and cleave to one another and that this cleaving is of such force that the man even forsakes his

---

50. Claude Levi-Strauss, *Elementary Structures of Kinship*, trans. J.H. Bell and J.R. von Sturmer (New York: Beacon Press, 1971).

family of origin in order to cleave to one with whom he has become one flesh. This union of desire and delight is not itself questioned but rather affirmed by Jesus. Thus it is marriage as an institution and not the erotic attachment of people to one another that is abolished by the resurrection of the dead.

Perhaps this will also help us to see the sense in Jesus's attitudes toward adultery. On the one hand, Jesus is quite nonchalant about adultery in the legal sense: refusing to condemn the woman caught in the act and shaming her accusers into ignoring the biblical command to stone her; or even commissioning the Samaritan adulteress in John to be the first apostle to the Samaritans. Adultery, as legally defined, depends on the ownership of a woman's body by her husband. If another man encroaches upon the exclusive right of the husband to possess the woman's body, then he is an adulterer, and if the woman collaborates in this theft of her body from her husband, then she is an adulteress. Without the ownership of women's bodies by men, adultery is simply an impossible legal concept. (It does not help to compound the difficulty by making ownership of one another's bodies mutually reciprocal, since this merely disguises the structure of masculine domination while continuing to pervert relations between persons into relationships of property ownership.)

Indeed, adultery can only have new meaning if we transpose the question of adultery into a context of freely chosen commitment. Then the abrogation of such a commitment is a betrayal of another who has come to rely upon the loyalty of the other. And it is precisely this that Jesus denounces when he condemns the ways in which men absolve themselves from their freely chosen commitments in order to take possession of another woman's body.

On the other hand, in Matthew, Jesus redefines adultery as any attempt or even desire on the part of a man to take possession of a woman for his own uses—that is what looking at a woman lustfully means, after all. It is the first stricture against what in modern times is called "sexual harassment": treating others as objects of one's own desire without mutuality or consent.

The Lucan version of the conflict between Jesus and the Sadducees appears more radical in keeping with Luke's rather more severe strictures against marriage and family values. It is in Luke after all that Jesus says: "Whoever comes to me and does not hate father and mother, wife and children, brothers and sisters, yes, and even life itself, cannot be my disciple" (Luke 14:26). What Jesus says to the Sadducees is: "Those who belong to this age marry and are given in marriage; but those who are considered worthy of a place in that age and in the resurrection from the dead neither marry nor are given in marriage" (Luke 20:34-35). Now the plain meaning of this saying is that anyone who has hope of entering into the reign of God avoids the institution of marriage entirely. This is a saying about what it means to live now as if one hoped to enter into the life to come, the reign of God, the resurrection from the dead. Astonishingly, we are quite ready to ignore the clear teaching of Jesus on this matter, while insisting on following isolated scraps from Leviticus as the literal law of the church. This is surely a staggering example of sheer bad faith.

Again, let us recall that the problem is posed as one of possession or ownership and that marriage law is always and everywhere based upon, and in service to, property law. What is abolished by Jesus, at a minimum, is anything like traditional or conventional marriage. But does this mean that suspicion is cast upon the erotic or sexual character of human existence: Of course not, for salvation is not a repudiation, but a restoration, of creation.

An Alternative Model: Same-Sex Erotic Friendship

Our problem then is the following: We accept and celebrate the desire and delight that brings people together in love and mutual loyalty as an essential part of what makes us human. But we must reject the age-old structure of marriage as the ownership of women by men. Is there a model for relationships of desire and delight that does not depend on the structures of ownership of one person by another, that does not make the erotic subservient to questions of progeny and property, that is not unilateral domination at heart?

In antiquity even as today, the answer is that, yes, there is available such a model: the relationship between two persons of the same sex. In antiquity, this (idealized, to be sure) model was the relation between males, a relationship born of physical attraction and desire but which did not entail ownership of one by the other, or even of one another, nor did it aim at the use of sexual desire to create children as property or to assure the transmission of name and property. It was indeed what might rather be termed erotic friendship: producing lifelong companionship, loyalty and the encouragement to greater virtue and justice.

One of the ways one can see this taking shape is in the work of Plutarch. Like many other thinkers of the Hellenistic world, he produced a dialogue on love comparing the merits of same-sex vs. cross-sex relationships. And as is generally the case, the same-sex relationships come out as superior in terms of equality and mutuality. But Plutarch takes this a step further than most in that he seeks then to re-order marriage to reflect the values inherent in same-sex relationships, making of marriage something that has nothing to do with masculine domination or property, but rather the partnership of equals. This is a (partial) subversion of marriage and family values as these were instantiated in the legal structures of antiquity through the humanization (one might almost say the homosexualization) of marriage between a male and a female.

Is this not also what Aelred of Rievaulx does when he attempts to make the paradigm of Jesus and his beloved, or David and Jonathan, into a model for cross-sex (or heterosexual) relations, turning on its head the usual interpretation of Adam's rib to argue for the equality of the male and the female who then come together in mutual desire and delight? Of course Aelred could have even strengthened this argument by pointing to the biblical model of the relationship between Ruth and Naomi. So compelling a love story is their relationship that we sometimes use the words of Ruth in our wedding services:

> Do not press me to leave you or to turn back from following you
> Where you go I will go
> Where you lodge I will lodge
> Your people shall be my people
> And your God my God.
> Where you die I will die, there will I be buried
> May the Lord do thus and so to me, and more as well
> If even death parts me from you. (Ruth 1:16-17)

These words of commitment beyond death are spoken by one woman to another. Nor is the erotic element lacking, for the narrator uses the same word that Genesis 2 uses for the coming together of male and female: Ruth "cleaves" to Naomi. To be sure, the women must struggle to protect their love under the conditions of patriarchy, so they conspire to seduce old Boaz into providing shelter to Ruth, and so also to Naomi. And when a son is born, the village women rejoice that Ruth has given a son, not to Boaz, but to Naomi! Ruth is then recalled as the ancestress of David and in the Gospel of Matthew is listed along with Tamar, the cultic sex worker, Rahab, the prostitute, and Bathsheba, the adulteress, as ancestors of Jesus.

In *Jacob's Wound*, I suggest that the relationship between Ruth and Naomi serves as a parallel model to the more predominant male-male erotic and sexual attachments that proliferate in the literature of ancient Israel. More clearly than most of the male-male relationships in this literature, the relationship between Ruth and Naomi heralds a new and more just way for human beings to structure their erotic and sexual attachments. Furthermore, as I point out, the relationship between David and YHWH is also portrayed as a homoerotic romance ending in a sort of marriage that also includes the whole of David's people within the ambit of YHWH's steadfast love, a love that continues for the sake of YHWH's love for David. In other words, same-sex loving is not only a model for faithful marriages of all types but also of the divine-human relationship.

I think it fair to say that if heterosexual marriage is somewhat more humane today than in antiquity, it is precisely because of this homosexualization of marriage. That is, heterosexual marriage has already been positively transformed through the imitation of same-sex relationships. It is indeed only because of this transformation that one could dare to say an affirmative word about an institution so thoroughly rejected by the Jesus tradition.

Further, the rejection of same-sex unions is nothing other than an attempt to make marriage once again into the very institution repudiated by Jesus and the Gospels. It is an attempt to make women once again the private property of men, to make them to be the breeding cows of masculine pride and self-perpetuation. It is of course no accident that those who are today incensed by gay and lesbian unions are also those who suppose that men and institutions controlled by men get to tell women how their bodies must be made to serve men's interests, that choices about reproduction are to be made by men and their institutions, not by women themselves. The same voices insist that biological parents own their children, that biology trumps love in disputes about a child's welfare. They even sometimes claim that sexual harassment legislation is a woman's conspiracy against men (as if men had an inherent right to impose their sexual advances upon women).

That people maintain these things is not surprising, given the weight of traditions of male supremacy and domination. But that Christians lend their support to any of this can only be regarded as collective amnesia regarding the foundations of our faith in Christ. And this amnesia results in what may be termed apostasy from the Gospel of Jesus Christ.

Clearly, these reflections on the Bible and on church tradition are relevant for the question of the celebration of same-sex unions within the community of faith. At the same time, the critique of the social institutions of marriage and family in the Gospels makes me rather dubious of the entanglement of these blessings, whether of "gay" or "straight" relations, in the legal structures of what the state recognizes as marriage. Perhaps it is well past time for us to resolutely separate Christian marriage or union celebrations from the legal structures ordained and governed by the state.

Let me simply quickly indicate some of the cautions against an uncritical affirmation of same-sex unions, concerns that are rightly raised within the gay and lesbian community itself.

First, we must not so concentrate on the recognition of same-sex unions that we make them simply mirror images of straight relationships. This would mean missing the opportunity for gay and lesbian relationships to offer a transformative model for other relationships. Insofar as conventional marriage models ownership rather than friendship, or domination rather than equality, these models require the transformation offered by the celebration of same-sex relationships.

Moreover, there is a very real danger that the press for same-sex unions may have the unintended consequence of marginalizing those, whether gay or lesbian, who are not in such long-term committed relationships. It is already the case that the single are marginalized within congregations and society through the focus on family in the compulsory heterosexism of many of our institutions. It would be a bitter irony if the press for the recognition of same-sex unions only made this marginalization more severe.

There is finally a real danger that focusing attention on the question of long-term committed relationships will only serve to perpetuate the marginalization of other sexual styles within the gay and lesbian community. By trying to be equal to the heterosexual majority, it is quite possible that some gay and lesbian people, those who can successfully imitate heterosexual lifestyles, will join in devaluing the sexual lifestyles of other gay and lesbian people, indeed perhaps the majority of gay and lesbian people. A strategy of assimilation may wind up amputating from the community the majority of gay and lesbian people. This will only perpetuate the marginalizing of people for the practice of gay and lesbian sexuality. The Jesus tradition is remarkable for its refusal to condemn people because of unconventional sexuality. I fear that there is a real danger that the current struggle may find itself, even if successful, only echoing the sexual moralism of the church and society it wants to join.

It should be clear, then, that gay and lesbian people are divided over the question of marriage or holy unions, whether as a legal contract or as a religious celebration. One of my students, for example, who has been and continues to be in a long-term committed relationship with her partner, both of whom are also committed Christians, has nonetheless written essays that strongly oppose the efforts of LGBTQ people to normalize their relationships, either through legal contract or through religious ceremony. I mention this to make clear that on this issue it is not a matter of straight versus gay, but of finding ways in an ambiguous world to be faithful above all to the Gospel of God's redeeming and liberating love.

In a broken and fragmented world, there is every reason to celebrate the love that people find growing between them. The Jesus tradition that invites us to such a celebration also warns us against making our celebrations into a cause of suffering for those who are left out or excluded, and urges us to oppose ties that bind people into destructive structures of domination and division. The challenge that faces us then is to find appropriate ways of celebrating love without erecting new walls of division and domination.

Let me end with some fairly simple and, I trust, by now obvious theses for discussion. The traditions concerning Jesus as well as some of their antecedents in the literature of ancient Israel make it clear:

- that there is a much stronger case for celebrating same-sex unions than exists for the celebration of traditional heterosexual unions;
- that marriage as an institution of ownership and domination is abolished by the Jesus traditions;
- that the only way we could possibly affirm what is called marriage between a man and a woman is by also celebrating same-sex unions that model mutuality and freedom;
- that our refusal to celebrate same-sex unions while continuing to celebrate traditional marriage is a direct and open repudiation of the Gospel;
- that the celebration of unions between lovers in the community of faith must be rigorously separated from the legal institutions of marriage; and
- that any such celebration should take care not to marginalize either those who are not in such relationships, or those whose sexuality does not fit into this mold—that is, the celebration of love and loyalty must not become a new tool of oppression and division within the church that seeks to be faithful to Jesus.

If these statements are persuasive, the need to transform our practices around the celebration of both same-sex and cross-sex relations should be clear. And, joining in the struggle to make such changes, we may yet become a more faithful reflection of the mission and ministry of Jesus that makes love rather than law the measure of right relationship.

Chapter Five

The Trouble with Marriage

In the foregoing consideration of same-sex unions and their relation to heterosexual marriage, we have been focusing on the religious institution of marriage, rather than the civil institution currently sanctioned by the state. I have, in fact, argued that these should be separate, that religious celebration should be distinct from state involvement and sanction. And so we now return to a consideration of the civil, state-sanctioned institution of marriage.

As I indicated, much of the energy behind the push for state-approved marriage came from the trauma caused by AIDS in the gay and lesbian community. When the lack of rights associated with marriage came into focus, it became clear that there are in fact quite a large number of rights and privileges granted by the state to married persons that are not available to those who are not permitted to marry. Understandably, if unfortunately, then, LGBTQ political advocacy groups devoted a majority of their resources and energy towards winning access to state-sanctioned marriage for gay and lesbian couples as a matter of civil rights.

While I do not believe that it is at all justifiable for the state to grant the availability of rights and privileges to a sector of the population that happens to be heterosexual (that is, to those who, because they are heterosexual, may be able to marry) and to deny those rights to those who are not, this by itself need not mean that the extension of marriage rights is the only way to achieve the ends of a more fully democratic state.

A Queer Critique of Marriage Rights

In any consideration of same-sex marriage, it is important to listen to the perspectives of those who, in the name of queer affirmation, reject the politics of marriage. Of these, one of the most persuasive is Michael Warner in his book, *The Trouble with Normal: Sex, Politics, and the Ethics of Queer Life*. There are several difficulties with the way the LGBTQ movement has been taken over by the politics of marriage rights, he suggests. The first is that the determination to focus on marriage rights has actually been counter-productive. Just as Clinton's push to include gay and lesbian people in the military resulted in "Don't Ask, Don't Tell," so also the push for gay marriage resulted in the Defense of Marriage Act.[51]

But what if the movement to establish same-sex marriages were actually to succeed? The result, Warner suggests, would actually be catastrophic for queer sexuality. It would lend legitimacy to the view that sex without or outside marriage is a matter of reproach or shame. Thus it would function to further marginalize all those sexualities that do not conform to the current ideologies of marriage. He points out that this is not incidental. This is precisely the argument for gay marriage offered by church advocates like John Shelby Spong and by gay opinionators like Andrew Sullivan (110-13).

Warner notes that "marriage sanctifies some couples at the expense of others. It is selective legitimacy" (82). He refers to the French institution called PACS (pacte civil de solidarité) "that bestows benefits on households of all kinds, including cohabiting siblings" (85). The later development of this institution, endorsed by many French intellectuals, including Jacques Derrida, also includes insisting on doing away with the restriction to two; that is, a pact of civil solidarity, regardless of number or gender.[52] This sort of civil legitimacy (involving rights like inheritance and so on) would not discriminate between kinds of households. But marriage does. Warner notes that already in 1972 the National Coalition of Gay Organizations in the U.S. "called for repeal of all legislative provisions that restrict the sex or number of persons entering into a marriage unit and extension of the legal benefits to all persons who cohabit regardless of sex or numbers." He further notes that the Coalition called for "the elimination of tax inequities victimizing single persons and same-sex couples" (90). With the focus on the right of some to marry we have not exactly moved forward after fifty years!

Moreover, the agitation for same-sex marriage may simply take as a given the association of multiple societal and governmentally bestowed benefits on married as opposed to other relationships. Warner maintains that the best way to deal with this is to dismantle the packaging of such rights and privileges so that they can be distributed more fairly to single persons as well as persons who live in unconventional households (siblings, long-term companions, and so on).

In addition, there is the implicit—and sometimes explicit—message that people ought to want to "get married," that maturity, including sexual maturity,

---

51. Michael Warner, *The Trouble with Normal: Sex, Politics, and the Ethics of Queer Life* (Harvard: Harvard University Press, 1999), 128. Subsequent references to this text in this chapter will be given in-text.

52. Jacques Derrida, *Learning to Live Finally: The Last Interview*, trans. Pascale-Anne Brault and Michael Naas (Hoboken: Melville House, 2007), 42-44.

can take only this one form. Thus sexual styles that rupture the containment of stereotypically monogamous relations are regarded as illegitimate or shameful, or immature. But as Warner recalls, the point of gay liberation, before the marriage frenzy took hold in the '90s, was the affirmation of multiple and changing sexual styles and formations.

The difficulty here is that when LGBTQ people choose to marry, it may have unintended social effects: It stabilizes the invidious distinction between the married and those who have a different sort of relationship—polyamory, for example, or open marriage, or sexual friendships (that is, friends with benefits—one of many forms of what is quaintly called promiscuity). Moreover, seeking social respectability serves to further distance queer folk from disreputable sexual formations: sex workers and their clients, the single, the "underage."

I have argued that same-sex love is crucial for making what is called marriage. But it is by no means clear that it will have a similarly subversive effect if it assimilates to the institutionalized marriage of church and state. Indeed it is the association with the state that is especially problematic in Warner's view because of the myriad ways in which the state has come to supervise sexual life through a series of carrots (benefits for those who marry) and sticks (punishment for those who do not).

Warner points to the real effects of involving the state:

> As long as people marry, the State will continue to regulate the sexual lives of those who do not marry. It will continue to refuse to recognize our intimate relations—including cohabiting partnerships—as having the same rights or validity as a married couple. It will criminalize our consensual sex. It will stipulate at what age and in what kind of space we have sex. It will send the police to harass sex workers and cruisers. (90)

Moreover: "Even though people think that marriage gives them validation, legitimacy, and recognition, they somehow think it does so without invalidating, delegitimating, or stigmatizing other relations, needs, and desires" (99). He maintains he is not condemning those who get married but that "marrying should be considered an ethical problem" (107).

What, then, is possible? Warner suggests the following: One could insist on not only ending "the discriminatory ban on same-sex marriage" but this requires one also to:

> say that marriage is a desirable goal only insofar as we can also extend health care, tax reform, rights of intimate association extending to

immigration, recognition of joint parenting and other entitlements currently yoked to marital status. [We] would have to say that marriage is desirable only insofar as we can eliminate adultery laws and other status-discriminating regulations for sexuality. It might well also involve making available other statuses, such as expanded domestic partnership, concubinage, or something like PACS for property sharing households, all available both to straight and gay people alike (146).

This seems a reasonable approach. The difficulty will be that in order to get marriage equality, it is likely that these suggestions may receive, at best, only lip service. The value of Warner's approach is that he suggests not only that marriage is an ethical problem but also that there are obligations that fall upon those who pursue it. The struggle for marriage equality then carries with it the obligation to struggle to overcome the ways in which marriage will always tempt us to marginalize those on the outside.

This is something that already occurs. When in a church service those who have been married for several years are celebrated, it is virtually impossible for this not to be a judgment upon those who are not or who are no longer married. (Just as when we honor the women who are mothers on Mothers Day, we unintentionally marginalize all those women who are not mothers.) Ironically, this valorizing of a long-term committed relationships seems to occur at least as often in congregations in which lesbian and gay people are heavily represented. This is quite understandable, given the desire to counter the stereotype that same-sex relations are always and only promiscuous, but it may have the (unintentional) effect of marginalizing those who have not chosen to form their relationships after the model of something like marriage.

In the midst of all the excitement about same-sex marriage, it is important to find concrete ways to ensure that the possible victories in this regard do not allow us to overlook the profound moral ambiguities involved.

Warner's polemic may unfairly criticize those who have been engaged in the struggle for marriage equality by charging them with the unintended consequences of a one-sided emphasis on marriage. What is valuable about his perspective, however, is that it does suggest alternative avenues for exploration on the part of all who are concerned with a more just social order, whether or not marriage plays the dominant role in that agenda.

Domestic Partnerships

Recent events suggest that there may be a better way forward to move toward full civil rights for LGBTQ people that will also benefit non-LGBTQ people (thereby offering opportunities for building alliances) and will have a less harmful effect on persons for whom marriage may not be an option.

In 2009, voters in Maine overturned a legislative act that would have opened marriage to same-sex couples. This came as something of a surprise—as well as a bitter disappointment—for marriage advocates, since Maine has a reputation for approaching these issues with a "live and let live" attitude (the same voters approved a significant relaxation of drug laws regarding the use of marijuana, for example). It seems clear that marriage equality has been extended primarily through court and legislative action and that it is much more difficult to win in the realm of a direct popular vote. In fact, thirty states have managed to outlaw same-sex marriage, often by way of constitutional amendments supported by popular vote.

At the same time, voters in Washington State approved an extension of rights to same-sex partners in domestic partnerships. The absence of the word "marriage" may have facilitated this victory. In the months following the election of Barack Obama, the federal government moved to increase the rights of same-sex couples in domestic partnership arrangements within its ranks, extending to them many of the same benefits that are associated with marriage. These moves have not provoked a significant outcry against the erosion of marriage and family values.

What can we learn from these developments? Is it possible that the emphasis on marriage has worked against the goal of extending rights to some LGBTQ people, while at the same time further marginalizing those for whom marriage is not an attractive or even viable option? This has by no means been the intention of most of those who have struggled for marriage equality. Many have been engaged in this struggle at great cost to themselves and to the movements and churches which they represent, and they have often had to bear the brunt of the homophobic reaction that meets any attempted advance in the rights and recognition of lesbian and gay people.

Perhaps a more effective strategy would be to promote domestic partnerships within the sphere of civil society while leaving the question of marriage to the religious sphere, where it may in fact better belong. In the thirty states where marriage has come to be exclusively defined as relationships constituted by one woman and one man, there still may be significant opportunity to open discussion about domestic partnerships inclusive of LGBTQ persons. Such partnerships are not specifically forbidden by law, and many major corporations already offer substantial benefits to domestic partnerships and thus could be allied to the struggle. Moreover, such an emphasis would include non-LGBTQ persons and so allow for the building of alliances with members of the heterosexual majority.

Further, this strategy could build on growing sentiment for non-discrimination against LGBTQ persons. There was a very strong popular support for extending hate crimes legislation to protect LGBTQ persons, and the U.S. House of Representatives was able to pass non-discrimination legislation as well (the Employment Non-Discrimination Act, or ENDA) which also enjoys majority support in the general population. (The Senate, as usual, has stalled out even though ENDA seems to enjoy majority support.) The hate crimes bill as well as ENDA not only have enjoyed significant popular support, but also benefit all LGBTQ persons, not just those who seek to be conventionally married.

Building on ENDA would make it possible to strengthen the rights and privileges that can be associated with domestic partnership arrangements. For example, health benefits are not currently taxed for married couples, but are for domestic partners. Joint tax return advantages, such as they are, are restricted to married couples. These and other privileges could be extended under the rubric of non-discrimination to domestic partners, including same-sex relationships. The goal, then, is to increase the availability of domestic partnership status to a variety of households while more widely distributing the rights and privileges currently attached to marriage at the state and federal levels.

Ultimately, domestic partnerships could be extended in something like the way contemplated in the French movement toward PACS in that a variety of arrangements might be covered. For example, when siblings, such as two unmarried women who are sisters, choose to live together, they could be partners in the meaning of the law. This separates partnership from any necessary connection with sexual expression. Moreover, adult children could be similarly covered.

But this may allow even further modification. For example, I know women who are unrelated but have chosen to live together over many years. They do not identify as lesbian and their relationship is probably not sexually expressed. (Whether it is, is of course nobody's business but theirs.) One such couple I know in California has been together since they were college roommates nearly sixty years ago. They are now able to live together in a nursing home. Almost certainly they have never had "sex," but even so, their relationship, and others like it, is a domestic partnership that should have available state protections and guaranteed rights.

From this, it is not too big a leap to include domestic relationships that are not restricted to two people. Why shouldn't people enter into civil partnership arrangements of three or more? At one end of the spectrum we could have parents and an adult child, or a parent and two or more adult adopted or biological children. (Bear in mind that recognized households already include underage children, and health care legislation now includes them up to twenty-six years of age.)

But what of other arrangements? In my home, we have had young adults who become a part of our family. Some of these are short-term arrangements, but others are domestic relationships that last for years. Again, the question of sexual expression does not enter the discussion. But the possibility of extending, for example, health benefits, education benefits, or tax benefits (or even immigration rights) would be a great advantage to many people in longer-term and committed relationships that may not look like marriages but entail similar emotional, financial and other types of healthy human bonds.

The point here is that it is possible to extend the notion of "family" to include people we choose rather than only those to whom we are biologically fated. In the Gospels, Jesus is recalled to have responded to the members of his "biological family" who sought to have him reinstated in the institution of family for his own good by saying, "Who are my mother and brothers and sisters?" (This was not a reassuring question for the family members who thought he was out of his mind.) And then Jesus continued in similarly perplexing fashion, saying of the motley crew following him and listening to his teachings: "These are my mothers and sisters and brothers." Certainly the experience of many lesbian and gay people is that their real family is made up of friends and lovers who share experiences and values and commitments that together constitute a life-giving and life-enhancing bond.

Much of society, not only lesbian and gay people, might benefit greatly by a more ample understanding of what makes a family, or, as we are now saying, what constitutes the basis of a domestic partnership. Moreover, this would assist those who live within "conventional" nuclear families (a minority of the U.S. population) to sense solidarity with those who also struggle with the commitments of family life outside the conventional norms.

To return to where we began, a movement to broaden and strengthen domestic partnership legislation may have greater chance for success than the current focus on marriage rights. This does not necessarily mean an end to the struggle for marriage rights. There is evidence to suggest that once domestic partnerships inclusive of LGBTQ persons are accepted, then there is greater support for the expansion of marriage rights. For those who want marriage at all costs, this could actually be a pretty good short-term strategy. At the same time, it would be possible to broaden the appeal of the struggle to include numbers of others who might benefit from strengthened domestic partnership possibilities.

Such a project would go a long way toward answering the question raised by Warner about marriage as an ethical problem. For such a movement would seek to extend rights outside the conventional marriage bond rather than stigmatizing those who remain outside.

Trouble for Heterosexuals, Too

As I hope the previous discussion has made clear, heterosexual marriage as traditionally constituted is itself beset by ethical as well as theological problems. These problems have first of all to do with the property structure that serves as the background assumption of the marriage contract. Much of the advance in ethical understanding has to do with the growing sense that persons should not be understood as another person's private property. The abolition of slavery crucially depends upon this insight. And the advances in the rights of women are also dependent upon the recognition that men must not be understood as the owners of women as private property.

However, in the case of heterosexual monogamy and relationships that take this structure to be paradigmatic, it is commonly supposed that one party has exclusive rights to the other person's sexual expression and practice. Originally it was only the male who owned the sexuality of the female. This is the supposition of the various legal codes concerning adultery in ancient Israel, for example. This also appears to be true of virtually all other cultures as well. (The situation is unchanged in the case of polygamy, where the male has ownership of the sexual expression of the women under his control.)

One of the most significant changes in the understanding of this relationship was to make the ownership of another's sexuality reciprocal. That is, today we tend to think of the marriage bond as entailing that each person has exclusive rights to the sexual expression and practice of the other (except perhaps in cases of masturbation, where one of the parties has the right to sexual enjoyment of her or his own body). The violation of this assumption is typically called adultery. The official remedy for this ownership of one's sexual expression by one's spouse is divorce, which has accordingly become extraordinarily common wherever it has been made legally and socially acceptable.

The prevalence of divorce, however, is but one of the indications that marriage is, as some LGBTQ activists maintain, a failed institution. Marriage, as traditionally practiced, has also been recognized as a scene of violence, both physically and otherwise. The incidence of spousal abuse (typically the violence directed against women by their husbands) as well as the very high incidence of the sexual abuse of children (again, perpetrated most often by their male "owners" or fathers) show that something is terribly wrong with this institution. It is therefore not difficult to justify the extremely critical view of marriage and family that we see in the New Testament Gospels.[53]

These are not the only signs that something is amiss in our understanding and practice of marriage. The marriage contract as commonly understood may be constantly violated even when there is no divorce or violence. Laura Kipnis in her *Against Love* points to the extraordinarily common practice of some sort of "adultery" as well as the perhaps even higher incidence of suspicion that "something" may be going on.[54] Here there may be even more than the structure of implicit ownership at work. It may also have to do with suppositions about the significance of romantic love.

The idea of romance as the basis of marriage is itself rather odd. In the West, the ideal of romantic love began as an explicitly anti-marriage sentiment. The troubadours of the Middle Ages sang of the joys of romantic love as the desire for a person who was "off-limits" in terms of the marriage contract. It was, in short, a celebration of adultery. (Think of the love triangle of Arthur, Guinevere, and Lancelot.) It was perhaps a significant advance when persons were enabled to choose their own life partners without the intervention of extended families. But one must say "perhaps" here, since in many cases still today persons who have had their marriages "arranged" are often no less satisfied by their relationships than those who have chosen for themselves. In modern India, it seems relatively common for young adults to enjoy the freedoms afforded by city life and multiple relationships, while at the same time assuming that one day they will settle down into an arranged marriage.

In some modern Asian cultures, I have been assured, most spouses simply quit having sex with one another soon after any children are born. Sexual fulfillment, if any, is found outside of that bond. Might it be the case that the lifelong partnership of a "marriage" with or without children is itself a good thing, aside from the expectations of romance, sexual adventure, and so on? To what extent is the mixing of expectations of companionship and partnership (perhaps in child raising but also in life projects) with those of romance and sexual fulfillment itself a recipe for the disasters of broken homes or the mutual recrimination and suspicion that plague even marriages that "last"?

If there is any truth in this questioning of marriage assumptions, it might be the case that talk of "domestic partnerships" rather than of marriage, with all the suppositional baggage that entails, might also be liberating for heterosexuals, and thereby prompting discussions of open relationships and polyamory.

---

53. For a discussion of the critique attributed to Jesus in all of the Gospels, see my *The Man Jesus Loved*.

54. Laura Kipnis, *Against Love* (New York: Pantheon Books, 2003).

Chapter Six

Beyond Marriage

In this chapter we will discuss two of the ways in which it is possible to think "outside the box" with respect to lifelong committed relationships. First, we will look at open marriage, a way for a lifelong commitment to be intentionally inclusive of other sexually mediated relationships. We will then turn to the discussion of what is sometimes called polyamory. As we will see there is some overlap in these two ways of trying to think and act beyond marriage, as well as important differences, but both entail a common sense of the importance of lifelong committed relationships.

Open Relationships

In the discussion of marriage we have come upon the problem or issue of marriage as "possession" of another's sexuality or sexual activity. The move toward a model based not on private property but on partnership and friendship raises the question of primary relationships that do not preclude either or both partners from engaging in additional sexually expressed relationships. Where this is an opening to similarly long-term and somewhat exclusive relationships, we are dealing with what is called polyamory, which we will subsequently discuss. But where the additional or supplementary sexually mediated relationships are of a distinctly different sort than the primary relationship we may best use the term "open relationships."

To put it another way, open relationships are those in which two persons form a long-term and committed relationship yet leave space for additional sexual expression for one or both partners of a lower degree of commitment. Where heterosexual couples are concerned, the literature has often characterized this as "swinging." Sometimes this involves another couple, or sometimes one or both partners have additional relationships.

The challenge of such relationships is that they be developed in ways that do not adversely affect or threaten the primary commitment. Often people speak of "fidelity," but what is at stake here is the meaning of fidelity or faithfulness. Obviously we suppose that one can be a faithful friend to more than one friend. But is the faithfulness involved of a different order when the friendships are sexually expressed?

In some circles we are dealing with what at least used to be called "adultery," that is, sex outside and alongside the primary affectional bond, especially if this is normalized by church and/or state. (Astonishingly, there are states in which adultery remains a crime!) Raja Halwani notes that "All such relationships are adulterous; they all involve at least one spouse engaging in sexual activity with someone other than his or her spouse, and this, no matter how one defines 'sexual activity,' is adultery."[55] But he adds, "Adultery is not wrong by definition, even if the word has negative connotations." The problem rather comes when adultery involves deception or lying.[56] Thus, if we remain wed to the language of adultery, in "open" relationships, we are speaking of something like "consensual adultery."[57]

The difference between what has conventionally been represented as adultery and the open—or better, hospitable—relationship, lies in the transparency that is necessarily involved here. It is not a unilateral or a hidden decision. If it is to work, it requires a very difficult level of honesty and trust and risk. For many folk, this will simply not be possible. The intimacy and vulnerability that often goes together with a primary bond of sexually expressed love is something that lovers learn to depend upon for emotional stability, comfort, and solace. Primary bonds entail a degree of interdependence (hopefully not what is sometimes diagnosed as 'co-dependence'), such that even when they "go bad" and end in divorce, the pain of separation can be quite horrific.

We are trained to suppose that engaging in extramarital relations is a threat to that primary bond or a precursor to its dissolution. The need to possess another person is strongly embedded in our ways of institutionalizing love and in our ways of fantasizing about it. We are taught to suppose that fidelity entails exclusivity.

To venture beyond this way of thinking requires considerable trust in one another, and this means that transparency is a must. It means that when partners decide upon embarking on such a course they need to understand fully one another, trust one another, and keep communicating with one another. Of course, it helps if this is something that has been talked about and understood

---

55. Halwani, *Virtuous Liaisons*, 226.

56. Halwani, *Virtuous Liaisons*, 227.

57. Halwani chooses to develop his views in dialog with the position of Bonnie Steinbock, "Adultery" in *The Philosophy of Sex: Contemporary Readings* 2nd edition, ed. A. Soble (Lanham: Rowman and Littlefield, 1991). Steinbock argues against the possibility of open relationships in this essay and Halwani takes her as making a cogent case that must be contested.

together from the very beginning of the relationship. It is very much more difficult to move from a closed to an open relationship. This is sometimes considered to be a relative failure of the initial commitment, a diminishment of its intensity or primacy. This may especially be true if one but not both partners have the view that extramarital sex is necessary for sexual fulfillment. Others may, as Halwani notes, "believe that being sexually monogamous is a way of conforming to socially oppressive norms, and so the spouses attempt to lead their relationship in nonconformist ways. And what better way is there than nonmonogamy."[58]

Testimony:

> I have been in a faithful, committed, and open relationship for more than thirty years. I think our relationship is much stronger because it has been open to other sexually expressed relationships from the very beginning. It has not been easy. Sometimes it has been very scary for each of us, in different ways and at different times. But it was an integral part of our commitment to one another from the beginning. It even made its way, surreptitiously, into our wedding vows: We promised to make our relationship a hospitable place for other friendships; our friends knew what the words meant, but our mothers did not. And there have been differences: She rolls her eyes at my enjoyment of football in much the same way she rolls her eyes when I spend a night at the gay baths. How can you do that? she asks with puzzlement—and some disdain. Must be a guy thing, I reply. We are both what is sometimes called "bisexual," that is, our attractions and desires are not very predictable but fluid, changing, diverse. She has a healthy libido, but I have had a rather excessive one. We have each had to wrestle with fears of abandonment, but we have done so together. If a relationship with another person went beyond the initial encounter, we have both welcomed the other person into our home and friendship. Our lives have each been enriched by friendships with the other's sexual friendships. When bad things have happened (and over the course of so many years they are bound to)—the death of the man I loved for me, the ending of a long-term sexual friendship for her—we have been there

---

58. Halwani, *Virtuous Liaisons*, 228.

for one another knowing that we could depend on one another no matter what. In all of this we have had to make it up as we went along; none of our friends have done this, and we have no role models. But for all these years, we have made a point to go out to dinner once a week to talk over our lives. At first we did this so that we would have to get out of bed, put on our clothes and behave in public while we talked. But it also became the indispensable way to make sure we have the time and place to say: This is what is happening in my other relationships (if there are any at the time); this is how it seems to me, how does it seem to you? Every week, for more than thirty years.

Part of the problem has to do with illusions about what is possible in a primary relationship. Lovers sing romantic phrases such as "you are my everything" while gazing into each others' eyes, but most realize the absurdity. No person could possibly meet all of one's emotional or affectional needs. In heterosexual partnerships, men generally need their night out with the guys, and women, perhaps even more, need the emotional support of circles of girlfriends. Through work or other activities, we also tend to develop social groups comprised of both men and women. Couples develop sets of friends that sometimes overlap and sometimes do not. And this is actually healthy, for placing upon one other person the burden of being the whole of one's relational life means making impossible demands.

This may even extend to the sexual expression of relationships, either as an extension of intimacy of friendship or simply as a way of having sexual adventure that supplements, without supplanting, the primary bond.

How might this be negotiated? One of the challenges is that of signaling the ongoing primacy of the primary bond. How is this to be achieved? For some, this will mean that if there are to be additional sexual outlets or experimentation, this be something that they always do together or not at all. Maybe this means exchanging partners with a friendly couple, participating in a sex club, hiring a sex worker, cruising together, or sharing together with a friend. The first of these are more common for heterosexual couples, others work fine with same-sex partnerships or those in which one or both are bisexual.

In some cases, the primacy of the bond is expressed by limiting outside relations to one-night stands, anonymous (public sex) venues, or commercial sex. This seems to be the preferred case in the discussion offered by Halwani. In other cases, there may be greater flexibility about levels of duration and personal involvement, which may open the door to possible forms of polyamory.

What are the ethical issues here? As I have indicated, it is essential that there be honesty and transparency between the primary partners. But this also means honesty with those others with whom one becomes sexually involved. There must be no illusions about the character of the primary bond. This often will make potential lovers very nervous. They may have a strong desire to have their own primary bond and decide that they don't want to be "second fiddle" or supplemental. Thus there is a cost when it comes to honesty with persons outside the primary bond.

While it is important that the partners in a primary bond be open with one another, it may not be necessary that they wind up with the same rules or guidelines. They may, for example, have very different levels of need for sexual experimentation. One may like to do this a lot, the other only a little; one may be comfortable with the other partner having relations only with persons of the same sex as their partner, the other without such a limit. The point is that the partners in a primary relationship don't have to be the exactly the same in their other relationships as long as they are open with one another about what they are doing and how it supplements, without supplanting, the primary bond.

A life together of this sort is one of constant improvisation, of continual communication and, though I hate to use this word, of continual re-negotiation. It requires time to regularly check in with one another and test how the other person is feeling about one's other relations, trying to be honest about what is going on and open to discover that there are new limits or new desires. Of course, there are things a partner may not need or want to know. There is such a thing sometimes as too much information, but you know this only by checking in. And that means that the other person gets to ask questions, sometimes searching ones, and that you try to be as honest as possible with yourself, with your partner and with the other parties to your sexual life.

Testimony:

> I didn't have sex until I was twenty-four years old. I was no prude, but I also wasn't willing to risk a good marriage and eternal damnation for a little sex. That's not to say I wouldn't have naked time with many a male friend, often with a good deal of touching, licking, hugging, and (depending on how powerful I wanted to feel) sucking. But sex? The real kind— the "penis in vagina" kind? No, couldn't do that until marriage. God and mom said so. And so it was that I made it to age twenty-four before I did the deed (We jumped the gun a little. I

figured God would understand if I did it while engaged). And so it was that I was married at twenty-five to the only man I'd ever had sex with.

Now I am twenty-nine, have been married for four years, and have sex with other people in addition to my beautiful husband. How it came to be that we opened our marriage is a longer story than can be transcribed here, but the gist is this: Seminary has taught me not to accept just any idea that comes your way, no matter how many people before you have. No idea is created in a vacuum and some of them are just plain bad ideas (not that marriage or monogamy are bad ideas; they are fine choices if they are indeed choices). I've often heard that a childlike wonder is a necessary component of spiritual life. I've found it horribly helpful when exploring societal norms and expectations. "Why?" has become, once again, my favorite question.

So why did I wait until marriage to have sex? And why should I only share my body with my husband? And why should I have dominion over his? And why is it assumed that extramarital sexual activity is inherently evil? We do not lie to each other. We do not keep secrets. We do not have to pretend to be anything other than what we are with each other. I have seen marriages fail. I have witnessed the secrecy of affairs, the painful agony that accompanies finding out that you're not the only one in her life, the debilitating guessing game of "Is he cheating on me?" That, my friends, is the concept of marriage that I was introduced to and saved my body for. I am thankful that I was awoken to new concepts and encouraged to childishly ask "Why?" of my life because that is not the marriage that I will damn my future with.

Like the student who came to reconsider what makes a marriage, Warner notes that in debates about sex:

the implication tends to be that those who favor sex, especially casual sex, are opposed by those who favor romantic love. But queer culture is the last place where this opposition should be taken for granted. One of its greatest contributions to modern life is the discovery that you can have both: intimacy and casualness; long-term commitment and sex with strangers; romantic love and perverse pleasure.[59]

Warner also cites *The Male Couple: How Relationships Develop* by David P. McWhirter and Andrew Mattison. In this study of 172 male couples, none of those who had stayed together five years or more were totally monogamous.[60] He also cites Carol Card, who reports a trend among some lesbians of "more than one long-term intimate relationship during the same time period."[61]

If the male couple example may lean more toward some variation on the open relationship model, the lesbians reported by Card may lean toward the polyamory model. But this doesn't mean that all male coupled relations are open, nor does it mean that no lesbian relations are.[62]

I am trying to emphasize the value of the attempt to get beyond jealousy that springs from the fear of abandonment. What living on the basis of such a fear robs us of is the continual surprise and the gift of the other person in our lives, a presence that is not controlled or taken for granted, but received for what it is: an astonishing gift, new every day, yet at the same time indispensable.

The confusion of love with private property runs very deep. If it were easy to break that connection, a lot more folk would have done so already. This is yet another arena in which same-sex love may be able to overcome some of the ways in which the privileging of marriage may marginalize other sexual lifestyles. It may also be a way in which lovers become more than lovers; lovers may become, as well, best friends.

Polyamory

Polyamory is another way in which the convention of monogamy comes into question. Polyamory involves the question of the viability of engaging in more than one primary committed, long-term relationship during the same period of time.

---

59. Michael Warner, *The Trouble with Normal*, 73.

60. David P. McWhirter and Andrew Mattison *The Male Couple: How Relationships Develop* (Englewood Cliffs: Prentice Hall, 1984), 252 -259; cited in Warner, *Trouble with Normal*, 172.

61. Carol Card, "Against Marriage and Motherhood," *Hypatia* 11.3 (Summer 1996): 8.

62. Warner also indicates the existence of porn stores catering to lesbians and of radical lesbians who are promiscuous for periods of their lives: *Trouble with Normal*, 152.

In the West, and increasingly in industrial democracies of Asia, the prevalence of divorce has led to what some call "serial monogamy," in which persons move from one marriage to another. While about half of all marriages in the U.S. (and other western countries) end in divorce, a much higher percentage of divorces end in marriage. The values of long-term committed relationships as a context for intimacy and nurturing of life seem to be more deeply ingrained than divorce statistics would suggest. At the same time, the ease with which society and many religious groups have accommodated themselves to divorce and remarriage suggests that people are not as governed by religious tradition and authority in this connection as their views about same-sex love might lead one to expect. One agitator for same-sex marriage has indeed proposed that in those states that prohibit same-sex marriage that ballot measures be introduced (with religious arguments adduced) to ban divorce, or at least remarriage. This would at least have the advantage of exposing the utter hypocrisy of those who forbid same-sex marriage on religious grounds (something on which the New Testament is silent) while permitting divorce and remarriage (which the Jesus tradition seems to strictly and explicitly forbid).

In the case of divorce and remarriage, we have not only serial monogamy, but also something like a sort of extended polyamory distributed across time. One person falls in love with and enters into committed relationship with more than one person in the course of a lifetime.

In more traditional societies, there has been a tendency to suppose that men (and, in a few cases, women) may have more than one spouse at the same time. With respect to ancient Israel, for example, the patriarchs and the kings seem to have regularly engaged in what is called polygamy. Abraham with Sarah and Hagar is one example, Jacob/Israel with several wives by which he fathered the twelve tribes of Israel is another, and then there is David, and above all Solomon, for whom the numbers approach the astronomic. The change from a permitted polygamy to an expectation of monogamy comes not from the emergence of Christianity but from Christianity's adoption of Roman custom and law. In turn, Roman law applied basically only to elites (other people's living arrangements were not supervised by the state) and even then permitted secondary wives as regulated under laws of concubinage. Judean custom adopted Roman custom and this served as the background for Christianity's adoption of monogamy as its way of thinking about marriage.

Islam, which arose in a later and distinct cultural sphere in which polygamy was widely practiced, limited polygamy to four wives. This may have had to do with making sure that the wealthy and powerful did not have a monopoly on women. When Islam entered African traditional cultures, which had wider polygamy practices, Islam imposed the limit of four, while Christianity sought to impose the limit of only one wife.

In Islam, wives are not regarded only as the property of the male. There are expected to be bonds of affection, respect, and shared endeavor among the wives. Nevertheless, it is only males who may have more than one spouse and the rootage of marriage in property law has not been abolished. Women are still regarded as the property of fathers and husbands, and adultery on the part of the woman is often punished by stoning (as is also required under the laws of the Torah). The literal application of this law in some contemporary Islamic states has been the occasion of outrage. In Pakistan, for example, there seems to have been strong revulsion against the Taliban when it carried out this punishment. (I mention Pakistan in order to make clear that this is not merely a matter of western views vs. Islamic ones, but indicative of a divide within Islam itself.)

The basis for the persecution of Mormons in the nineteenth century was precisely their permission of polygamy, and most Mormons have adjusted their beliefs and practices to conform to the U.S. prohibition of polygamy. I am completely unclear how the government handles the situation of visitors from Muslim or traditional societies in this regard, but immigrants must conform to U.S. law rather than to traditional social arrangements or religiously permitted relationships in Islam, for example. In my own view, the prohibition of religiously sanctioned polygamy (on the part of Muslims or Mormons) is very difficult to justify. At the very least, it is an infringement on religious liberty as well as liberty of conscience. Perhaps there is an opportunity here for a very odd alliance between queer folk and those most often thought to be their enemies.

Contemporary discussions of polyamory, however, are not attempts to argue for polygamy or even polyandry as traditionally practiced. The "poly" in this case means more than two people in a relationship. But it turns decisively away from the notion of property and especially the idea of male property rights with respect to women. Polygamy has traditionally meant the right of the male to control or "own" the sexuality of more than one woman. But the idea of control or ownership is replaced in this term by the idea of love (hence, poly-amor-y).

The love that is being emphasized here entails, first, that all parties to the relationship freely choose the relationship and have equal rights and responsibilities. Thus the exclusive right of one party to the relationship (the male) to initiate and terminate the relationship, or to dictate its terms (with the approval of the social order established by and for men) is replaced with notions of freedom, mutuality, and equality.

In general, then, polyamory will mean that more than two persons enter into a committed and faithful relationship that is expected to endure through time. This appears at first to be similar to what actually happens in many families with the addition of children. The difference here is that the relationship(s) are open to non-coercive, freely chosen sexual expression. The relationships are entered into by persons capable of choosing the relationship who are not typically related to one another through a traditional family structure.

Testimony:

> One day, I announced to my partner, "I think I am in love with someone else, but I don't want to leave you. I want a relationship with another person." Serial monogamy is one thing, but this request crossed into the new territory of polyamory. The new relationship led me half-way across the country to various cities and hotel rooms every four to six weeks to meet my new lover.
>
> Both therapists and friends asked, "What do you need in these relationships?" It was an appropriate question for which at the time I could not produce a coherent answer. Two years later, as my new lover and I began to part ways, two things came to the forefront: home and family. By addressing these issues, the ethical concerns of relational needs began to emerge. First, intellectual and sexual compatibility is attractive, yet due to my emotional disposition, I discovered a home base creates a foundation. I longed for "hearth and home" to legitimize the relationship. Secondly, as my partner and lover vied for relational primacy, I discovered my lack of jealousy and ability to remain emotionally engaged with both. The triangulated conflict demonstrated ways my separate relationships created an extension of my affectional self, and formed a type of family unity, albeit in competition with one another.
>
> Equipped with a better idea of my relational (sexual, intellectual, and emotional) needs, I am presently building relationships with a couple to form a family unit. The goal of the relationships includes individual relationships, alongside a relationship as a triad. We are presently forming relationships of mutual respect, love, and shared and individual space. This is not an easy

endeavor, yet all three of us share the same vision and values of a polyamorous loving home and family.

What is different here from the families we know traditionally is that the relationships are chosen by all parties and, it is supposed that they will be sexually expressed relationships.

In our previous discussion of the trouble with marriage, we noted that there are lesbians who have more than one stable committed relationship at a time. For purposes of illustration, we may suppose that the commitment means that the sexual relationship of person *a* to persons *b* and *c* are closed relationships and that moreover *b* and *c* may or may not also be sexually involved with one another. What if the relationship is an open one? In that case, the commitment to one another of the parties to this polyamorous relationship would not preclude some other sexually expressed relationship distinguished from the primary relational triad. In fact, this may be the way the relationship developed. It may have begun as a dyad and, through openness to other sexually expressed relationships, found it appropriate to include another person who had in the meantime become a lover of one or both of the members of the original dyad. The result, in any case, is a triad or polyamorous relationship.

Or take the case of a woman who is in a relationship with another woman and becomes involved with a man as well. It may be that only the first woman finds the male sexually attractive but the second woman has no objection to the relationship between the man and the first woman. This opens up another sort of triad made possible by the "bisexuality" of the first woman.

Let us consider another case: A man is married to a woman and discovers that he sexually attracted to other men. In many cases, such a discovery has resulted in divorce, sometimes even more or less amicably. But what if it does not end in divorce? What if both partners agree to make space for the man to have relationships with other males, even including the possibility of finding a male partner in addition to the female partner? In this case the first "marriage" would continue, and if the man were bisexual, then his relationship to both partners would be open to sexual expression. The woman would be able to determine whether this meant an opening for sexual expression with other folk (including perhaps the man's new partner) or not. This would be something they would all have to work out or improvise.

Another example: Two persons form a committed dyad that is nonetheless an open relationship. One of them, say the man, winds up having a relationship with a man, who is not interested sexually in women, but who nonetheless becomes a part of the household. Say that the woman has a relationship with a woman and this also becomes an enduring relationship that also constitutes a household. In this case we end with four people in a nexus of committed and sexually expressed relationships but the sex occurs only in dyads.

Let us take this somewhat more complicated relationship (without supposing that it cannot be further complicated). The sexually expressed relationships are what we might think of as romantic relationships, while the relationships that aren't sexually expressed are more like friendship or even adoptive relationships.

If we ask about civil society, we may see that here we can suppose the possibility of domestic partnerships of the sort I discussed previously. That is, the persons would form a household or domestic partnership irrespective of the sexual dimension of some but not all of the relationships sheltered in this household. The financial and other benefits associated with domestic partnership (up to and including all those currently associated with marriage) could be attributed to all those within this household, if the parties all agreed.

What about religious celebration? It is becoming increasingly common for persons to seek ritual recognition of polyamorous relationships of the sort I have been describing. In some cases, relationships that have been celebrated as dyads subsequently come to be polyamorous through the addition of one or more persons to the relational complex. In other cases, especially those for whom ritual recognition was not possible because they are gay or lesbian, by the time they come seeking the blessing of the community of faith they are already, sometimes for a number of years, living as a polyamorous household.

The difficulty they will encounter is that even if they are gay or lesbian, churches that will celebrate gay and lesbian marriage are at a loss with respect to polyamorous relationships. Yet the very reasons that many gay and lesbian folk seek the blessing of their church is the same for the members of a polyamorous relationship: public acceptance, celebration of the miracle of committed relationships that last through time, and recognition of the status of their relationship among friends and family in the community of faith.

Indeed, one could suggest that the affirmation of such polyadic relationships may help to break the monopoly of monogamy in ways that are helpful in signaling within the community of faith that love is not only a private property relationship but that it stands outside the law of traditional marriage and family values. It thus may signal ways in which the law is superseded by the commitment to love one another.

This does not mean, of course, that polyamory is for everyone. For most of us, it may seem too complicated and too demanding of time, energy and commitment. Undoubtedly, most will continue to find that something like monogamy (whether open or closed) is by far the preferred option. Indeed, there are probably few persons who go out of their way to build a polyamorous relationship from scratch. It is rather something that "just happens." Its happening, however, may be regarded as a gift to the parties involved and to the community of faith, just as only some will be opera singers or athletes.

What about the ethical issues that arise here? In general, this is not an exception to the valuing of long-term faithful relationships. No such relationship can or should be lightly entered into (as they sometimes say about marriage in wedding ceremonies). Multiple commitments require considerable emotional maturity to balance inevitably competing claims and responsibilities. Recalling again Levinas' imperative of regarding the other, such relationships place us in a situation of radical commitment that always makes the appearance of a third into something of an ethical conundrum.[63] Finding ways to accept the inevitable hurt feelings and to engage in practices of forgiveness is important in all relationships, and all the more, perhaps, in polyadic ones. Having a community of friends who understand and support this adventure in relationship is important here as in all relationships of commitment. A willingness to grow, to be corrected, to forgive and be forgiven, to be attentive to the needs and desires and pleasures of one another in contexts of intimate vulnerability—all this is essential. And yet not different from what may be necessary in any relationship.[64]

---

63. Levinas, *Totality and Infinity*, 212-214.

64. One of the most helpful discussions of the ways in which persons can learn to handle the inevitable problems that surface with respect to jealousy and honest and open communication is Dossie Easton and Catherine A. Liszt, *The Ethical Slut: A Guide to Infinite Sexual Possibilities* (Eugene, Ore.: Greenery Press, 1997).

Part Three

Sex Work

Chapter Seven

From Prostitution to Sex Work

The Priority of Prostitution

At first blush, an extended discussion of prostitution may seem odd in the context of a treatment of queer sexual ethics. Prostitution may seem to compose a relatively small sector of queer sexual behavior, but the discussion of prostitution intersects with all the issues that are important to a treatment of queer sexual ethics. Furthermore, in the construction of a biblically informed sexual ethic, prostitution has an important place in that there is, or appears to be, far more biblical evidence to deal with in discussing prostitution than any of the other themes we reflect upon elsewhere in the book. Thus the principle biblical category that represents what we might term radical horizons for sexual ethics is that of the prostitute. Of course there is the disadvantage from a queer perspective that this evidence, in general, seems to deal with female prostitutes available to heterosexual men. This is true also of the considerable body of literature that since the nineteenth century has been devoted to prostitution. Indeed much of the treatment of prostitution in gay-friendly discussions—as little as this may be—also focuses on women selling sexual services to men.

However, there are a number of intriguing relationships between a treatment of prostitution and other queer sexual practices. In many languages, including Greek, the term for prostitute is the same as the term for fornicator. Thus issues of promiscuity and prostitution have an important overlap. In addition, the term "pornography" basically means "writing (about) prostitutes" and was developed as a genre for the description of the lives of prostitutes in connection with French proposals to introduce government regulation of this activity. Moreover, the legal regime imposed upon prostitutes is co-terminous with important legal regimes in the modern period imposed upon homosexual practice. Thus the English Criminal Law Amendment Act of 1885, which criminalized same-sex practice even between consenting adults, was originated in connection with laws regarding prostitution. Finally, as we shall see, much of the literature that is now surfacing about male prostitution involves issues of the age of consent and cross-generational sex—which, in turn, anticipates the discussion below on pederasty.

The discussion of prostitution serves as an opening to, or review of, many of the other issues with which this study deals. However the most important reason for an emphasis on prostitution is the exigency of constructing a theological ethic of radical sexuality that takes biblical reflection into account. In particular, this will mean taking into account the saying of Jesus in the Gospel of Matthew that prostitutes enter the reign of God first.

That prostitutes have priority is important for our purposes because it points to the place of unregulated sexuality over against the regulated sexuality of the "righteous." It thus serves as a paradigm for the discussion of "outlaw" or radical sex that is implicated in the theme of "frontier" questions or horizons in queer sexual ethics. Of course, many cultures of antiquity integrated prostitution as an institution within the overall social structuring of sexuality. But even there the prostitute as such was regarded as a marginal or disreputable character. This attitude serves as the background for many of the biblical references to prostitution.

In approaching the question of prostitution, it is important to be aware that in prostitution we encounter a place in which a number of issues of great importance for any consideration of ethics today intersect and complicate each other. When I was getting ready to teach a seminar on sexual ethics a decade ago, a story appeared in the press that made this all too clear.

"Neighbors Join Forces to Keep Out Prostitutes"[65] appeared in the *Chicago Tribune* and reported on incidents in the "rapidly gentrifying" neighborhoods of Wicker Park and Bucktown. The police had greatly stepped up their arrests in the area of prostitutes: 153 arrests as opposed to 31 in the same time frame (August to September) of the previous year. The neighbors gleefully joined in on the "clean-up" campaign. "We chased a girl for six blocks in 6-inch heels" said one of the women who was engaged in the activity of "cleaning up the neighborhood." "Basically we have them running—into buses, into taxicabs or into squad cars, but they are leaving our neighborhood. This is thrilling," she said. New businesses had joined in the "fun," including Home Depot and AT&T, which both sent employees to participate in the anti-prostitution rallies. All this occurred against the background described by the reporter as characterized by "younger and more upscale residents moving into the neighborhood..."

This report, which is echoed in hundreds of other such newspaper reports, represents an astonishing confluence of class, race and gender oppressions joined by family-ism, gentrification, and even corporate America. Note that no one reports talking to the prostitutes. Nobody takes any interest in their lives,

---

65. Heather Vogell, "Neighbors Join Forces to Keep Out Prostitutes," *Chicago Tribune*, 15 Oct 2000, 1-2.

still less their livelihood; they should just leave. Nothing is thought of chasing people or yelling abuse at them. The newspaper speaks of vigilance but it is more like legalized vigilantism.

The press makes invisible any implication of race but class is there for all to see. The wealthier new residents want to chase out those who are presumably holdovers from when these were neighborhoods of the poor. It might be argued that neighbors are uncomfortable having prostitutes working the neighborhood streets. Whatever might be the reason, does anybody suggest cleaner, safer, working environments? Of course not—prostitutes are only trash to be "cleaned up" like so much litter. Neighborhoods of the poor are invaded by middle-class folk, who then drive out poor sex workers. A neighborhood that had been inhabited by persons of color and migrants is becoming increasingly white, and so prostitutes (who in this case are primarily persons of color, women and transgender alike) must be driven out. Race and class stratifications and oppressions, gender anxieties and sex panics converge in mob action enforced by the police, abetted by corporations. This is no isolated incident. It happens in neighborhoods all over America.

What is perhaps even more chilling is that many of those who engaged in this vigilante activity—supported, of course, by the police—may regard themselves as upstanding Christians. This is one reason that a consideration of prostitution is so important for a treatment of queer sexual ethics.

I should also mention another reason that I have placed an emphasis on this topic: I am no neutral outside observer. I have the very good fortune to have friends who are prostitutes. Some of these are male hustlers whom I have known for years and grown not only to like, but to respect as persons of integrity. Some others are MtF transgender prostitutes of color who have contributed in important ways to discussions of this topic in my seminars. Whether male or female or transgender, these are people who have enriched my life and my thought. That these good people are the object of social stigma and self-righteous religious rejection, and are hidden away like dirty secrets even in liberative discourse among LGBTQ and LGBTQ-friendly discussions in church and society greatly pains me. I am committed to being an advocate for them, in solidarity with them. I am persuaded that the gospel demands no less.

One of the most daring contributions to liberation theology is that made by Marcella Althaus-Reid, an Argentinean theologian who taught at the University of Edinburgh until her untimely death of breast cancer a few years ago. In *Indecent Theology*,[66] she takes particular note of the erotic lives of the

---

66. Marcella Althaus-Reid, *Indecent Theology: Theological Perversions in Sex, Gender, and Politics* (New York: Routledge, 2000).

poor, especially poor women but also all those who engage in survival sex or who otherwise live outside the boundaries of religious and social respectability. Among her claims is that theology, including liberation and feminist theology, has too often sought respectability at the cost of ignoring the "indecent" lives of the poor and of the women in whose name they sought to speak. While her reflections are pertinent for all the topics taken up in this reflection on queer sexual ethics, they are especially important for a consideration of those who are often most stigmatized: those who survive (and occasionally—but rarely—thrive) by selling sexual services to others. Perhaps this may even be extended to those who are their willing accomplices in this trade (clients and facilitators), at least those whose participation takes seriously the welfare and dignity of the sex worker as well.

In order to approach this set of issues, we will first consider some of the biblical texts that may have relevance for the discussion of prostitution. These texts are generally concerned with female prostitution, women who sell sexual services to men. I will argue that it is clearly consistent with biblically informed ethics to stand in solidarity with prostitutes and to be an advocate for their cause and for their dignity. Then we will turn to a consideration of recent debates that also focus on contemporary sex work. This literature is vast and it will be necessary to deal only with representative samples of the discussion. The contemporary discussion has generally focused on the question of whether sex work should be decriminalized because it is simply work, or whether prostitution should be opposed because it involves the perpetuation and intensification of male domination of women. This discussion also primarily focuses on female prostitution. Little attention is paid to the gigolo, the male sex worker whose clients are women. Even less attention is paid in this literature to women who sell sexual services to (other) women. Nevertheless, this will help us to subsequently reflect on the distinctive features of the work of men who sell sex to men. As we will see, this topic will suggest some important modifications for our understanding of prostitution. Finally, we will turn to the currently controversial topics of sex tourism and sex trafficking to see what light our overall approach may shed on these practices.

In order to prepare ourselves for this set of discussions, it may be helpful to indicate some features of the general perspective that will inform the subsequent discussions. It is a perspective consonant with that which informs all our discussions of new horizons in queer sexual ethics.

Perspectives

The general point of view of these discussions closely parallels that of Martha Nussbaum, as well as that of Raja Halwani and of many sex workers themselves.

I believe there are several reasons for the marginalization, stigmatization, and even criminalization of sex work that need to be strongly contested. The basic ground for such attitudes is a profound, though often covert, erotophobia. It is on the grounds of such erotophobia that sex workers are regarded as being either degraded people or as being uniformly coerced. That is, sexual activity is so scary or repugnant that only a person who is morally depraved or who is forced could conceivably engage in sex for money. We have already maintained that erotophobia must be contested, but it is often some version of erotophobia that makes sex work a special case, as opposed to other forms of work that, depending on circumstances, may or may not be degrading.

It is true that female sex workers, as opposed to "wives" under conditions of patriarchy, do not have the same sort of "security" as those who set up long-term or putatively lifelong contracts that involve the exchange of sexual attentions for material support. On the other hand, they may have a certain independence from any one client and therefore may more easily be able to escape the degradations attendant upon a bad contract. To be sure, the occupation does not provide lifetime security or tenure. (In many cultures marriage does not either, certainly not in cultures where males have exclusive and uncontestable rights to dissolve the contract at whim.) Prostitutes also have to be clear that this is not a job one will be able to earn a living at forever. Even if a number of sex workers seem to be able to do well into their 40s or 50s, they, like others who sell bodily services (professional athletes for example), will be faced with the need to change careers. Moreover, as currently practiced under regimes of criminal law and social marginalization, prostitutes, especially female prostitutes, are exposed to significant risks of bodily harm. Moreover laws against procuring clients, disorderly houses, and so on are regularly used to prevent women from moving into management positions in the sexual service sector of the economy.

What I want to emphasize is that there is nothing so awful about sex that makes sex work more degrading than, say, working in construction or caring for the children of others or harvesting fruit in season. Of course, not everyone enjoys sex, or sex with strangers. But some may. Some may even have a vocation for it. Some may enjoy cleaning other people's houses, or being filing clerks, or even being administrators—but not everyone. Some may find sex work preferable to cleaning others' houses or being secretaries or even, say, academic deans.

In general, almost all work is a function of economic necessity. That is, if one were independently wealthy, one might spend at least part of one's time differently. As much as I am one of the lucky ones who gets paid a comfortable wage to do things I mostly enjoy, this would also be true for me. I would probably still read and write and lecture and hang out with colleagues and students, but I might spend a lot less time doing things like grading papers or attending committee meetings. But most people, the overwhelming majority, live a far more economically marginal existence than seminary professors do. And they must perform work that does not provide emotional or intellectual stimulation, even work for which they often are not at all suited. This situation is not helped by reducing the options people have by criminalizing some of their economic opportunities that do not entail fraud or force.

Another issue has to do with an ideological separation of money (payment) from sexual pleasure. In the first place, we must be clear that the exchange of financial support for sexual access is a characteristic of the marriage contract for many people. One of the aspects of this arrangement increasingly being exposed as supportive of male dominance is the undervaluing of the "free" domestic labor provided by women in such arrangements. As a man, I may expect my wife to make my breakfast, clean my house, iron my shirts, care for my children, etc., but it is unclear how the decision to pay for these services is more dehumanizing than expecting them to be provided free of charge. In these illustrations, the payment for services otherwise taken for granted is a positive step forward.

It is conceivable that even married people desire certain sexual services that their partner is unwilling or unable to provide. Would not the contractual arrangement for these services be less problematic than "having an affair," at least under certain circumstances? There are many others, for example the unmarried, who might contract for sexual services, just as they might contract others to prepare their meals.

A set of issues specific to female prostitution has to do with the attitudes toward unregulated sexuality deemed threatening to certain forms of social order, including some forms of patriarchy. In the discussion of biblical texts we will see that "loose women" seem to undermine the claim of men to sexual ownership of women. These women may be free of the primary institutional form of male dominance: marriage and family. They also escape some of the stereotypes of women's sexuality: that women have no sexual desire, no independent sexual interest. To be sure, prostitution is ambiguous in these regards. Prostitution may also provide a safety valve that functions to stabilize arrangements of sexual power for men. And female prostitutes may be used as the counterpoint to the "good" woman as mother/wife (or virgin). But stigmatizing prostitutes only collaborates in these negative functions of prostitution; it does not undermine them.

Those like Barry,[67] as well as Carter and Giobbe,[68] who underline the horrors to which all too many female prostitutes are subjected, do well to remind us of the very real power of male domination and violence in the world of prostitution. To be sure, this also characterizes the situation of all too many women in conditions of marriage. While it is possible that some progress has been made in delegitimating male violence against women through the exposure of domestic abuse and the development of laws against sexual harassment, there is considerably more needed. Any progress here may positively affect the life chances of prostitutes as well.

Further, the evidence indicates that prostitutes with the worst experiences are those who have a history of being sexually abused as young children. This leaves people open to collaboration in their own abuse later in life, or inhibits the development of survival strategies. Perhaps the most important thing that could be done to positively affect the worst forms of prostitution would be to make significant inroads on the incidence of childhood incest abuse.

In addition, it may be that models of a somewhat more humane style of prostitution are suggested by a consideration of the literature on male prostitution. The much lower frequency of violence on the part of clients, the virtual absence of pimps, together with the greater sense of control reported by male prostitutes, may help point the way forward toward the betterment of the relations between clients and prostitutes, including female prostitutes and their customers.

Policy

What, then, should be done on the level of policy regarding prostitution? A basic principle is that the determination of good public policy should be dependent upon careful attention to the perspectives of those most affected: sex workers themselves.

Laws that protect people from coercion, including coercion in sex, are clearly in the interests of a just society. However, the best approach to prostitution would be simply to abolish all forms of criminalization. Decriminalization is preferable to the regulation characteristic of European approaches. This, at least, is the perspective of many sex workers. Regulation is often done in ways

---

67. Kathleen Barry, *Female Sexual Slavery* (New York: New York University Press, 1984).

68. Vednita Carter and Evelina Giobbe, "Duet: Prostitution, Racism and Feminist Discourse," in *Prostitution and Pornography: Philosophical Debate About the Sex Industry,* ed. Jessica Spector (Stanford: Stanford University Press, 2006), 17-39.

that perpetuate the stigmatization of sex workers, such as assuming them to be carriers of disease. (Mandatory testing is quite different from the provision of free health care.)

Laws against "living off the earnings of a prostitute" should be abolished or severely amended so as to criminalize only clearly exploitative working conditions. The average CEO of a major company makes 500 times the wage of an employee; this is clearly exploitation. Most pimps and madams are far less exploitative. Laws against "disorderly houses" should be repealed. Such places should be subject only to reasonable laws regarding health and safety that apply to other service establishments (restaurants, for example). Unionization of sex workers should be encouraged so that they are in a better position to bargain for improved working conditions.

Perhaps the most detailed set of recommendations about public policy in this regard, which also offers a case for significantly more regulation than I have envisioned here, is found in Kuo's work.[69] It seems to me to be also a very important and promising place to begin consideration of policy proposals. In her final chapter, Kuo notes, for example, that decriminalization alone will not address the need to develop police sensitivity to and commitment to the well-being of prostitutes. Thus some sort of re-training of the police would be imperative. Kuo also agrees that prostitutes "must be permitted to migrate for work" with the same protections as other workers.[70] While several of her suggestions seem to me to be unrealistic, they are nonetheless carefully thought out and thus worthy of discussion.

Now, this may sound like a simple (or modified) libertarian agenda. But I believe that it also entails a claim upon the church. The churches have provided the ideological framework within which prostitutes are made to be the prey of police and criminal exploitation as well as of social stigma. We bear direct responsibility for the degradation and dehumanization of prostitutes. And this is in conflict with not only a general ethic of solidarity with the marginalized and vulnerable, but is also in direct conflict with the attitude taken by Jesus as represented in the Gospels. It is time for acts of repentance and of restitution.

A Question of Ethics

Much of what I have thus far said refers to what can or should be done on the legal and political fronts. But that is not the end of the matter, for we must

---

69. Lenore Kuo, *Prostitution Policy: Revolutionizing Practice through a Gendered Perspective* (New York: New York University Press, 2002).

70. Kuo, *Prostitution Policy*, 154.

also consider in what way ethical reflection can be brought to bear on the situation of those who offer or who seek sexual services within the framework of prostitution.

First, with respect to the "client" for sexual services: The horror stories told by some sex workers about the levels of abuse and danger to which they are subject from at least some clients makes clear that there is some urgency to this question. The ethical danger for the client is to suppose that the offering of a fee gives rights over the person of the prostitute that reduce her or him to sub-human status. Clearly, physical violence is legally ruled out in any case (or should be), but reducing the other person to a mere means for the satisfaction of certain sexual needs without basic decency of interaction is also fundamentally unethical. This is not something that applies only to prostitution, of course. Indeed, the point is that the same considerations that apply to all interactions with others, including commercial ones, should apply here as well. Unless some mutually explicitly agreed upon fantasy scenario is being enacted (see the discussion of BDSM below), the expectation that people should be treated decently and with respect holds true. Indeed one might argue that it may be even more important here on account of the physical and psychological vulnerabilities in play. Obviously, the client should not insist on sex acts that prejudice the health of the worker (for example one should not insist on unprotected sex).

It is important to underscore the importance of taking care that the work does not damage the worker. That is, one must have appropriate care for one's own body as well as that of the other. In his essay on "The Uses of Money," John Wesley proposed that workers should not endanger their own health or that of others.[71] Reasonable care about the transmission of STDs, especially HIV, should of course be taken. Beyond this, it is important to find ways of respecting the client as a human being and not simply as a money machine.

In general, I agree with Halwani's claim that sex work is not in itself incompatible with being a morally good person exhibiting the virtues of courage, temperance, and care, as well as wisdom and other virtues.[72] But as he also recognizes, there are conditions attendant upon the work of many sex workers that may significantly damage human flourishing and moral formation. It would be naïve to suppose that women, especially poor women and women of color, have the same opportunities for moral agency and human flourishing

---

71. John Wesley, "The Uses of Money." Edited by Jennette Descalzo, student at Northwest Nazarene College (Nampa, ID), with corrections by George Lyons for the Wesley Center for Applied Theology. < http://wesley.nnu.edu/>

72. Halwani, *Virtuous Liaisons*.

in this context as others might. Attending to these constraints may also help us think more clearly about how sex workers' lot might be improved in ways that would make flourishing more possible. This includes attention to the macro issues of race, class, and gender in our societies, but it also means attending to legal and other conditions that diminish or increase the chances for flourishing, including making sure that there are viable alternatives for those who seek to escape from a situation that seems to them to be hopelessly abusive.

While more might be said about other agents involved in prostitution (managers, "pimps," and so on), it is also the case that those not involved in prostitution have the responsibility to act with care and decency to all those who are involved in prostitution. This involves things like not stereotyping prostitutes, clients, and pimps, without informing oneself of the multiplicity of ways people engage in prostitution from these roles. It also means not romanticizing in ways that prevent solidarity with those who are damaged within this context. It also means not acting in ways that demean the prostitutes themselves in an effort to "clean up the streets." Finally, it would mean that churches in particular must reverse their prejudices against persons who engage in sex work and seek to become inclusive of these persons not as sinners in need of repentance but as those who may have much to teach all of us about the human condition.

Chapter Eight

Biblical Perspectives on Prostitution

The discussion of prostitution presents us with the opportunity of attending to the wealth of biblical data in which prostitutes play a significant role. The difficulty, however, is precisely the abundance of material that could be included in this discussion. In this chapter, I will not attempt to be exhaustive but instead indicate a number of passages that offer fruitful possibilities for further reflection and discussion. Of course, biblical literature does not speak with a single voice on this topic. What has generally happened is that the texts that convey a negative view of the prostitute are the only ones that come to be cited in Christian ethical discussion, thereby leaving aside those texts that offer a different voice and view. Accordingly, I will attempt to rebalance the discussion by offering reflections on texts that either take the practice of prostitution for granted or that accord dignity to the prostitute.

Matthew (Jesus)

Biblical reflection on this topic begins necessarily for the Christian theologian with the odd saying of Jesus in the Gospel of Matthew in which he addresses the religiously respectable by saying "tax collectors and prostitutes enter the reign of God ahead of you" (Matthew 21:31).

The saying follows immediately after the parable of the two sons: one who said he would do what his father asked but did not and one who said he would not obey but did (21:28-31). The prostitutes and tax collectors are those who openly refuse obedience, but then act in accordance with justice, or as Matthew's Gospel regularly says: justice and mercy. That they act in accordance with justice (as opposed to the religious and respectable) is shown by their belief in or loyalty to John the Baptizer, who came in the name of justice, in spite of his rather disreputable appearance and irregular message and practice. Meanwhile, the religious and respectable refuse to believe John, in spite of (or perhaps because of) the response to him on the part of the disreputable of Judah. They are then like those who profess to do what God requires but substitute obedience to pious regulation for heeding the call and claim of justice and mercy.

In a very helpful discussion Avaren Ipsen (whose book *Sex Working in the Bible* is the product of biblical study with sex workers in California) notes that in Luke, John responds to tax collectors and soldiers who ask what it would mean in their cases to practice the requisite justice.[73] He says, "Collect no more than is appointed to you," and "Rob no one by violence or false accusation." The obvious conclusion, then, would be that something similar would apply to the prostitute; not that she (or he) must leave the profession but that this profession should be one within which to practice justice and mercy.

But why should it be specifically prostitutes who have priority over the religious and respectable? It is often (and perhaps correctly) supposed that this signifies that the reign of God gives priority to the marginalized and the vulnerable, and that, in any case, Jesus is criticizing the pious for their presumption of privilege.

While the tax collector may stand for all those who violate the norms of social and public (or national) respectability, it may be that prostitutes violate more intimate norms of reputability. But is there even more at stake here?

To be sure, in this Gospel Jesus has things to say about other sexually marginalized persons, notably eunuchs, and this has been taken in some cases as a primary opening for discussion of "homosexuality."[74] This clearly has certain advantages, as it is in fact the case that there was marginalization of eunuchs on the basis of gender stereotypes. As Wilson demonstrates, there is considerable biblical material about eunuchs that provides interesting parallels with the situation of "homosexuals" in the modern period.

But there are also disadvantages to trying to force the parallel between eunuchs on the one hand, and lesbian and gay people on the other. In antiquity, eunuchs were often reputed to be sexually active with both men and women. As eunuchs, they were capable of sex but not procreation, so there was no danger of unwanted pregnancy in relations between women and eunuchs. If anything, then, the eunuchs might be described as bisexual or even omni-sexual. Moreover, eunuchs were exclusively male and so not a good fit for lesbian aspirations. Thus, while the texts concerning eunuchs may help with a general concern about "sexual minorities," they are less directly helpful in making immediate parallels to the situation of modern lesbian and gay people. However this text is understood, it is clear that Matthew's gospel is a rich resource for the affirmation of sexual minorities.[75]

---

73. Avaren Ipsen, *Sex Working and the Bible (London: Equinox Publishing, 2009).*

74. Nancy L. Wilson, *Our Tribe: Queer Folks, God, Jesus and the Bible* (San Francisco: Harper San Francisco, 1995).

75. For further discussion of the passage on eunuchs and a discussion of the case of

To return again to our immediate question, what is it about prostitutes that connects them to Matthew's overall emphasis on justice and mercy? One way of getting at this is to say that they were persons who escaped the regulation or institutionalization of patriarchal heteronormativity. Of course there were others who also escaped the most direct forms of patriarchal regulation, such as virgins and widows, categories of persons much more favored by the Pauline tradition. In the first centuries of Christianity, there were sizeable groups of widows and virgins in most congregations. However, the difference between prostitutes and these more reputable characters is that prostitutes were sexually active. Indeed, the term *pornae* functions indiscriminately to name women who were sexually active outside the strictures of male ownership, whether what is involved is "prostitution" or "promiscuity." Thus in street language, a person (female or male) who is promiscuous may be called "a whore" whether or not they charge for sexual favors. It's not the money; it's the unregulated sexuality.

However, it is probably the case that those who are thus labeled are those who support themselves (and their children) through whatever they receive in exchange for sexual availability (in distinction from women who receive more stable economic support in exchange for being sexually owned by males in the proprietary relations of marriage).[76] In most cases, these prostitutes may have been women who were at the lowest end of the economy and who were "unmarriageable" perhaps because of being unwed mothers (a fate from which Joseph rescued Mary) or victims of rape. We do, however, know of famous cases at the time of upper-class women who made themselves available as "prostitutes" in Rome.[77] The outrage expressed by Roman historians about this had to do not with prostitution, but with the fact that elite matrons who were married to elite men were engaged in the practice.

There is some reason to suppose that these prostitutes to whom Jesus gave priority were poor. However that does not seem to be the basis for their being singled out. They are, after all paired with tax collectors, who were not poor but

---

the centurion's boyfriend in Matthew 8, see my *The Man Jesus Loved*. On the latter passage, see also the essay that I co-authored with Tat-Siong Benny Liew, "Mistaken Identities but Model Faith: Rereading the Centurion, the Chap, and the Christ in Matthew 8:5-13," *Journal of Biblical Literature* 123.3 (2004): 467-94.

76. On male ownership of women see Gayle Rubin, "The Male Traffic in Women" in Rayna Reiter, ed., *Toward An Anthropology of Women* (New York: Monthly Review Press, 1975).

77. See Tacitus, *The Annals: The Reigns of Tiberius, Claudius, and Nero*, trans. Anthony A. Barrett and J. C. Yardley (New York: Oxford University Press, 2008); Cassius Dio, *Roman History, I–IX* (London: Loeb Classical Library, 1914-1927).

despised. These women were despised regardless of their poverty or lack of it. They were sexual outlaws.

But is that all that should be said of them? It is not the case that they are simply destigmatized. They are said to enter the reign of God ahead of the religious and respectable. Why might that be so? At the risk of romanticizing a bit, let me suggest a factor that may account for the plausibility of this privileging of the prostitute. Above all, the prostitute is one who knows intimately all sorts and conditions of men (and perhaps women as well). In this context they provide a measure of comfort, solace, and even pleasure to "all comers." They risk a certain vulnerability in order to provide a degree of "hospitality to the stranger." This "romanticized" version of the trade is not so very far from the description I have heard from an organizer of female sex workers in Brazil.[78] It is certainly recognizable in the stories of O. Henry and in the images of the women of bordellos in the Wild West, both in movies and the TV series *Gunsmoke*, which featured the owner of the local bordello, the remarkable Miss Kitty.

Rahab

Perhaps more important for our purposes is the way in which this description actually connects with the most famous prostitute of biblical literature: Rahab, the harlot of Jericho. The story takes up the second chapter of Joshua. The most significant action of the story is Rahab's protection of the strangers who had come to her house; her house, let us recall, of prostitution (and so of hospitality). We are told, rather laconically, that the spies "spent the night there." When the king sent soldiers to arrest the spies, Rahab applied to the spies the laws of hospitality: She refused to give them up (like Lot in Sodom). Instead, she hides them on her roof. [79] She then gives a speech in which she basically says that she believes that the spies will be able to conquer Jericho because of the success that they have had in previous guerilla attacks. Rahab and the spies make a mutual protection pact that includes the protection of her entire "household" (perhaps other prostitutes and her and their children). Perhaps the crimson

---

78. See Gabriella Leite, "Women of the Life, We Must Speak," in Gail McPheterson (ed.), *A Vindication of the Rights of Whores* (Seattle, Seal Press, 1989), pp. 288-93.

79. It is possible to read this as a consorting with the colonizer, and so a betrayal of her own people and this is the way the story may be read through the lens of a post-colonial interpretation. The sex workers who contribute insight to Ipsen's bible study suggest that Rahab however may be rebelling against the bad treatment so often accorded to "working women" (Ipsen, 86).

cord she ties in the window of her house on the walls of the city marks her house as the first "red light" district in history.

In the sequel to the story (Joshua 6:17, 22-23, 25), Joshua "fights the battle of Jericho," the walls come down, and he orders the slaughter of all the inhabitants (as a dedication or sacrifice to the Lord) with the exception of Rahab and her household. In consequence they are all spared, and her family dwells in Israel "to this day." Note that in each case she is identified as a prostitute whether or not her name is used.

The story of Rahab does seem to suggest that the Greeks were not entirely wrong in supposing that engaging in prostitution (as the seller) rendered questionable one's loyalty to the city. This, at least, was the argument concerning men who offered themselves for sale or rent in the speech of Timarkhos studied by Dover in his landmark study of Greek homosexuality.[80] If such male sex workers were citizens, they would presumably lose their rights to participate in the assembly of the polis: "Anyone who prostituted himself, whether out of economic necessity or greed (sexual desire is never mentioned as a possible motive), indicated by that gesture that his autonomy was for sale to whoever wished to buy it. The city as a collective entity was supposedly vulnerable in the person of such a citizen—vulnerable to penetration by foreign influence or corruption by private enterprise."[81] Rahab's story would amply substantiate these fears for the citizens of Jericho, at least. This may also suggest a further connection between prostitutes and tax collectors in the Jesus narrative: Perhaps they are linked because of their suspect loyalty to national integrity. Prostitutes, as we have said, are "loose" in the sense of being loosed from the immediate bonds of patriarchy—but they are also loosed from the bonds of "patria" by which patriarchy and patriotism are joined.[82]

At least for the Christian, the narrative in Judges is by no means the end of the story. Rahab shows up in the genealogy of Jesus (Matthew 1:5); she is the mother of Boaz, who marries another disreputable woman—Ruth the Moabite—to become the great-grandfather of David, who in turn appears as the "husband" of another "shady lady": the "wife of Uriah" (this designation

---

80. K.J. Dover, *Greek Homosexuality*, rev. ed. (New York: MJF Books, 1997).

81. Dover, *Greek Homosexuality*, 97-98.

82. See also the quoted remarks in Martha Nussbaum, *Sex and Social Justice* (New York: Oxford, 2000): "There are two natural disasters in the world: prostitution and riot" (443). Cited from Alain Corbin, *Women for Hire: Prostitution and Sexuality in France after 1850*, trans. Alan Sheridan (Cambridge, MA: Harvard University Press, 1996), 373.

makes clear that Bathsheba is an adulteress and David is an adulterer). In addition to these three women, there is yet another prostitute: Tamar, who gives progeny to Judah and so also has a place in the Matthean genealogy of Jesus. In this line of remarkable women (which concludes with Mary), there is a strange priority given to women who are sexually disreputable—and to Rahab above all.

But we are not yet at the end. Rahab appears again, not once but twice: first in Hebrews 11:31 and then in James 2:25. First Hebrews: "By faith Rahab the prostitute did not perish with those who were disobedient, because she had received the spies in peace." Note that Rahab is not identified as the wife of Salmon or the mother of Boaz. She is simply the prostitute—and not the ex-prostitute. And her "faith" consists in doing what any prostitute would presumably do: welcoming strangers in peace. Now James: "Likewise, was not Rahab the prostitute also justified by works when she welcomed the messengers and sent them out by another road." Her acts of kindness (and sexual expression can be an act of kindness, even if it receives generosity in return) and of loyalty to the guest are her works, the works of faithfulness that mark her as exemplar not of law but of justice. Hebrews calls it faith, James calls it works, but both call it justice, and blessed.

What these texts underline is precisely the prostitute's hospitality to the stranger, her risk of openness to the alien, the strange, the unforeseen. They also underscore her loyalty to those she welcomes at the expense of loyalty to the *polis*, the city, where she stands outside the regulated and protected space of the household.

These are important characteristics of the welcoming of the reign of God in the Jesus tradition. It means, among other things, being open to what is new, different, and strange. It means not being loyal to the ties of family that hinder an opening to the new and unexpected. In the Jesus tradition, faith is regularly associated with this letting go of ties to the social order, with the welcoming of what is strange and new—in short, with risky behavior. In this, the prostitute is quite different from those who live within the boundaries of respectability and rectitude, and who are often unforgiving of human weakness and unwelcoming to the stranger, the outsider, and the alien.

Other Hebrew Bible Texts

Before returning to the New Testament, it may be useful to briefly look at other Hebrew Bible material that deals with prostitutes. First we may consider other narratives that make reference to prostitutes. The first is the story of Tamar, already noted in connection with Matthew's genealogy of Jesus, a narrative found in Genesis 38. Tamar poses as a prostitute (or cultic prostitute) in order to produce heirs for her first husband after his two brothers had failed. She succeeds in seducing her father-in-law by presenting herself as a prostitute. The twin progeny of that roadside encounter become the progenitors of the tribe of Judah and so of Rahab's "husband" and so of Ruth's and so of David and so finally the ancestors of Jesus. In the story Tamar appears to be condemned to death for playing the role of the prostitute, thereby demonstrating the extreme vulnerability of sex workers, but especially the vulnerability of "respectable women" who take up the trade in defiance of household duties. But her daring, cleverness, and foresight (in keeping the pledge of payment left her by Judah) save her from that fate and in fact earn her an honorable place among the ancestors of Jesus.

The second narrative is in Judges 16:1-3 and concerns Samson, who in his adventurous life manages to spend the night in Gaza with a prostitute. When the men of Gaza seek to trap him he escapes, taking the doors with him. This sets up, as it also summarizes, the whole narrative concerning Delilah (who is not said to be a prostitute but certainly seems to be portrayed as one). What is intriguing for our purposes is that there is no explicit or implicit condemnation of prostitution as such in these narratives.

There is another narrative in Judges 11 that is instructive. It concerns Gilead's son Jephthah, who was born of a prostitute. Because of this fact he is ostracized by his "legitimate" brothers when his father dies and is driven into a life of banditry. However, when the Philistines threaten the existence of the people, his countrymen seek to persuade him to return to lead their forces against the enemy. He reluctantly agrees to do this after reminding them of the shabbiness of their treatment of him as the son of a prostitute. The moral of the story to this point seems quite compatible with what is briefly indicated in the Jesus tradition: There should be no discrimination against prostitutes and their progeny. (The tale continues in the much more frequently remarked-upon episode of Jephthah's own daughter; but that is, as they say, another story).[83]

In this rapid survey of biblical texts, we should also mention the story of Solomon and the two prostitutes who come to him to seek justice in a dispute between them about a child. There are many ways to understand this story. One is that we are reminded that prostitutes are often mothers who care deeply about their children. Indeed, it is often for the sake of children that women may become prostitutes. Another lesson that can be drawn from this story is that prostitutes have a claim on justice. They are not simply outlaws, but have the right to approach the law seeking redress of grievances. Whatever we may think about Solomon's resolution of the conflict between them, we should

---

83. For further reflection on this story, see Chapter 11 of my book, *Jacob's Wound*.

above all be keenly aware that in our society prostitutes cannot approach the law with any hope of justice because they would simply be arrested as criminals. What is perhaps most astonishing about this story is the way Christians (and other readers) have managed to ignore the fact that the women involved are actually prostitutes. Although the narrative is often found in illustrated bibles for children and youth and is often a text for preaching and teaching, the designation of the women as prostitutes in the text is simply hidden away like a dirty secret—a fate common to sex workers of all descriptions.

Further, in the law codes of the Bible, there seems to be no condemnation of prostitution as such. We do find that priests are not to marry widows, prostitutes or divorcees—that is, women who have had sex with another man (Leviticus 21:7, 14). And the men of Israel should not sell their daughters as sex slaves (19:29).[84] In addition, the wages of prostitutes should not be dedicated in the temple, although that is probably related to debates—quite complex ones—about "temple prostitution" (Deuteronomy 23:18). Similarly, there is to be no temple prostitute from the sons or daughters of Israel (Deuteronomy 23:17). Does this mean nobody should be a prostitute or that nobody should be one connected to a temple?[85] We may note that temple prostitution may have minimal sacral function: It may simply be that prostitutes congregate there as in a public space and that they may enjoy some protection there.[86]

Prophetic literature contents itself with condemning the way in which Israel sells her/himself to foreign powers rather than relying upon YHWH. That too is a complex story that does not bear directly on our inquiry, even though it has been adduced as evidence of a negative attitude toward prostitution. We may also mention the warnings against spending all your money on prostitutes in Proverbs (e.g. 6:26 and 23:27), but that seems a counsel of prudence; we will return to this theme when we discuss the parable of the prodigal son below.

---

84. This text may be useful also in reflecting on the modern sex traffic trade, where poor families sell their children to sex traffickers. There is a growing body of literature about this practice in Southeast Asia and elsewhere. See Chapter 11.

85. I have attempted to deal with the much vexed question of male temple prostitutes in *Jacob's Wound*, especially in the chapter on "Holy Hustlers."

86. See the point and location of prostitution in Solon's legal reform according to Dover, *Greek Homosexuality*, and David Halperin, *One Hundred Years of Homosexuality: And Other Essays on Greek Love* (New York: Routledge, 1989).

Luke (Jesus again)

To return to the New Testament, we may briefly consider a couple of passages in the book of Luke that may be useful for further reflection. Luke does not have the saying about tax collectors and prostitutes, but does contain a narrative concerning a tax collector: Zacchaeus, who restores whatever he has defrauded. Does Luke also have a story about a prostitute, a person who might be categorized as *pornae*?

There is some possibility that the woman identified simply as a "sinner" in Luke 7:36-50 is to be understood in that way. If so, we must note that Jesus says she is forgiven or set free—but how is this so? Is she set free of the stigma attached to her way of life? It is also said of her that she has shown "great love" (47). But in her case, this love is demonstrated through intimate bodily service to Jesus as she pours ointment on his feet, bathes his feet with tears and dries them with her hair. Indeed Jesus says, "She has not stopped kissing my feet." We might also recall the difficult problem of determining what counts as a sex act; does this intimate bodily contact with the aim of producing bodily pleasure or comfort count as a sex act? That is, does a sex act require orgasm or penetration? And we may recall that in the Gospel of John, Jesus is said to perform a similarly intimate (and erotic?) service in washing the feet of his followers and friends. In her case, the act of love precedes the pronouncement of forgiveness. Note that it is her faith that has saved her. What faith? Is it her simple yet extravagant compassion? Or is it her audacity in approaching Jesus in the midst of these respectable and reputable men, reclaiming him for the marginal and disreputable people he had come to "save"? Certainly there is no confession of sins reported here. Nor is there any word of repentance. Jesus does not even say, "Go and sin no more"—as many versions of another story of Jesus, a prostitute and religious authorities in John 8 has it—but only, "Go in peace." It is her dignity that is restored. In that way she is made whole.

On the basis of this passage and the saying in Matthew, a case has sometimes been made that Jesus counted prostitutes among his most devoted followers. This would be little different from what we know of some other philosophical schools: Nussbaum, for example, recalls "the two women recorded as students in Plato's Academy were both *hetairi* [courtesans, or high-end sex workers], as were most of the women attested as students of Epicurus, including one who was apparently also a wealthy donor."[87]

Traditional depictions of Mary Magdalene have often supposed that she was a prostitute. Of course, when this is suggested, she is cast not as a practicing

---

87. Martha Nussbaum, *Sex and Social Justice*, 442, n15.

but as a former prostitute. But when prostitutes accept the characterization of Mary as a prostitute, they turn the tables on that traditional view and see in her a valorization of the prostitute as a particular friend of Jesus. This interpretation does not seem to me to violate the tenor of Gospel narratives that depict Jesus as a friend of sinners, a descendent of prostitutes, and their defender.

In Luke 15, we have the tale of the "prodigal" son. While there are two or three ways to describe his loss of "substance," the one most interesting for our purposes is that he spent all his money on prostitutes. Note that no special moral problem is indicated here beyond that of a waste of resources through an extreme form of extravagance analogous to the saying in Proverbs noted earlier. Perhaps the problem is not giving money to prostitutes, but doing so in such a way as to impoverish oneself, and perhaps to risk becoming a slave.

It appears, in fact, that slavery may be the fate of the prodigal son. Out of money, he becomes dependant on a gentile, a pig farmer. He is reduced in status by the need to engage in menial labor. This also entails the social stigma of working with unclean animals. His position is certainly no better than that of a slave. And as was customary in the context, his status as slave may also have entailed the requirement that he provide sexual services for the farmer on whom he depends.

The texts we have been considering from the Hebrew Bible and the New Testament seem to be generally accepting of prostitutes and their profession as a morally neutral way of life. But there are other texts from Paul, that appear to cast a much more negative light upon prostitution.

Paul

In a consideration of Pauline texts, we may begin with a note on 1 Corinthians 5:9-13. Paul warns against association with *pornois*. He is clarifying something he says he wrote in a former letter, trying to make clear that this does not apply to those outside the community but only within.

Who are the pornois? This appears as the masculine form of pornais, which we have seen refers to female prostitutes or at least to women whose sexuality is unregulated by patriarchal family (they are loose women in that they are not owned—although they are possibly rented). Normally this is translated as fornicators or as (sexually) immoral persons. The latter, though meant to be kinder, is nonetheless perhaps worse: It becomes rather more inclusive than it may have been for Paul and his communities. Commentators do not generally understand *pornois* literally as a reference to male prostitutes, although this should be at least entertained as a possibility. As Dover notes, in classical Greek, *pornos* "applied to men or boys who submit to homosexual acts in return for money."[88] Further noted is the distinction between *porne* and *hetaira*, where the former is lower-class and probably in a brothel, and the latter is more like a mistress.[89] The speech of Aeschines explains the distinction between *hetairekos* and *pornos* as that between having a partner from whom one accepts financial support (a kept boy) and taking it from many men (a hustler), respectively.[90] Thus, we must look closer to see if the language use changed by the time of Paul, roughly four centuries later.

The association here, as well as in the vice list of 6:9-10, with swindlers and abusive persons suggests that the form of unregulated sexuality (if that is the common denominator) attributed to men is an abusive sexuality that takes advantage of the other person. It would then be a form of sexual exploitation and abuse, much as swindling is economic exploitation, as I discuss elsewhere. Moreover, there are good reasons for supposing that the other category of offender in which sexuality is involved, *arsenokoitai*, may involve sexual violence or rape.[91] Thus one possibility would be to suggest that pornois may refer to men who sexually harass people, especially women. It would thus be in some continuity with those who leer at women, as in Jesus's extension of the meaning of adultery in Matthew 5:27.

Another intriguing text from Paul is found later in the same letter. In 6:12-20, Paul begins by saying that all things are lawful but not all are helpful. This then leads to a warning about excessive preoccupation with food and drink. This, in turn, leads Paul to advise against joining oneself with a *pornais*, or a female prostitute. Ultimately, Paul puts forward as an alternative the licit joining with a "virgin." The whole discussion is rather complex and provocative. But ultimately, however we mitigate Paul's views as somewhat "enlightened for his culture," it seems unlikely to be reconcilable with the view of the prostitute that we have in Matthew or the reference to Rahab in James or Hebrews. That joining the body with a prostitute is somehow in competition with joining one's body with Christ, however, is wonderfully suggestive, queer even: Union with Christ is imagined as a (quasi-)sexual union.

We may also note that Corinth had a remarkable reputation for prostitutes connected with the temple of Aphrodite. Halperin notes: "In Roman times (according to Strabo, 8.6.20) the famous and wealthy shrine of Aphrodite owned more than a thousand temple slaves who worked as prostitutes, making

---

88. Xen. *Mem.* 6.13 and Ar. *Wealth* 153-9, qtd. in Dover, *Greek Homosexuality*, 20.

89. Dover, *Greek Homosexuality*, 20-21.

90. Dover, *Greek Homosexuality*, 21-22; cf. 146 (citing Aristophanes' *Wealth*).

91. On this see Jennings, *Plato or Paul?*

Corinth the Amsterdam of the ancient world."[92] This may well explain the odd disjunction between relations with a prostitute and relation with Christ, if Paul assumed that relation with a *pornae* in this case meant relation with Aphrodite. Once again we may have in view an indictment of the practice of kidnapping girls (and boys) to make them sex slaves for brothels, including those clustered in the public precincts of temple areas. This would be an ancient equivalent of the modern sex slavery that is so rightly denounced in contemporary literature. At the same time, we should avoid conflation of real sex slavery with other forms of sex work that may be entered into voluntarily. We will come back to this later in the modern discussion about whether prostitution should be regarded as the equivalent of sex slavery or, more benignly, as sex work.

Where does this review of Pauline texts leave us? The only attempt to prohibit a relationship with a prostitute appears to be Paul's brief and problematic advice in 1 Corinthians 6:12-20. This text is most often used in the tradition to indicate why remaining unmarried is best (since apparently any sexual relation competes with the relation to Christ). Paul's logic drives him in this direction, but he is at pains to make at least grudging concessions to permit marriage in Chapter 7 of his first letter to the church at Corinth. Ironically, if we follow the surface character of Paul's argument about why it would be better not to be married, we would have to conclude that non-marital sexual expression might actually be better from that point of view than a marital relationship. The oddity of Paul's advice makes it rather precarious to derive *any* sex ethic from it, let alone any prohibition of prostitution.

Indeed, we might say that Paul's more direct and clearly thought out view of "calling" or of one's place within the world would have a far different application with respect to the prostitute than what we may have gathered from these texts. Paul simply says that if you are slave or free, don't seek to alter your status as a condition of participation in the messianic project; the same is true for one who is a Jew or a Greek (1 Corinthians 7: 17-24). It would seem at least plausible to suggest to Paul that he ought to adopt a similar view with respect to those who find themselves under the necessity of supporting themselves as sex workers, and even to adopt a sort of empathy for them, given that he has himself undertaken the rather degrading occupation of tent-maker. I hope that in this way Paul might have been persuaded to have adopted a view rather more in keeping with what seems to have been the perspective of the one he called "Lord."

---

92. David Halperin, *One Hundred Years of Homosexuality*, 106.

Reflections

On the whole, the biblical traditions do not seem to be especially horrified by prostitution. Prostitution seems generally to be regarded as an unremarkable part of the everyday life of society. There appears to be no good grounds for an attempt to abolish prostitution or to criminalize prostitutes.

But these are only negative results. Far more important in my view is the strong case that can be made for the acceptance and destigmatization of prostitutes—and indeed the honoring of prostitutes within the community. Here, I am especially struck by the narrative traditions, which range from matter-of-fact acceptance of sex work as an occupation to a profound preferential option in the Rahab and Jesus traditions.

In any discussion of prostitutes and prostitution that is undertaken in communities for which the Bible has an important role, it is crucial that the texts that accord dignity to the prostitute be taken with real seriousness. It is also the case that the help we may gain from a consideration of this horizon of queer (or, at least, non-normative) sexuality may inform approaches to other varieties of sexual expression that have been subjected to religious and social stigma.

Chapter Nine

Sex Work: Contemporary Questions

We turn now to a consideration of the situation of the contemporary sex worker. The bulk of literature in this area consists of reflection on female sex work, but a consideration of some of this literature will also serve as background to consideration of the specificity of male sex work.

First, the very term "sex worker" will need to be understood and perhaps questioned. Tracy Quan notes that the term was coined by Carol Leigh (a prostitute-activist) in the late 1970s to promote solidarity among "peep show dancers, strippers, and prostitutes." In the 1980s, porn actors were also included under this umbrella term.[93] Many of those, including Leigh, who work as prostitutes prefer to keep the old term for themselves and to use terms like "whore" or even "ho" to make clear that they are neither ashamed of their role nor do they desire to sanitize or objectify it in ways that the seemingly more clinical "sex worker" might, if simply substituted for "prostitute." As with any identity marker, the terms used to describe the practice of exchanging money for sexual services or practices will be contested and evolving. When (male) erotic dancers came to speak to the seminar I was conducting on queer sexual ethics, they shied away from the term sex worker because it had become exclusively associated in their minds with the provision of specific sexual services, services that they did not provide (they did of course not only dance but also "make out" with customers, who gave them "tips"). Thus a term that had been invented to be inclusive had become exclusive.

In a consideration of prostitution, it is important to take some account of the changing nature of prostitution across time and between cultures. In the United States, for example, rather dramatic changes in the character of (female) prostitution occurred at the end of the nineteenth and especially the beginning of the twentieth century, when, as Priscilla Alexander says, "One state after another passed laws prohibiting prostitution." At the same time,

---

93. Tracy Quan, "The Name of the Pose," in Jessica Spector, ed., *Prostitution and Pornography: Philosophical Debate About the Sex Industry* (Stanford: Stanford University Press, 2006), 342.

there were attempts to control diseases like syphilis, along with the panic about "white slavery" that produced the Mann Act of 1910.[94]

Alexander continues: "Despite the wave of reforms of sexual law during the 1970s and 1980s that included repeal of laws prohibiting fornication, adultery, and in many states, sodomy, no state reversed the prohibition of prostitution, and instead, many have increased its intensity."[95] As a consequence, "all 50 states in the United States define prostitutes as criminals through laws prohibiting both soliciting and engaging in prostitution, which is defined as sex in exchange for money or other consideration or compensation. All states also prohibit a range of activities associated with prostitution including living off the earnings of a prostitute (pimping), and running a sex work business (pandering, procuring, running a disorderly house)."[96]

Alexander contrasts the United States to Europe: "Since the late eighteenth and early nineteenth centuries, the traditional 'public health' approach has been either to regulate prostitution with mandatory licensing or registration and testing of female prostitutes (the nineteenth-century European model), or to close brothels and prohibit prostitution (the U.S. model)."[97]

Changes in legal and regulatory regimes certainly affect the reality of prostitution. Other authors have noted that female prostitution in the U.S. in the nineteenth century (before criminalization) seems to have permitted greater movement in and out of prostitution for women, with somewhat less stigma attached, and certainly less danger than associated with criminalization.[98] Others have noted a change in prostitution in the U.S. in the 1970s or thereabouts: Some forms of prostitution have become more routinized, losing

---

94. Priscilla Alexander, "Bathhouses and Brothels: Symbolic Sites in Discourse and Practice," in *Policing Public Sex: Queer Politics and the Future of AIDS Activism,* ed. Dangerous Bedfellows (Boston: South End Press, 2008), 222.

95. Alexander, "Bathhouses and Brothels," 222.

96. Alexander, "Bathhouses and Brothels," 227.

97. Alexander, "Bathhouses and Brothels," 227.

98. A rather striking difference in the prostitute population is also noted by Timothy Gilfoyle, who reports about late nineteenth-century prostitution: "When investigators counted 187 women in 32 boardinghouses and brothels in the Tenderloin, only 13 percent were American-born. Over half were Jewish, and more than a third were French." Gilfoyle also notes that between 1912 and 1916 prostitution became furtive as a consequence of criminalization due to the passage of the Mann Act. See Timothy Gilfoyle, "From Soubrette to Show World: The Contested Sexualities of Times Square: 1880-1995," in *Policing Public Sex,* ed. Dangerous Bedfellows, 269.

some dimensions of human warmth between clients and sex workers that may have been more common earlier.

In addition to this variation between even similar cultures (U.S. and Europe) and across even relatively short periods of time, another variable that may need particular attention is that between different forms of prostitution even in the same culture and time frame. For example, Kuo notes in her comparative reflections on prostitution in the Netherlands and the U.S. that there are multiple ways of engaging in prostitution and that these distinct forms have significant consequences for the way prostitutes feel about their work, as well as how they fare in other ways. For example: About a quarter of women prostitutes are doing far worse in life than non-prostitutes, about half are in a more or less comparable situation, and about a quarter are faring better than non prostitute women. Of the worst-off group, many were street prostitutes, had a high incidence of childhood sexual abuse (typically, in the family), used heroin (although use often began prior to prostitution), and experienced violence on and off the job. Women who worked in bars, some brothels, or in escort services tended on the whole to have far better life chances and far greater job satisfaction.[99]

Kuo concludes:

> The experiences of prostitutes cannot be generalized into one coherent and consistent picture....For approximately 25 percent of prostitutes, the experience ranges from bad to nightmarish. But the vast majority of this group represents a population that was especially vulnerable prior to their entry into prostitution. These are women most likely to have suffered childhood or adult non-prostitution violence and sexual assault, to be poor, to be unmarried while having a greater-than-average economic burden, to be immigrants, to be drug-dependent, or to use weak survival strategies.

They also "must deal with a relatively high number of clients, spend less time with each, and receive less pay per client."[100] When we discuss prostitution or study the literature about prostitution, therefore, it is important to be aware of the diversity of prostitutions. Generalizations from one part of the population of prostitutes ought to be viewed with some suspicion. That is, one needs always to ask: Which prostitutes are being described or are describing themselves, and how might this relate to other sectors of sex work?

---

99. Kuo, *Prostitution Policy*, 95-100.

100. Kuo, *Prostitution Policy*, 100.

Additional variables to be taken into account will include very diverse cultures (which we will explore in dealing with men who sell sex) as well as the significant differences between male and female prostitution.

Objections and Responses

By far, the most interesting debates surrounding prostitution in the last twenty-five years are often cast as a dispute between feminists who deplore prostitution as an especially egregious case of masculine domination, and liberals (also often women) who insist that free persons in a free society should be free to engage in prostitution if they choose, and that therefore society should decriminalize prostitution in the name of protecting the rights of women (and men) to engage as sellers or buyers of sexual services. Moving somewhat unpredictably between these positions are the views of (female) sex workers who engage in and speak about prostitution. Most of these seem to favor the liberal perspective, but there are eloquent examples of those who take up and develop the feminist discourse, including Carter and Giobbe.

While these discussions can be quite uncompromising in their rejection of alternative views, there is nonetheless a good deal that does appear to be common to the views most often encountered in this literature. First, most are agreed that the primary concern should be to protect prostitutes from coercive practices that amount to slavery. Whether this behavior is engaged in by parents, pimps, traffickers, police, or clients, there is a general abhorrence of practices that no one doubts affect a great many prostitutes. All are agreed that violence against women in or out of the domain of sex work must be prohibited by laws that are strongly and effectively enforced.

While some early feminist rhetoric may have stigmatized prostitutes as sellouts to patriarchy and masculine domination, there seems to be much greater care these days even among those who hope to abolish prostitution to take into account the voices of women prostitutes themselves and avoid (re-)victimizing those who may already be regarded as victims of the exercise of the "male sex right." The fine collection of essays in the previously noted volume *Prostitution and Pornography*, edited by Jessica Spector, presents some of the most thoughtful essays on this subject.[101] In what follows, I will draw on many of these pieces, as well as other book-length works to try to provide a representative overview of the contours of this debate.

---

101. Subsequent references to the Spector volume in this chapter will be given in-text.

First, we should consider the perspectives of those feminists, sometimes self-identified as radical feminists, who seek the abolition of prostitution. The indictment of contemporary prostitution in the U.S. by Carter and Giobbe describes prostitution as exhibiting the worst forms of sexist, racist, and classist degradation of women, especially women of color and poor women. This searing charge by those who have first-hand knowledge of the dehumanizing experiences shared by many in prostitution makes it impossible to treat this theme in a purely academic way. The trajectory from childhood sexual abuse to being pimped by fathers and other male family members and the exposure to violence, both physical and psychological, at the hands of clients, cops, pimps, and sex business managers and owners is a powerful testimony to the ways in which prostitutes are often made to bear the brunt of massive social structures of domination and degradation. From this point of view, the only way to be of any assistance to those who are caught in this web of violation and violence is to help them to escape. Certainly this must be a basic ingredient to any approach to prostitution: enabling persons to reclaim dignity and integrity, either by abolishing these structures or enabling sex workers to escape, or both. In Chicago, for example, the work of Genesis House is of great importance in providing ways for women who have in this way been victims of the sex industry to escape from its clutches and to find alternative ways of life that are less threatening to bodily and psychological integrity.

While Giobbe and Carter believe that prostitution as a system is incapable of reform and so must be abolished by whatever means necessary, I remain dubious of this claim. The structural evils of racism, sexism, and classism they deplore undoubtedly exist, but they exist outside prostitution. Male domination of women has not yet disappeared from systems of marriage, for example. The view that men have a right to do what they want with certain women's bodies (the "male sex right") must be combated strenuously, whether in dating, marriage, parenting, or prostitution. But just as I do not believe that opposition to childhood sexual abuse (something these writers and Margaret Baldwin find at the origin of many life stories of prostitutes) should mean the abolition of all parent-child relationships, or that the abolition of spousal rape and abuse should mean the termination of all heterosexual erotic partnerships, I doubt that the abolition of prostitution is truly the only or even the best means of combating the abuses to which many prostitutes are subjected.

Carole Pateman's essay explores the question of the male sex right as standing behind the contract for services that liberals suppose would govern the case of prostitution. While her essay goes on also to explore questions of surrogate pregnancy, I believe that her observations about the structures of sexism and male domination are quite helpful in that they make clear that we must be aware of the ongoing effects of male domination of women when we discuss prostitution. Women in prostitution do not enter into these "contracts" as fully free actors. They and their clients are profoundly affected by sexism. The explicit identification of the constraints of sexism on women's choices, it seems to me, is an important corrective to some of the liberal perspectives that appear to think of individuals in these situations as atoms without embeddedness in social history. Of course, the same is true of what is sometimes called the marriage contract. Why should prostitution be a special case? Pateman does recognize at least in passing that this situation may be more complex since there are also male prostitutes (something radical feminists tend to ignore) and that at least some of these are available to women. As the essay by Julian Marlowe about gay male prostitution makes clear, taking this into account greatly complicates the ways in which we should understand how prostitution is situated in relation to systems of male domination.

The essay by Norma Jean Almodovar stands in remarkable contrast to that of Carter and Giobbe. Almodovar entered prostitution as an adult, indeed after spending time as a cop in the Los Angeles Police Department. She is a fierce advocate for the right of women to engage in prostitution and thus for the decriminalization of prostitution. She rejects the view that all prostitutes are victims who need to be rescued. Rather, in her view, what is crucial is the right of prostitutes to enjoy the protections of civil society, protections that would eliminate the very abuses decried by the feminist "abolitionists."

In general, I find myself in substantial agreement with the position taken by Nussbaum in *Sex and Social Justice*. Nussbaum begins by destabilizing the boundary between sex work and other forms of work: "All of us, with the exception of the independently wealthy and the unemployed, take money for the use of our body."[102] She continues, "Some people get good wages and some do not; some have a relatively high degree of control over their working conditions and some have little control; some have many employment options and some have very few. And some are socially stigmatized and some are not" (276). Nussbaum also notes that gaining rational clarity about these issues will require dismantling certain prejudices that she characterizes as irrational: "When we consider our views about sexual and reproductive services, then, we must be on our guard against two types of irrationality: aristocratic class prejudice and the fear of the body and its passions" (280).

While some feminist writers have characterized prostitution as supportive of patriarchal attitudes and institutions, Nussbaum notes that some feminist

---

102. Nussbaum, *Sex and Social Justice*, 276. Subsequent references to this work in this chapter will be given in-text.

arguments fail to note that prostitutes are generally regarded with horror by supporters of patriarchy (286-87). And in response to the strict "abolitionist" perspective of some of these writers, she notes that "a woman will not exactly achieve more control and 'truly human functioning' by becoming unemployed" (290). Moreover, as Nussbaum points out, "Prostitution is hardly alone in being shaped by, and reinforcing, male dominance" (294) and "More generally, one might argue that the institution of marriage as most frequently practiced both expresses and reinforces male dominance" (295). Against the argument about commodification and alienation, she argues: "It seems implausible to claim that the prostitute alienates her sexuality just on the ground that she provides sexual services for a fee. Does the singer alienate her voice or the professor her mind?" (291). As we shall see, there are certain interesting objections brought against this analogy, but how serious they are will have to be considered.

Nussbaum's argument touches here on one of the core concerns of the present work: "So our moral question boils down to the question, Is sex without deep personal knowledge always immoral?" She says such an affirmation "seems officious" (292). She also notes that addressing this issue means grappling with "the influence of our heritage of romanticism" (293). In this connection we may also recall the perspective of Halwani, who maintains that the ideology of romantic love may seriously distort reflections on sexuality. This is, he suggests, because the idea that only romantic sentiment can legitimate sexual practices not only represents a confusion about both sex and romance, but also because romance may not be necessary to human flourishing in the same way that sex is. Indeed romantic attachments may blind us to important questions of virtue (in ourselves and others), in contrast to, for example, notions of friendship.[103]

In terms of the proper regulation of prostitution, Nussbaum concludes that "What seems right is to use law to protect the bodily safety of prostitutes from assault, to protect their rights to their incomes against the extortionate behavior of pimps, to protect poor women in developing countries from forced trafficking and fraudulent offers, and to guarantee their full civil rights in the countries where they end up" (295).

The essay by Scott Alexander in Spector's edited volume raises an important question about one aspect of Nussbaum's argument concerning contract, in which he maintains that the law against prostitution does protect a person's sexual autonomy. He argues that sex is a special case (unlike dancing or teaching) that should not come under the rule of contract, and offers a number of illustrations of possible consequences to buttress his view. I wonder, however, if these illustrations do not entail supposing sexual services to be an implied

---

103. Halwani, *Virtuous Liaisons*, 89-168

codicil to an overt contract. I agree that a person's sexuality is not precisely the same as their singing voice, or what have you. In discussing theological sexual ethics (see Chapter 3), I have argued that sexuality is a locus of temptation and vulnerability. This would not seem to me to mean that it cannot therefore be made use of to "earn a living." Since Alexander does not want to argue against some forms of promiscuity, it is unclear to what extent "taking money for it" serves to drastically change the activity.

In addition to the more philosophically sophisticated perspectives advanced by Martha Nussbaum on prostitution, we should also take note of perspectives advanced by sex-positive radicals more in the line of Gayle Rubin. One of these is Pat Califia, whose book covers a number of the subjects to which we have been or will be attending. Califia notes in particular the ways in which prostitutes are victimized by the police, a victimization licensed by the criminalization of prostitution. She writes, "It would take a massive public outcry to alter the public policies that allow this cruel farce [corruption by vice squads, etc.] to continue. But the impetus for a social experiment in decriminalization of prostitution will not come from the woman's movement."[104]

In contesting the views of one of the strongest feminist opponents of prostitution, Califia writes: "The most reprehensible thing about this book [*Female Sexual Slavery* by Kathy Barry, 1979] is the way it encourages feminists to view prostitutes as their enemies, as women who contribute to the oppression of all women because they have allowed themselves to be victimized."[105] As we have seen, most feminist critiques of prostitution, including those who seek to abolish prostitution altogether, have sought to greatly nuance the perspective offered thirty years ago by Barry.

In a section titled "Whoring in Utopia,"[106] Califia maintains that some form of prostitution would remain even if the various structures of oppression were eliminated, meaning that even in a just world the sex industry would flourish. After all, not everyone can maintain a long-term relationship, not everyone wants to, and not every such relationship is sufficiently erotically exciting to preclude other activity. Why not pay or be paid for it?

Califia also agrees with some of the perspectives offered by Nussbaum when she writes, "The notion that a woman might prefer hooking or nude modeling to being a secretary or cleaning hotel rooms is beyond" the understanding of at

---

104. Pat Califia, *Public Sex: The Culture of Radical Sex* (San Francisco: Cleis Press, 1994), 136.

105. Califia, *Public Sex*, 136-37.

106. Califia, *Public Sex*, 261-68.

least some radical feminists.[107] That is, a certain class bias may enter into some of the discussions.

Priscilla Alexander, writing in the collection *Policing Public Sex*, maintains that "When a society names and condemns the prostitute, again through its law enforcement apparatus, it robs women of the right to say yes to sex."[108] This view is echoed by Carol Leigh: "My Mantra… LAWS THAT PUNISH PROSTITUTES ARE CRIMES AGAINST WOMEN."[109] Leigh's views are shaped by working with prostitutes as an activist for prostitute's rights. She acknowledges that experiences of prostitutes vary considerably: "Attitudes are diverse. I have spoken with a number of prostitutes who worked in their teens and do not think back on this part of their lives with horror. I have met others who do."[110] In general, she maintains that there is an important difference between legalization and decriminalization, and maintains that for most prostitutes:

> Decriminalization, or repeal of all laws prohibiting prostitution, was clearly a more fruitful area of study than 'legalization,' offering more autonomy and less surveillance. Legalization usually refers to licensing or zoning systems, which inspire numerous human rights and labor rights abuses wherever they have been put into effect."[111]

She also warns against over-broad anti-pimping legislation. Legally, pimping is defined as "living off the earnings of prostitution….All my call-girl friends and I are legally defined as pimps if we do so much as share clients."[112] (This caution also enters into the suggestions of Kuo, who speaks of prostitution facilitators.) Leigh maintains, "Although police should enforce laws against persons who abuse, coerce, force, kidnap, or commit violence against prostitutes, criminalizing "living off the earnings" makes it impossible to spend one's money on family, friends, or lovers."[113]

A position that takes very seriously the way in which multiple societal oppressions come to bear upon the situation of prostitution and that recognizes

---

107. Califia, *Public Sex*, 112.

108. *Policing Public Sex*, ed. Dangerous Bedfellows, 237.

109. *Policing Public Sex*, ed. Dangerous Bedfellows, 260.

110. *Policing Public Sex*, ed. Dangerous Bedfellows, 252.

111. *Policing Public Sex*, ed. Dangerous Bedfellows, 253.

112. *Policing Public Sex*, ed. Dangerous Bedfellows, 256.

113. *Policing Public Sex*, ed. Dangerous Bedfellows, 261-62.

that prostitution is itself quite a varied phenomenon is to be found in Julia O'Connell Davidson's *Prostitution, Power, and Freedom*.[114] I think it fair to say that Davidson regards prostitution in a strongly negative light. She characterizes clients as those who are in the position "to use their economic power to transform another human being into the living embodiment of a masturbatory fantasy."[115] In a certain sense, then, her position is a kind of abolitionism, but a very nuanced one that places prostitution in a wider framework, recognizes variations within prostitution, and takes into account a number of ways in which both abolition and regulation (that is, legalization) unintentionally may make matters worse for the persons they purport to help. Although she dreams of a day when prostitution will disappear, she sees no simple or simple-minded solution to the ills that she details.

The debates about abolishing, legalizing, and decriminalizing prostitution provide a rich resource for ethical reflection. In general, I side with those who believe that an important step toward improving the lives of prostitutes would be the decriminalization of prostitution. I also believe that laws against fraud and coercion should be vigorously enforced. Moreover, I am persuaded that it is imperative to offer assistance to any who seek to escape abusive and demeaning forms of prostitution. Finally, it is important that sex workers have every opportunity to seek redress in courts of law without fear and that they be protected and allowed to protect themselves against harassment (whether by police or others)—and that they have the same rights as other workers to organize themselves in the search of better working conditions.

Whatever stance is taken with respect to sex workers, I believe it is essential to attend closely to the views and experiences of sex workers themselves. If we do this, we will also become aware of the vast differences in the experiences of sex workers and so be less inclined simply to generalize from restricted samples.

It is also important to attend to the way in which sex workers, perhaps especially female sex workers, bear the brunt of a social order still characterized by masculine domination, white supremacy, and a marginalization of the poor. Thus, here as elsewhere, a concern for sexual ethics cannot be limited to what is sometimes thought of as the private sphere, but must engage all the ways in which the humanity of our neighbors is demeaned, their dignity compromised, and their very being threatened.

---

114. Julia O'Connell Davidson, *Prostitution, Power and Freedom* (Ann Arbor, MI: University of Michigan Press, 1999).

115. Davidson, *Prostitution*, 209.

Communion

When I was in Brazil with faculty, students, and trustees from several other seminaries, we were housed for a time at a religious retreat center on the outskirts of Rio. Our host was the resident Catholic bishop. One afternoon, the invited speaker was a remarkable woman who headed a movement of prostitutes. She said the church had wanted to appropriate her for the purposes of talking about "getting out" of prostitution. But she had no desire or inclination to get out, nor did many of her constituents. She joined the communists, but they wanted the same thing. Nobody was interested in what she and her co-workers wanted: respect and dignity.

She spoke of the way her work was in part a reparation of the damage done to men's sexuality by the teachings of church and society, and how it sometimes meant giving solace and comfort to those to whom this was denied. But more remarkable was this: While she was speaking to us and answering our questions, out on the veranda overlooking a sunny mountain top, the bishop brought out coffee (*cafezinho*) and small cookies. Unobtrusively he passed among us, pouring coffee into small white cups and handing out the sugar cookies—while this remarkable sex worker and activist spoke. At some point it was as if time and space were suspended and I knew that we were having Eucharist. It was clear that the presider/prostitute and the server/bishop were in on this together, and that in that moment, it was Christ who was the host. It seemed certain that the one who was the descendent of whores and their defender and friend was veritably present in the passionate words she spoke, and in the humble service he performed. In the *cafezinho* and powdered sugar on cake, the sunlight on our bodies, and birdsong in our ears, the reign of God drew near.

Advocacy for prostitutes is not an option for the church. For those who gather in loyalty to the One who was a son of prostitutes, One who was their friend and advocate, this must be a mark of our identity, a sign by which our faithfulness to him is recognized.

Chapter Ten

Hustlers

From our previous discussion of prostitution, focused where the biblical and contemporary literature points us, namely, on women as "sex workers," we turn now to the population of men who sell sex to men. The basic approach that has been developed in the previous chapters about prostitution guides also these reflections. That is, I can see no reason for being more restrictive with respect to male prostitution than with respect to female prostitution. If anything, the plausibility of the argument of some feminist writers concerning the way in which prostitution reproduces male dominance of women is challenged with respect to men who sell sex.

One of the reasons that a discussion of male sex work is necessary is that some of the discussion of Christian sexual ethics that has seen itself as "gay-friendly" has tended to exegetically deflect the presumed target of Paul's references among his lists of those who are immoral (sexually and otherwise), especially the terms *malakai* and *arsenokoitai*, from homosexuality as such to passive and active prostitutes, or passive prostitutes and their active clients. That is the result, for example, of one of the most well-known and influential gay-friendly discussions of those terms in the groundbreaking work of Robin Scroggs.[116] He proposes: "If the *malakos* points to the effeminate call-boy, then the *arsenokoites* in this context must be the active partner who keeps the *malakos* as a 'mistress' or who hires him on occasion to satisfy his sexual desires." Scroggs's claim is that same-sex relationships of mutuality may exist and that Paul, far from condemning such relationships, condemns instead "a very specific form of pederasty, one the entire literature agrees is evil." While appreciative of Scroggs's work in support of LGBTQ inclusion in the churches, his argument is flawed in my view, stigmatizing prostitution in order to exonerate homosexuality. This is a paradigmatic example, then, of the assimilation by amputation strategy that we have identified as a basic problem with an assimilationist rhetoric and strategy with respect to the gay rights movement.[117]

---

116. Robin Scroggs, *The New Testament and Homosexuality* (Minneapolis: Fortress Press, 1983).

117. I have offered a very different interpretation of these terms in *Plato or Paul?* I

There has been virtually no attempt to include sex workers and their customers within the discussion of gay or queer liberation, or the LGBTQ human rights movement. The normalizing discourse so fashionable in our time pretends that gay males are interested only in monogamous relationships. Even when it is admitted that men may have sex without the idea of marriage uppermost in their minds, the prospect of "paying for it" is sure to preclude prostitution from reflection. The admission that one pays for sex, at least for the gay male, is redolent of the loss of sexual attractiveness that is deeply threatening to the gay male ego—probably more so than to the heterosexual male. In this vein, while the heterosexual male has the excuse of the difficulty of finding willing women partners, the gay male has presumably a world of gay bars with their denizens to choose from. That the plethora of available sex partners does not provide a partner can only suggest failure. This may be why some gay men feel an antipathy even toward the hustlers they contract.

In addition, much of the literature (little as it is) and the popular discourse often identifies "hustlers" as young men who are actually straight but make money from gay men. This certainly makes for an unattractive stereotype, one that is false and decidedly unfair on several grounds. It is false because many men who sell sex are exploring their sexuality or are themselves gay. It is unfair because the hustler is after all providing a service that the client has sought out. This is also unfair because it is another instance of the way in which an emphasis on "gay identity" and the "gay community" may become a principle of exclusion and marginalization. After all, hustlers and their clients are an important segment of the men who have sex with men, and therefore are also targeted by the laws and stigmas attending to male same-sex practices.

In any case, the gay rights movement has tended to ignore the existence of gay male prostitution. This is deeply ironic, since a perusal of most gay-oriented magazines and newspapers discloses that a significant proportion of the revenue supporting the existence of such mainstays of the gay culture is derived from escort services, masseurs, and freelance models—that is, from men who are actively selling sexual services within the gay community.

I must also say that I have a certain stake in this discussion. Some of the people I regard as dear friends are or have been "hustlers." These are people for whom I have respect and affection, and I find their exclusion from the emancipatory discourse of gay rights and religious liberalism very troubling.

---

am quite confident that Scroggs, with whom I taught for several years, would have retracted these statements had he encountered some of the male sex workers—effeminate or not—whom I have known.

We will now attend to some of the recent work that has begun to appear about this population, and will deal with the question of ethical relationships between hustlers and their clients, as our concern is not merely with legal and attitudinal reform but also with ethical reflection.

Male Sex Workers in the Developed World

A convenient place to begin reflections on "hustlers," rent-boys," or male sex workers is the essay in Spector's *Prostitution and Pornography* by Julian Marlowe. There he reports his own entry as a graduate student into the world of prostitution, or accepting money for sexual encounters. He had understood himself to be sexually attracted to men and was somewhat surprised that he could actually make money from having sex. His subsequent activity took different forms and included the development of the occasional longer-term friendship.

One very extensive study, undertaken in England but with some cross cultural reference to San Francisco and Thailand, is Donald J. West's *Male Prostitution*.[118] This study was based on a series of extensive interviews with men in the sex trade in London. The largest sample is a group of 50 young men who were engaged in "street prostitution," supplemented with others who had been involved in this work in the past. In addition, West interviews those who engage in prostitution either as employees of a "massage parlor" or as freelance workers who advertise their services independently. In this way, West attempts to provide at least a limited cross-section of the variety of sex work available in London at the time.

In general, the youths who sell sex on the streets were from abusive homes, had little opportunity to make money in any other way, and often were homeless or nearly so. However, most (about 60 percent) identified as gay or bisexual and had either entered into prostitution accidentally, having been surprised that they could make money this way, or else had entered the scene upon hearing of this. That is, they were not forced into this work in any but an economic sense.

While some men detail experiences of violence from clients, this appears to be rather rare (in contrast, perhaps, to the experience of female prostitutes at a similar socio-economic level). Moreover, the incidence of violence appeared to be similar to that reported in non-prostitution settings by gay males generally. Of particular interest is that there is no exposure to the violence of abusive pimps. Thus even at this level of socio-economic dysfunction and

---

118. Donald J. West, *Male Prostitution* (New York: The Haworth Press, 1993).

deprivation, their situation appears significantly better than that of women in similar circumstances. This may suggest that the levels of violence experienced by women in some forms of prostitution is not a function of prostitution per se but of the wider culture of male violence against women.

Sex workers who do not have to walk the streets but find clients in other ways generally report much better social and economic functioning and job satisfaction. They also may come from more stable backgrounds and have more options. In their case, selling sex is much more of a free choice. The incidence of self-identification as "gay" is much higher, nearly 100 percent. The greatest problem stems from the potential for police harassment and arrest (though British police are far less corrupt and violent than their U.S. counterparts), but the independent contractors are virtually exempt even from this. Also they are far less likely to have drug or alcohol dependence.

West also maintains that childhood sexual abuse does not seem to be a factor. While the street workers did report a relative high incidence of domestic childhood sexual abuse (by males or females), West finds this to be simply part and parcel of the dysfunctional family environments from which folk on the street tend to come. There was no such incidence of sexual abuse on the part of the "off-street" sample.

Comparison with the more recent collection of material in Peter Aggleton's edited collection *Men who Sell Sex*, especially for the U.S. and Europe, may help to fill in this picture.[119] The first essay about Cardiff (South Wales) and London updates some of these findings. As to the sexual orientation of hustlers, all in South Wales identified as gay and represented a broad cross-section of class structure. In the London sample of forty-one hustlers, only five identified themselves as not gay (5). This represents an increased percentage in both cities and may be a result of greater acceptance in society of a gay identity. Note that in Cardiff a wide class representation was found, whereas street hustlers in London were still of the disadvantaged strata. This may have to do with the big-city character of London, where accessible hustlers are also very marginal (homeless), although it also has to do with the access through the "Streetwise" social service agency of the earlier study by West.

We also should notice that the average age for entering the work for street hustlers appears to be 14-16. For other forms of male prostitution, most entered as adults. As to the question of what sorts of relationships with clients (called "punters" in the U.K.) these young men sought, the writers note that

---

119. Peter Aggleton, ed., *Men who Sell Sex: International Perspectives on Male Prostitution and HIV/AIDS* (New York: Routledge, 1998). Subsequent references to this text in this chapter will be given in-text.

"contrary to the popular stereotype, male sex workers do not cater solely for the anonymous." This means: "In practice, sex workers distinguish clearly and consequentially between casual and regular clients" (8). From this the authors conclude: "These young men evidently often seek friendship and support as well as sex from their punters" (11).

The authors of *Men who Sell Sex* also reflect on a dynamic that has also motivated our study of queer sexual ethics:

> Sex workers form a part of that community [the gay community], yet this is routinely denied or ignored by its opinion leaders. There is a range of reasons for this. Many feel that the existence of organized sex work in the gay community will be regarded by those who would deny their civil rights to gay men and lesbians as further reason to diminish their precarious freedom under the law. Others feel that sex work has no place in the gay community since it represents a form of sexual relationship which that community seeks to eradicate. (18)

It is all too clear that the prejudice against sex workers among the heterosexual population tends to be mirrored in the LGBTQ community.

Perhaps we might listen to the testimony of a young sex worker in Chicago:

> I had dropped out of college and gotten into drugs. I took up sex work, which I think of as "gay for pay," in order to support my drug habit. Later, it helped pay for methadone and therapy as I struggled to get clean. But the most important thing for me is that I met really nice people. Of course there were some jerks, but also some really fine people. I had been very scared and suspicious of people, but I met very kind and generous guys, some of whom have been friends for a long time. Although some day I would like to get out of the gay for pay business, so I wouldn't have to charge money all the time, I think being a hustler has been really good for me in my development as a person.

As the sociological studies have suggested, young male sex workers develop lasting relationships with some of their clients and often report very positive experiences.

The authors of a study on male sex work in the Netherlands note that in the 1970s "the age of consent for homosexual behavior was lowered from

125

21 to 16 years" (24). The basic venue for sex workers in Amsterdam is the "boy brothel" that is regulated by city authorities. However, as in other cities, we note that sex work varies widely here, too. In addition to the boy brothels that are quite famous in Amsterdam, there are also street workers and escorts, representing the opposite ends of the economic and social scale. Further, many of the sex workers report identification as gay or homosexual, but this doesn't seem as high as in the British samples (29). One advantage that some may find in sex work is that "They are able to experiment with their homosexuality without permanently identifying themselves with a particular sexual preference" (32). With respect to the brothel population, it is noted that there had been some coerced sex trade but "On the whole … even East European boys work voluntarily in sex work" (31). The Czech boys who populated the brothels were openly recruited in Czech Republic. In another chapter we will have to attend to some of the complexities involved in what is called sex trafficking.

As is true in many of the contexts that are studied in this volume, we may note that: "Frequently clients are regarded as their friends, lovers, social workers, or providers of sleeping accommodations" (34). Thus the mixture of quasi-romantic and friendship connections with sex work seems to significantly differentiate male sex work from what we have encountered in the literature on contemporary female sex work.

In the sample from France offered by Laurindo da Silva, the age of beginning in sex work seems to be 12-17, lower than that which we have seen in Britain. There are also differences in sexual identity: "Of the 53 garcons interviewed, 22 defined themselves as homosexual, 18 as bisexual and 13 as heterosexual" (58). Again a considerable majority self-identify as homosexual or bisexual, although not as high as in the more recent British sample. In the French sample, there seems to be considerable difference between those who identify themselves as *gigolos*, those who are more generically garçons, and those who think of themselves as *trasvestis*. Of the gigolos, the author says:

> By affirming that they only engage in insertive sex, these young men (gigolos) seem less concerned with avoiding being labeled homosexual than with finding a way of ensuring that their virility is not called into question. This is equally true for those who define themselves as gay or homosexual and for those who see themselves as heterosexual. (47)

As will be increasingly common when we look at other parts of the world, the relation to a "cash for services" structure seems rather loose. After referring to Mauss on gift exchange, da Silva notes that the exchange is not necessarily for cash but something of at least symbolic value (48). Nevertheless, cash may serve an important purpose in helping to reduce the risks (on both sides) of emotional entanglements that might be counter-productive. Da Silva writes, "Emotional risks are professional risks: money is the third party protecting the sex worker and client from this possibility" (50). Thus there may be a tension between cash as a protective barrier and other forms of exchange that blur the distinction between sex work and more "romantic" or perhaps patronage relationships. It seems to be true in a variety of cultures that cash for services may represent a somewhat more distant relationship (advantageous to the seller of services who must remain free to engage multiple clients), while the relaxation of the cash nexus in favor of gifts of clothes, electronics, or payment of school fees may suggest a stronger desire for emotional attachment (as well as a way of warding off whatever stigma or criminal penalties that may be associated with the payment for sexual services). While friendships between clients and workers are not uncommon, romantic attachments with concomitant possessiveness and jealousy represent a threat to the livelihood of the sex worker.

Two findings highlighted in the study of Canada by Allman and Myers may be of particular interest. The first is the estimate that "25% of sex workers in Canada were male" (64). This percentage would certainly make it imperative that any discussion of sex work be balanced between discussions of female and male sex workers. The other suggestion is that "male sex workers earned much less than their female counterparts" (64). This corresponds to what I have found in studies of other societies, and it may stem from the wider availability of free sex in gay venues. As in other samples discussed thus far, the majority of male sex workers identify as gay or bisexual (70). A further point of great interest is that "the Badgley Committee stated that the proportion of younger male sex workers who reported sexual abuse was similar to the proportion reported by males in the general Canadian population" (71). Again this may indicate a difference between male and female sex workers, but the absence of good comparative studies makes it hard to be certain. This may be contrasted with the findings in the U.S. of frequent reports of physical and sexual abuse, especially among those who work the streets (87). However, it is not clear whether the abuse is greater than that which would be reported among a comparable population (for example, homeless or runaway youth).

The need for further study of male prostitutes in the West is abundantly clear. Comparative studies of the experience and circumstances of female versus male prostitutes is also indicated. Both are necessary if we are to develop a grounded and compassionate ethic to guide policy decisions in relation to this vulnerable population.

Male Sex Workers in the Developing World

The material provided in the Aggleton volume covers 15 countries. Space considerations preclude attending in detail to all the contexts covered, so I will focus on Mexico, Brazil, and India in order to indicate some of the range of cross cultural material available for reflection.

In the report on Mexico, Liguori and Aggleton focus on two populations identified as *trasvestis* and *masajistas* (givers of massage). The former identify as gay, the latter as straight. The *trasvestis* are quite similar to the group in Neza (a large city attached to Mexico City) portrayed in the wonderful book *Mema's House, Mexico City: On Transvestites, Queens, and Machos* by Annick Prieur.[120] This full-length and in-depth ethnographic study provides a very rich picture of one of the gay subcultures in Mexico from which some sex workers derive.

One of the findings of the Aggleton study echoes a study of male sex workers in the U.S.: "It is not unknown for young men detained by the police to be accused of being sex workers if they are carrying condoms at the time" (122; see page 91 on the U.S.). Again, in Mexico, the *trasvestis* identified as gay, while the *masajistas* all identified as "heterosexual, and did the work out of economic necessity" (115).

The studies situated in Mexico City may not be representative of all parts of the country. For example, in Acapulco, the informal sex workers identify themselves as *mayates*. Since gay identity is regularly associated with effeminacy, many would not identify as gay, although others are yielding to the term as employed in the U.S. The following testimonial deals with this population.

> I have known many *mayates* over the years. The relationships include sex, to be sure, but often the exchange is not for cash, but for things like school supplies, tennis shoes, even cell phones. It very much mirrors a sort of patronage system, which can easily also become friendship. One young man I have known for over a decade. He introduced me to his "boyfriend" (a young *trasvesti*) and later to his wife. Eventually I would hang out with my friend, his wife, and their kid, even doing occasional childcare (the exchange items then were things like beans and diapers). I have also visited several *mayates* who got into trouble with the law in Acapulco prisons. This isn't to say that all such relationships become friendships. But some

---

120. Annick Prieur, *Mema's House, Mexico City: On Transvestites, Queens, and Machos* (Chicago: University of Chicago Press, 1998).

do and that is what makes life on the beach with these guys so rewarding.

The material on prostitution in Brazil is very rich, in large part because of the work of organizations and unions of prostitutes. However, the material on male prostitution is not as great. In addition to the essay in Aggleton by Larvie, however, there is a remarkable ethnographic study by Don Kulic titled *Travesti* that traces the lives of transgender prostitutes in the city of Salvador.[121]

In reporting on Brazil, Larvie notes that "the group of male sex workers … were indistinguishable in many ways from the so-called general population" (160) often because the vast majority of Brazil's population is very poor.

Because the *miches*, or young sex workers, are generally quite poor, those who have some success are able to cross the very marked class divisions which are also largely matched with racial differentiation. Larvie suggests therefore that "in a society which is extremely hierarchical and unequal, this form of sex work serves to provide opportunities for cross-class and cross-race sexual contact" (163).

Not all are very successful in sex work, however. Only half had *programas* (or tricks) the week before they were interviewed: "For most of the interviewees, sex work offers little in the way of either sex or money" (167). Nevertheless, sex work does enable some to compensate for the stigma of identifying as gay: It operates as an institution that provides a ritualized exchange (material or symbolic payment) that justifies otherwise stigmatizing sex acts (168).

Larvie argues that progress can be made in raising the status of these male sex workers but that this would entail some significant societal transformations:

> For male sex work to function as a service—much as other legal commercial services operate—the symbolic and material inequalities between client and provider would have to be mitigated in some form, either through real improvements in the provider's socio-economic status and the diminution of stigma associated with homosexuality, or through access to state-sponsored mechanisms for conflict resolution. (163)

We now turn to the South Asian context. Shivananda Khan writes about young male sex workers in India and Bangladesh:

---

121. Don Kulic, *Travesti: Sex, Gender, and Culture among Brazilian Transgendered Prostitutes* (Chicago, University of Chicago, 1998).

For the vast majority of people, sex work, or whatever name you give it, is a survival strategy. For most, it is a practice enforced by poverty, degradation, homelessness, hunger, and powerlessness, a form of slavery to economic, social and cultural deprivation, stigmatization, and marginalization. (196)

This description echoes some of the studies in the U.S. about survival sex among homeless or nearly homeless youth. But it is necessary distinguish the economic pressures in the affluent West from the often far more dire situation of people in India and, perhaps even more, in Bangladesh.

He reports on a locale in Bangladesh, where about 150 "boys" (or *kothi*) gather at a shrine (a convenient semi-public place), ranging in age from eight to sixty, and getting at best a dollar or two for being anally penetrated (196). The author notes that not all are there to sell sex; others are there to hook up with men looking for fun and sex which might, or might not, involve also some sort of gift giving. Despite the predominance of poverty as the context for the discussion of sex work in South Asia, there are notable exceptions: There are the stories of college students who make considerable extra money by selling sexual services, something like the pattern of those in the U.S. who work in escort services or bars (198).

One of the best parts of this report are the individual stories of sex workers, stories that reveal the diversity as well as the challenge of male sex work. One of the most striking characteristics of sex life in this region is the very young age at which kids become sexually active. It is not only those who engage in sex work who often "begin sexual activity at the age of 10 or younger" (195). Obviously, this challenges Western assumptions about the "age of consent."

Reflections

A shortcoming of the information about sex work across cultures is that most investigation of male sex work comes under cover of HIV/AIDS work. This has the tendency to medicalize the issue and is reminiscent of the medicalization of female prostitution at the end of the nineteenth century. Nevertheless, this work offers many important insights, and the wealth of cross-cultural information helps prevent too-hasty generalizations concerning male sex workers. It is very important to attend to multiple perspectives if we are to make sound judgments.

One issue to which we will return is the relevance of much of this material in considering issues of pederasty. In a great many societies, male sex workers begin at a very young age, while in other societies, the sex workers are older adolescents. The "age of consent" may often be determined by important cultural factors.

Another shortcoming in this material is the paucity of reflection on the clients of sex workers. When the material focus on AIDS transmission, it makes it seem that only sex workers are a vector for the spread of disease. A corrective can be found in Stan Persky's *Boyopolis*, in which he reflects on his own experience with young sex workers in the course of his work as a journalist.[122]

One may also note that it appears that the majority of men and boys who sell sex are not bisexual or gay, if these words have any meaning in the different cultures. Many are selling sex to experiment with issues of "identity" or to escape from domestic persecution or to have adventure. In many cultures, to be "gay" means rather to have a feminized gender identity and performance. In these contexts, generalizations from the way people do or do not identify themselves as gay may be hazardous.

With the exception of Sri Lanka, the Aggleton volume does not describe forced boy prostitution, save in the way in which economic necessity forecloses options for many. However, there may be other studies (of Thailand, for example) that would reflect the growing possibility of coercion into the sex trade in response to the pressures of sex tourism. We will turn to this set of issues shortly.

However, it may be helpful to pause and see how the consideration of male prostitution may shed light on the discussions of female prostitution.

First of all, we may note that in both male and female prostitute populations, there are quite different forms of prostitution. There seems to be a significant difference between what might be termed street prostitution and other varieties: brothels, independent contractors (via internet, etc.), escort services, and so on. In general, it appears that street prostitutes are more often characterized by socio-economic hardship derivative from broken and abusive family systems and complicated by drug use (often it would seem as something that necessitates prostitution, rather than something that follows from it). Much of the literature focuses on this population (both for women and for men), as this is a population that presents fewer difficulties of access for researchers. For example, West, in his study of male prostitution, noted the difficulty involved in interviewing men in escort services. The ready access to the street prostitutes through social service agencies tends to skew the studies

---

122. Stan Persky, *Boyopolis: Sex and Politics in Gay Eastern Europe* (New York: Overlook Press, 1996).

toward the most at-risk population of prostitutes. This may be exacerbated in the case of male prostitutes, since there is little or no attempt to organize male sex workers in the way that female sex workers are organized in many countries. Organizations of sex workers may provide researchers access to interviews with upscale prostitutes, but I have found so far no comparable organization of lobbying groups for male sex workers. Recently, however, I have learned of attempts to develop an organization inclusive of male and female sex workers, their "facilitators," and their steady clients in Calcutta. If this succeeds, it would offer a ground-breaking paradigm for the invention of new forms of solidarity.

In general, street prostitutes appear to enter into sex work at a younger age and are more exposed to violence. However, it appears that the likelihood of violence for male prostitutes is much smaller than for comparably placed female sex workers. In general, male sex workers think of themselves as more in control of the situations in which they find themselves with clients. They tend to be far less likely to have pimps as intermediaries, and so are far less exposed to violence from that quarter. Rather than the spectacular cases of serial predators (John Wayne Gacy, for example), the violence experienced is more likely to come from homophobic predators who target both prostitutes and non-prostitutes in gay areas.

Moreover, there is far more likelihood that male hustlers find prostitution to be a way of exploring sexual identity or of cashing in on a desire for sexual adventure. There seems to be a diminishing percentage of male hustlers who identify as heterosexual, although this may vary significantly across cultures.

In addition, most samples suggest that male prostitution is also related to the quest for patrons, friends, and other relationships. That is, the cash-for-services nexus seems far looser than appears to be the case for female sex workers today. There appears to be far more scope for the development of interpersonal relationships based on sexual encounters, but extending to include a significant range of interaction. This may also result in the diminishment of the likelihood of violence.

It also may affect the motivations of prospective clients. Many clients may find prostitutes in various contexts to be a relatively convenient way of cruising. No need to stand around in bars for hour after fruitless hour, drinking too much. Hiring a hustler tends to work more quickly and efficiently without sacrificing human interaction and even creates potential longer-term relationships. An intriguing study by Joseph Itiel aptly titled *Sex Workers as Virtual Boyfriends* underlines the very real attraction of a stable relationship between male sex worker and client.[123]

---

123. Joseph Itiel, *Sex Workers as Virtual Boyfriends* (New York: Haworth, 2002).

At this juncture, we might consider what would have to change for female prostitution to incur some of the advantages that seem to accrue to male prostitution. This is one of the areas where gay practices may have something to teach a wider culture, just as I have argued above that same-sex unions may have important things to teach in the transformation of heterosexual marriage toward a more humane institution.

Chapter Eleven

Trafficking and Tourism

Over the last few years there has been an extraordinary amount of attention given in the press and in international bodies to questions of sex trafficking and sex tourism. What is most visible is, of course, the most lurid. Thus we hear of varieties of sex slavery in which girls (and perhaps boys) are kidnapped or sold into the hands of persons who take them from their home settings and countries in order to make them available in some form of sex slavery, either in the cities of their own countries or in more prosperous countries where the sex traffickers reap huge profits while keeping their slaves in the most horrid conditions that make other forms of slavery seem almost mild in comparison.

Sex tourism typically refers to those going to developing countries where sex is cheap and easily obtained. But sex tourism also takes place when people travel to Las Vegas or New York City, as well as Paris and Amsterdam. At its worst, sex tourism involves pedophiles who provide a market for very young (pre-pubescent) children who have been kidnapped or sold into virtual or actual sex slavery, especially in Southeast Asia. Sometimes persons are said to engage in this practice in order to diminish the chances of contracting AIDS if the sexual partners are virginal (apart from the vileness of this practice, it must also be regarded as incredibly stupid). Certainly as regards situations of force and the provision of a market for coercive and fraudulent practices, these complementary movements of sex workers and their clients in the global sex industry merit the outrage and the legal interventions that are being mobilized against them.

But because of the way in which sex is routinely made the object of panic in our societies, it is also necessary to ask whether the picture might be somewhat more complicated than some are prepared to admit.

Sex Trafficking

Here it is very important to try to make distinctions between coerced and relatively free behavior. Of course, this is not always easy in practice. As we have seen in the case of prostitution, many of those who become prostitutes do so in the absence of good or attractive alternatives for supporting themselves. For many, this may be the least bad of several bad options. However, others may have all options foreclosed. In the accounts we have read (for example, by Giobbe and Carter) of those who were prostituted at a young age by family members, there may well be stories of those who have been coerced and to have had virtually no option at all. Clearly those who have been sold by their families to sex traffickers, or who are offered transportation into another country in ways that place them in perpetual debt servitude to brothel keepers, or who are kept in prostitution by means of threats to their families, are experiencing clear and, unfortunately, not uncommon forms of coercion that should be treated precisely as slavery.

Of course, we should also bear in mind that there are other migrant workers who are exposed to similar threats and coercion whose work is not of a sexual nature. Slavery, whether for sex or other work, has by no means disappeared from the planet, and efforts to eliminate it are of great importance. (Just recall the virtual slavery of children making rugs in Pakistan or picking cacao in West Africa.) The amount of slavery, particularly child slavery, in the world is appalling. The recent study by Siddhartha Kara titled *Sex Trafficking: Inside the Business of Modern Slavery* is an extraordinarily helpful (and chilling) study that combines first-hand narration and cultural, economic, and geopolitical analysis in a very readable way.[124]

But a proper outrage about the proliferation of sex slavery should not lead us to suppose that all who cross national boundaries to engage in sex work are in the same situation. In the discussion of male prostitution in Chapter 10, we noted the example of young men working as sex workers in the Netherlands who came from the Czech Republic. They are recruited for this work and offered transportation and other assistance. So long as they choose this work freely and are enabled to pay off any debt incurred without usurious rates and have clean and acceptable working conditions, sex work is quite different from the slavery that so often makes the headlines. There is also considerable literature now about young women from Russia who are brought to Western Europe to work as prostitutes. The sudden influx of Eastern European sex workers, especially Russians after the fall of the Soviet Union, has occasioned considerable literature. Many suppose that this is related to the "feminization of poverty" in post-Soviet Russia and to the untrammeled macho style of post-Soviet Russia (although this would have to be expanded to account for the other Eastern European migrations). Certainly the rise of organized crime in Russia plays an important part and this also tends to exacerbate the levels of coercion that are involved, but this does not mean all such sex workers are coerced.

---

124. Siddhartha Kara, *Sex Trafficking: Inside the Business of Modern Slavery* (New York: Columbia University Press, 2010).

There is also considerable attention given to migrations of sex workers from China and from Latin America, especially Mexico, to the United States. What needs to be carefully distinguished here is the question of organized or facilitated migration from questions of coercion. These are quite often simply lumped together without distinction. Hence the importance of Nussbaum's insistence that coercion be outlawed (or rather, vigorously prosecuted) and that the rights of migrant sex workers be protected in the country where they wind up. Unfortunately, laws tend to make the plight of the migrant sex workers far worse. Sex workers are subject to detention and deportation if they come to the attention of the authorities, which places them at the mercy of police and pimps alike. In this connection, it is important to pay attention to the scandalous conditions that are involved in illegal immigration detention facilities today in the United States.

One of the features of globalization is the migration of persons for work. In our time, there are no restrictions placed on the flow of finance capital, hardly any on information, and few on goods.[125] But the ability of people to cross frontiers in search of work is highly limited—in this way, money has more rights under the law than human beings. The use of the sex panic rhetoric associated with human trafficking to further restrict the options of poor people to have access to work, including sex work, is morally questionable at best.

A very helpful study of these issues is provided by Laura Maria Agustin in *Sex and the Margins: Migration, Labour Markets and the Rescue Industry*.[126] She places this discussion in the context of migration and calls for breaking down the sometimes rigid distinctions between migration, tourism, and other forms of travel. For example, the outflow of persons from the imperial centers to "colonies" has only recently been reversed, but this reversal comes laden with fears of the loss of national identity and border controls on the part of the imperial states whose populations faced no such restrictions in their outward migration during the previous several centuries. She also notes that there is migration, whether short-term or long-term, for a host of reasons, many but not all of which are economic.

By placing the movement of sex workers or of those who engage in sex work in their country of destination in a wider context, Agustin helps to defuse some of the "sex panic" rhetoric that tends to control discussion of sex trafficking.

---

125. See Saskia Sassen, *The Global City: New York, London, Tokyo* (Princeton: Princeton University Press, 2001).

126. Laura Maria Agustin, *Sex and the Margins: Migration, Labour Markets and the Rescue Industry* (London: Zed Books, 2007).

Califia notes that the attempt of the U.S. State Department to modify an anti-trafficking proposal in international law:

> took the common-sense position that such trafficking should be opposed only when it could be proven that prostitutes were forced or coerced into selling their bodies. A coalition which included Patricia Ireland of the National Organization for Women, Ms. Magazine founder and long time supporter of the anti-porn movement Gloria Steinem ..., and Planned Parenthood President Gloria Feldt, sent a letter of protest to the White House, attacking this as a weakened policy on prostitution.[127]

This appears to have been the result of something like a sex panic influencing the discussion of trafficking. The resultant policy against sex trafficking has often had extreme consequences for the poor women who were the intended beneficiaries of this international regime. As we shall see, some of Kuo's proposals do aim at a more nuanced approach to anti-trafficking legislation, recognizing the important differences between migration for work and forced trafficking.

Men, as well as women, cross state lines in search of better lives. Sometimes this means escaping what is felt to be an impossible home environment—impossible, that is, economically or politically or socio-culturally. In seizing upon or seeking opportunities to strike out, they are not to be classified as victims (or as criminals). It should be noted that one of the largest sources of income for several nations comes from the money sent home by legal as well as "illegal" migrants. The economy of the Philippines, for example, as well as that of Mexico, depends very heavily on these remittances.

The facilitation of this travel or migration is indeed a large and growing business. This is especially true for those who face severe restrictions on their ability to get travel visas, let alone work permits. For them the cost of migration tends to be much higher. There are borders to be circumvented, and there is the need to secure in advance a safe place to arrive and a means to survive. So, for example, for those who wish to enter the U.S. from Mexico, the cost and the danger of crossing has grown over the last few years. It is necessary to borrow money at high interest rates with little or no collateral. This facilitates the growth of sometimes ruthless criminal enterprises, although it appears that the majority of those who facilitate migration are not unscrupulous predators.

---

127. Califia, *Public Sex*, 137.

It is in this context that the migration of persons who seek or agree to travel to engage in sex work is to be understood. Sex work, like domestic work, is a wide part of the informal economy in which persons can find temporary income without having visas or work permits. Sometimes travel and work is facilitated by networks of extended family, friendship, or village ties. In other cases, travel is facilitated by professional groups that operate outside and against the laws that restrict migratory flows.

That some persons are cruelly exploited in this context is undeniable. But that all are passive victims in need of rescue is a fantasy created by what Agustin calls the "rescue industry." In what may be the most provocative part of her book, she traces the development of the rescue industry to the nineteenth century as middle-class women used organizing to better the lives of the poor as a way to escape the stultifying confines of middle-class households. This was a part of what she calls the rise of "the social" and what Michel Foucault (whom she cites) termed the emergence of biopolitics. As with the "native peoples" of the colonies, so also with the "poor" of the cities, there developed a strong network of helping, educating, civilizing crusades. One of the things in common with these movements and some contemporary activist networks is that those who seek to help seldom ask those they are trying to help what it is that they in fact want or need. Agustin is able to deploy some of the best insights of post-colonial analysis to debunk some of the excesses of the "rescue industry."

In this domain as in others that we study, it is important to defuse the extraordinary loathing associated with sexuality in general and the sexual practices of "others" in particular. It may be the case that, here as elsewhere, we will need to identify those areas of genuine violence from overgeneralizations that serve only to legitimate renewed sex panics. Migrations that entail sex work or prostitution should be understood within wider contexts of migratory flows, with the temptations for exploitation and the exposure to violence that are not peculiar to prostitution. In this case it may well be that the best advice is that offered some time ago by Martha Nussbaum that kidnapping and fraud are to be vigorously investigated and prosecuted and that workers, whether documented or not, have the right to be treated as fellow human beings, not imprisoned by employers or by the state. Indeed, sex workers should be granted the right of refuge in the country in which they arrive, or repatriation to their homeland, as they choose. This is again to say that sex need not be made a special case.

Of course, the commitment necessary to reduce the restrictions on migration, including migration for work and that of ensuring the basic human rights of those who undertake travel and migration in this way is extraordinary. Jacques Derrida, for instance, promotes a genuine cosmopolitanism that would overcome some of the worst features of "globalization." In many of his essays, he argues fervently for the opening up of borders to welcome the stranger, the immigrant, as an essential aspect of a politics that has any relation to the ethical.[128]

One of the few treatments of the international sex trade that deals with this set of issues from the standpoint of theologically informed ethics is that by Susan Brooks Thistlethwaite and Rita Nakashima Brock titled *Casting Stones*.[129] While we differ in some of the conclusions we reach, the authors and I strongly agree that what is required is attention to the rights of others, especially those most vulnerable among us.

Sex Tourism

Sex tourism is in some ways the counterpart to sex trafficking. In this case, persons from well-off countries go to so-called third-world countries at least in part to enjoy the availability of sex and, perhaps, sex workers in those countries. In the most egregious examples, European or American men travel to certain countries where they can indulge their tastes for sex with prepubescent children in brothels that cater to these desires. The market, we are told, for this sort of travel had increased with the emergence of HIV/AIDS that made younger and younger persons seem attractive to those who wish to engage in unprotected sex. Some of the most horrific stories of this kind come from Thailand, although other Southeast Asian countries may be competing for this market. Sex tourists are complicit in coercing young boys and girls from their families and villages to be made available as sex toys for these travelers. At the same time, it is not at all necessary to deny the horrors that are sometimes encountered in some of these contexts in order to insist that the picture of sex tourism is considerably more complex than these images suggest.

First, it may be important to recall that travel or tourism has generally been associated with the erotic. Whether in the case of the small town traveler to New York, the Midwestern traveler to Las Vegas or South Beach or the

---

128. See Jacques Derrida and Anne Dufourmantelle, *Of Hospitality: Anne Dufourmantelle Invites Jacques Derrida to Respond,* trans. Rachel Bowlby (Stanford: Stanford University Press, 2000) and Jacques Derrida, *On Cosmopolitanism and Forgiveness* (New York: Routledge, 2001).

129. Susan Brooks Thistlethwaite and Rita Nakashima Brock, *Casting Stones: Prostitution And Liberation In Asia And The United States* (Minneapolis: Augsburg Fortress, 1996).

gay man heading to San Francisco, just to take a few obvious examples, the connection between tourism and sexual opportunity is widespread—and don't forget college students heading to Fort Lauderdale or Acapulco for Spring break! Those who travel abroad find similar possibilities for the combination of sexual adventure with other sorts of adventure afforded by travel (culinary, athletic, etc.). For most people, I suspect, sexual adventure is only a part, even if an especially exciting part, of the attraction of travel.

Among the attractions of travel is the lower prices possible (though not guaranteed) for things like accommodations, sporting, food, and—yes—sex. For some the perceived inconveniences of third world travel are off-putting, while for others they are the main attraction. (Others are prepared to pay in excess of first world prices for third world getaways.) In addition, many have the impression that sexual adventure is easier to come by in warmer climes, not only because travelers are free from the constraints of work and neighbors and routine, but also because other cultures may have less restrictive or oppressive views of sex than that which is experienced at home. Sometimes this may take the form of flirtation, cruising, or romance (here we might recall the shipboard romance stories of another era). In other settings, there may be a dependence on the availability of prostitution. Again, the line between romance and prostitution may not always be clear.

For areas that depend or wish to depend on tourism as a major industry, there are incentives to offer a variety of possibilities for adventurous tourists. This will often include a permissive attitude toward the local sex trade, whether institutionalized (as with escorts and brothels) or more or less freelance. This may often include male and female prostitution, especially of the freelance variety. Some tourists may find language and culture barriers so difficult that they prefer more formal arrangements.

In some cases, lasting relationships are established. In *Sex Tourism: Marginal People and Liminalities*, Chris Ryan and C. Michael Hall refer to Scandinavian women who go to Gambia and sometimes bring their "lovers" home to Norway.[130] A Chicago group called Asians and Friends is composed of some couples who met in places far from Chicago but who have made lasting friendships. Sugar daddy and kept boy arrangements as well as other kinds of relationships may develop. Not all of these develop from tourism. After all, one doesn't have to go to the Philippines to find a Filipino lover, or to Mexico to find a Mexican lover, or … the list is long, especially in places like Chicago. Nor does one have to stop with the stereotype of Euro-American sex tourists.

---

130. Chris Ryan and C. Michael Hall, *Sex Tourism: Marginal People and Liminalities* (New York: Routledge, 2001).

There appears to be a far higher incidence of Taiwanese, Korean and Japanese sex tourism in South East Asia than Euro-American, for example. All this is to say that sex tourism involves men and women, straight and gay, commercial and non-commercial, European and decidedly non-European, and so on.

Within this framework, there are abuses that properly alarm observers. Again, these have mostly to do with cases of coercion, fraud, and exploitation. These should be addressed for what they are: extreme cases requiring appropriate levels of legal intervention. Interventions, however, should demonstrate an adequate level of cultural sensitivity. Not all societies have the same attitudes toward sex and its dangers. Here as elsewhere, it is good to listen before speaking, especially to the folk one intends to help.

Many of the most lurid examples have to do with underage prostitutes who seem plausibly to be coerced into prostitution. In the available material on men who sell sex, we encounter a wide range of data that points to a wide variation in ages of those who sell sex or who are paid for sex. In another chapter, we attend to the question of pedophilia and pederasty, in part by attempting to distinguish these. But in general, it would seem fair to suggest that pre-pubescent children are never appropriate objects of sexual seduction, nor are they appropriate persons from whom to purchase sex.

One goes to a new place not as a conqueror but as a guest. One goes with curiosity, open to learning how others do things without imposing a set of expectations that derive from an alien culture. One seeks to enjoy the food, the atmosphere, the drink, the customs of another place. In a place that is economically marginal, one wants to be generous especially to those who may be most vulnerable, to be honest without making false promises. The sex is no different. It would also entail making sure that the agency of persons is respected, including refusing to frequent establishments where there is reason to suppose that fraud or coercion has been employed to provide sex workers.

But if sexual exploration means opening oneself up to the possibility of encountering a person of a culture different from one's own, of making friends, of engaging in solidarity, and even advocacy, for them and their people, then sexual adventures in other places or with persons from other places should have no stigma attached.

Migratory sex workers and sex tourists are only the final examples of persons who may force us to consider our attitudes toward prostitution. Recall the heroic prostitutes of the Bible, especially those in the genealogy of Jesus, and consider how sexual services freely offered and generously compensated may be ethical choices both for the sex worker and the client. Thus reconfigured, prostitution leads us into further reflection on more marginalized sex practices that constitute the discussion in Part 4.

142

Part Four

Alternative Sexual Styles

Chapter Twelve

Promiscuity

What previous generations may have termed "fornication" is now more aptly termed promiscuity. But this term is a fairly slippery one. In general it seems to be a comparative term: One writer defined a promiscuous person as anyone who has more sex or more sexual partners than the speaker. In other words, if you have more sexual partners than I do, you are promiscuous. It is relative or correlative. Where the paradigm of exclusive monogamy prevails, then sex outside such a relationship is promiscuous. For some, this would also be true not only of sex with a partner who is being courted or auditioned for such a relationship and sex during the development of a partnership that is "marriage-like," but even where marriage is precluded (for example, with retirees who would lose important economic support like Social Security benefits).

If, according to the traditional ideal of marriage, any sex outside of marriage is either adultery (if one of the parties are married) or fornication (if neither are), then the range of supposedly prohibited practice is quite broad. It will include those who are exploring sexuality out of curiosity (adolescents, for example), those who are "dating" in a way that includes sexual practice (and what counts as sexual practice may itself have wide variation), and those who are living together without "benefit" of matrimony. It may also include those who have no desire for marriage, either for a season of their lives or at all, but who are not committed to celibacy as the only viable alternative. Clearly in our society there is a growing acceptance of many of these forms of what an earlier generation would have termed promiscuity or even fornication. And so, clearly, the definition of, and moral evaluation of, so-called promiscuous sex must be re-evaluated.

But even today, sex within the bonds of marriage may be also understood as fornication or promiscuity. Contemporary Roman Catholic doctrine more or less approves only of marital sex that aims at (or, at least, involves the possibility of) procreation. However, even this is rather lax by the earlier standards of some of the Church fathers. Tatian, who was a Christian apologist in the second century, maintained that even marital sex was fornication. And Clement of Alexandria, toward the end of the second century, maintained that any sex that was not explicitly aimed at reproduction was fornication (even having sex in the daylight hours counted as fornication for him). This is quite different from Paul, who maintained that the proper use of sexuality in marriage was to satisfy desire, especially that of the partner (1 Corinthians 7:5). Paul's relatively relaxed view of sexuality, later adopted by the so-called Puritans in New England, would have been regarded as endorsing promiscuity by the long tradition of Catholic sexual ethics, extending from Clement to the contemporary Vatican.

With the sexual revolution of the 1960s, which was made possible by advances in contraception such as the pill, the opportunity to engage in sex without the dangers and opprobrium of unwanted pregnancy meant a much wider latitude for sexual exploration. When people in churches, especially younger people, attempted to suggest that it was time to open up a restrictive sexual ethic and to make way for the exploration of ethical guidelines for responsible but non-married sex, the result was a determined opposition. As a result, the churches became increasingly irrelevant to the real-life experiences and dilemmas of people, especially younger people. In fact the student and young adult movements of most major denominations were disbanded at this time in large part because of their desire to open up discussion of sexuality, resulting in the loss of the institutions that had been major pipelines for new generations of religious leadership. Furthermore, the philosopher Gianni Vattimo has suggested that the largest reason for the perceived irrelevance of the church and of Christianity generally has been precisely this hypocrisy and obduracy regarding sexuality.

The most likely use of the term "promiscuity" these days would characterize a sexual practice with persons who are not candidates for eventual marriage, or the development of multiple relationships inclusive of sex but otherwise without commitments of even temporary exclusivity. I have the impression that within the gay community, someone who has more than one partner with whom they are having sex may be regarded by some as promiscuous while others would call only those who have several such partners, or who have some partners in the relational mix who are one night stands or who are met in venues for recreational sex, "promiscuous." The mere detailing of the possibilities suggests that promiscuity is a comparative and therefore rather slippery term.

In this discussion, I focus on the case of multiple sexual partners where the aim is not to establish an exclusive relationship. That is, situations where both singularity (as in monogamy or having only one partner) and exclusivity are suspended. Here it is a question both of intentionality (one is not looking for Mr. or Ms. Right, but for shared pleasure of open-ended duration) and of practice (one in fact has multiple partners). I do not mean that promiscuity is incompatible with long-term relationships. As stated in the previous discussion of open relationships and polyamory, one may have multiple relationships and engage in other forms of sexual encounters that are not intended to supplant or add to the number of these more stable and committed relationships.

Issues to be considered here include the following:

1. The place of sex without further commitment, such as one-night stands.
2. The significance of multiple sexual partners for the development of cross-cultural, cross class and other alliances.
3. The possibilities for establishing a lifestyle that includes a mix of various kinds of sexual relationships.

Encounters Without Commitment

Let us begin then discussing the sexual encounter that does not entail commitment beyond the encounter itself. Of course the most radical paradigm of this form of encounter in gay male culture is what might be termed public sex, but here I want to turn to the casual sex of chance encounters: cruising or courtship that produces sexual satisfaction or pleasure for both, perhaps in bed at home and not in a space that is public and so open to the eyes—and perhaps to the participation of others (discussed below).

What is the value of multiple encounters leading to sexual pleasure? And what are the liabilities? We begin by responding to the latter question. We must acknowledge that forms of sexual openness may also become forms of sexual possession in the forming of "counting coup," of racking up partners as a sign of one's own prowess, one's own attractiveness, or one's own "ranking" in a competitive accumulation of sexual conquests that mirrors the capitalist accumulation of "money" as a sign of power or possession. Here the emphasis is not on connection but on consumption, not on community but on accumulation. Sexual pleasure is then not a humanizing ascription of value to life and body and mutual dignity but a self-absorbed calculation of advantage. Certainly this is the form that promiscuity is often seen to take in straight men who use women as a way of asserting male identity and prowess.

Moreover, there is the danger that multiplication of sexual encounters can serve as a substitute for and a detour from other forms of encounter. No number of casual encounters can serve as a substitute or compensation for the development of other kinds of life-enhancing relations; a quantitative measure cannot achieve a qualitative end. When this is attempted, the result can be a pursuit of sexual encounters as a surrogate for something else, a pursuit that by definition is endless and so obsessive. It is this endless— and finally unsatisfying—promiscuity that was sometimes diagnosed within the gay community as the danger of the sexual explosion of the 1970s. (Paul Goodman has also suggested that a certain obsession may be produced by the prohibition itself: "As with any situation of scarcity and starvation ... we become obsessional and one track minded about it."[131])

There are also those who regard their own behavior as a sort of sexual addiction that crowds out other forms of desired activity (work, friendships, etc.). The obsessive and compulsive sexuality that is experienced as self-destructive by the agents themselves is something that psychotherapy is prepared to address. It should be noted, however, that such a diagnosis and course of treatment is based on the fact that the person engaging in the activity feels distress, not that moralistic on-lookers ascribe this addiction to another.

In keeping with what I earlier identified as the systematic ambiguity of sexuality, I would suppose that these and other deformations always lurk at the edges—if not at the center— of a celebration of promiscuity. But I want here to emphasize the "other side": the positive features of promiscuity as the openness to sexual encounters that are not governed by the desire to set up a long-term relationship, but that seek to celebrate sexual pleasure and erotic connection.

Promiscuity and Democracy

Perhaps the founding testament of such celebration is to be found in the poetry of Walt Whitman. Whitman was and is the poet laureate of democracy, and more particularly, of a specifically American form of democracy; that is, a form of democracy that celebrates the sheer diversity of race and class. It was indeed this vision of a society of equals composed of radical diversity that constituted his vision of democracy, American style.

For Whitman, what makes such a society possible is, in large measure, casual sexual encounter and erotic tenderness among men, a form of gay male promiscuity. Whitman called this erotic/sexual connectedness "adhesion." In a certain sense, it is cruising that provides the connective tissue of society among diverse conditions of humanity. That is, it is not what we might call "homosexuality" as such, but same-sex promiscuity that makes the vision work. It is not a question of a society of couples as in Spartan or Theban male bonds among lovers, but an organism whose circulatory system is constituted by a shifting interplay of multiple, often casual encounters among men.

This contributes to democracy by making an erotic friendliness the solvent that overcomes the individualism of competing interests, and so dissolves the walls of isolated monads to make individuals capable of solidarity. It is the

---

131. Paul Goodman, "The Politics of Being Queer," in *Nature Heals: the Psychological Essays of Paul Goodman* (New York: Free Life Editions, 1977), 223. See also Lacan's discussion of Romans 7 in *The Ethics of Psychoanalysis*.

tenderness of mutual welcome of the stranger that breaks down the acids of pseudo-masculine aggression and the enmity of each against all and makes possible a society of brothers and comrades.

To illustrate this, we turn to Whitman himself. Here are three passages from "Song of the Open Road," "Native Moments," and "Calamus (Path Untrodden)," respectively:

> Here is adhesiveness, it is not previously fashion'd it is apropos;
> Do you know what it is as you pass to be loved by strangers?
> Do you know the talk of those turning eyeballs?[132]

> Give me libidinous joys only, give me the drench of my passions,
>   give me life coarse and rank
> Today I go consort with Nature's darlings, tonight too,
> I am for those who believe in loose delights, I share the midnight
>   orgies of young men,
> I dance with the dancers and drink with the drinkers,
> The echoes ring with our indecent calls, I pick out some low person
>   for my dearest friend,
> He shall be lawless, rude, illiterate, he shall be one condemned by
>   others for deeds done,
> I will play a part no longer, why should I exile myself from my
>   companions?
> O you shameless persons, I at least do not shun you,
> I come forthwith in your midst, I will be your poet,
> I will be more to you than to any of the rest.[133]

> Resolved sing no songs but those of manly attachment
> ...
> I proceed for all who are or have been young men
> To tell the secret of my nights and days,
> To celebrate the need for comrades.[134]

In his prose as well, Whitman envisions connections between men as the warp of the fabric of American democracy:

---

132. Walt Whitman, *Song of the Open Road*, cited in Richard D. Mohr, *Gay Ideas* (Boston: Beacon Press, 1992), 133.

133. Walt Whitman, *Leaves of Grass* (New York: Mentor Books, 1958), 110.

134. Whitman, *Leaves of Grass*, 112.

I confidently expect a time when there will be seen, running like a half-hid warp through all the myriad audible and visible worldly interests of America, threads of manly friendship, fond and loving, pure and sweet, strong and life-long, carried to degrees hitherto unknown—not only giving tone to individual character, and making it unprecedentedly emotional muscular, heroic, and refined, but having the deepest relations to general politics. I say democracy infers such loving comradeship, as its inevitable twin or counterpart, without which it will be incomplete, in vain, and incapable of perpetuating itself.[135]

Further, such democracy is cosmopolitan and global in scope. Writing of China, Russia, and Japan, he says: "And it seems to me if I could know those men I should become attached to them as I do to the men of my own lands."[136]

This theme is wonderfully elaborated in the longer poem "Salut Au Monde" in which it is also clear, as in other poems, that Whitman's celebration of masculine friendship is not based in misogyny, for he knows also to celebrate the female as well, and not only as companion to the male. The story of Whitman's lifelong love affair with lovely lads and with democracy is detailed in Gary Schmidgall's *Walt Whitman: A Gay Life.*[137]

A century later, Paul Goodman could also point to the positive values of multiple sexual partners as constituting a web of interconnectedness that promotes human flourishing. He writes that his quest for sexual encounter has "given energy to my anarchism, utopianism, and Gandhianism" and continues to say, "Queer life has some remarkable political values. It can be profoundly democratizing, throwing together every class and group more than heterosexuality does. Its promiscuity can be a beautiful thing."[138] Of his own experience, Goodman writes:

"I have cruised rich, poor, middle class, and petit bourgeois; black, white, yellow and brown; scholars, jocks, Gentlemanly Cs, and dropouts; farmers, seamen, railroad men, heavy industry, light

---

135. Walt Whitman, *Democratic Vistas,* cited in Mohr, *Gay Ideas,* 133.

136. Whitman, *Leaves of Grass,* 122.

137. Gary Schmidgall, *Walt Whitman: A Gay Life* (New York: Plume, 1997).

138. Goodman, "Politics of Being Queer," 219.

manufacturing, communications, business, and finance; civilians. Soldiers and sailors, and once or twice cops…"[139]

He adds, "There is a kind of political meaning, I guess, in the fact that there are so many types of attractive human beings."[140]

Richard D. Mohr, in *Gay Ideas*, also takes up the theme of the relationship between a certain gay male promiscuity and democracy, further elaborating the perspectives that we have found in Whitman and Goodman. Here are some illustrative quotations:

> Gay sexuality of the sort that I have been discussing both symbolizes and generates a kind of fundamental equality—the sort of fundamental equality that stands behind and is necessary for justifications of democracy.[141]

> A model for equal respect can be found in erotic, even promiscuous filiation between males.[142]

> Equality is the ideal, male homosexuality its model, and democracy the realization of the ideal in practice.[143]

Mohr is especially interested in what he terms "hypermasculine" gay male styles, the sort that might be witnessed among Leather folk. Mohr has developed the idea that gay-male promiscuity of what he terms the hypermasculine sort may be understood as an important foundation for a democratic politics. While maintaining that this is meant as a model, it need not be exclusive in the sense that all people need to practice this in order for it to serve as a model of democratic politics. Mohr's model needs expansion in at least a couple of ways. The first has to do with his suspicion that lesbian sexual relations tend to move too far in the direction of a communitarian ethic. Of Sarah Lucia Hoagland's *Lesbian Ethics*, he writes that "far from suggesting liberal individualism as an ideal, lesbian relations provide a basis for attack on this ideal and point toward the desirability of communal or communitarian

---

139. Goodman, "Politics of Being Queer," 219.

140. Goodman, "Politics of Being Queer," 220.

141. Mohr, *Gay Ideas*, 196.

142. Mohr, *Gay Ideas*, 196.

143. Mohr, *Gay Ideas*, 197.

structures."[144] Oddly, he makes the same claim about the promiscuous adhesion of which Walt Whitman writes so eloquently in his poetry. Mohr writes: "The emphasis here on unity and collectivity far outstrips any possible hint that what he is trying to ground is a principle of one man, one vote."[145] And he argues that this leads to "metaphors of multiplicity bound into permanent unity rather than of the establishment of autonomous individuals."[146]

What is going on here? It seems to me that Mohr may have in mind a particular image of democracy that leans toward what we might term a "republican" model, as opposed to a socialist one. He favors a sort of equality that leaves persons as more or less autonomous monads, without enduring connectivity among them. By contrast, Whitman tends to suppose that the encounters in which we engage can and should leave a lasting impact on, or connectivity among, each of the persons. Nevertheless, he aims at "just the right balance between self and other to provide the mutual respect needed to model democracy."[147]

In fact, I believe that Whitman's view is more accurate as well as more ethical. Democracy requires, I believe, not only numerical equivalence (one man one vote) but a sense of sympathy or attunement to one another. This does not at all mean that singularity is simply done away with. Rather, it means that the singularity is constituted in and through multiple sites of engagement. We are differently shaped by our encounters with one another. And it is this sense of reciprocal shaping that may be conducive to an ethos that seeks something like the common good, even the sense that good can be common. But this is the *sine qua non* of the political as such.

For example, through sexual encounter, I may come to know someone of a very different social location than my own. They may be of a different race, religion, language, or class. If the sexual encounter produces a friendly feeling, a camaraderie between us, then I may be inclined to think also of a political good that exceeds my own narrow interests and includes that of another who is differently situated.

Promiscuity and Vulnerability

Within the erotic culture of the many forms of promiscuous gay male sexuality in the 1970s and early '80s, men put aside the markers of class and distinction

---

144. Mohr, *Gay Ideas*, 197.

145. Mohr, *Gay Ideas*, 202.

146. Mohr, *Gay Ideas*, 202.

147. Mohr, *Gay Ideas*, 203.

and found a profoundly humanizing solidarity in surrendering to one another's touch. This has been the case with several of my lesbian friends as well. This is humanizing in a number of ways. It first restores us to our bodies, thereby bringing reconciliation between bodies that had previously been alienated by the stratifying structures of the social roles assigned to each. It moreover helps to bring into focus the possibility of trusting one another with our bodies. One of the remarkable things about baths and gay bars and similar venues is the extraordinarily pacific forms of sociality that they encourage. One can see this in other ways as well. In the Gay and Lesbian March on Washington in 1993, the streets of D.C. were saturated with (primarily) males, in the streets, in the bars, on the sidewalks: drinking, hanging out, moving about, laughing, often boisterous. And yet, unlike a male group of, say, football fans or frat boys, there was no violence. Aggressiveness was conspicuous by its absence. Perhaps an openness to touching and being touched—an erotic availability—diminishes the aggressive impulse. But notice that this is not the case with cross-sex behavior; there, the rules of possession and thus of competition and jealousy and control are mobilized.

Perhaps it is here that we may see what it is about promiscuity that contributes to life enhancement: It banishes feelings of possessiveness toward any one other. This means that the other's promiscuity is also not a problem— and this in turn means that I am not in competition with others for the possession of this scarce good. Without a sense of possessiveness, we can than share ourselves broadly, which, in theological terms, is the central meaning of *koinonia*, or ecclesial fellowship.

Let us take this rather standardized description: I meet someone, a stranger. It is on the street, or in a bar, or at a newsstand. By chance it happens that both of us are feeling sexy, horny, erotically available. Something I see in him and something he sees in me makes it seem that here might be an agreeable partner for a time of pleasure together. Some form of communication of interest takes place, is verified, and is negotiated. We go to his place, or to mine. We explore one another's body; slowly or swiftly we make ourselves available to this touch, this exploration of the body. Some or other sexual practice, for instance genital stimulation toward orgasm, is engaged. And afterwards? We may chat, tell a part of our story. We may want to see one another again. We may be quite satisfied with what we have shared and have no need or opportunity to repeat it or prolong it. But we are grateful to one another for the time we have shared. It would perhaps be too much to say that we have become friends, but the encounter has certainly been friendly. The closed-off-ness to strangers of our urban capitalist landscape has been strangely challenged. We know a bit of one another's life, in fact perhaps rather a good bit about what gives the other pleasure. And we part on friendly terms. We are glad of what has affirmed life and body and connection and pleasure—and friendliness that dissolves, at least for a bit, the isolation, the suspicion, the allergy for the stranger that the social nexus cultivates and nurtures in us like a poison.

What I have so far indicated is something of the positive value of promiscuity as such. But now I want to turn to the value of a certain kind of promiscuity: the kind that specifically crosses boundaries of class and race and culture. Certainly this is already important in Whitman's vision of adhesiveness. For we recall that what Whitman saw as the specific character of American democracy was the sheer diversity of people, class and race and age. And it is "adhesiveness" that keeps these social positions fluid and makes friendliness across the lines that are socially constructed possible.

What promiscuity makes possible (though not inevitable) is the development of "sympathy" of feeling with, feeling together (as Dorothee Soelle used the term), among persons of otherwise quite distinct and often unbridgeable social divides. In late nineteenth and early twentieth century gay fiction, what comes most to the fore, especially in British writing, is the overcoming of the rigid class divisions that fractured the social order. E.M. Forster's *Maurice* celebrates the love of a middle-class protagonist with a male servant.[148] The relinquishing of class position on the part of the former is the "storybook ending" by which the author signals the possibility of a new social order. Similarly, Oscar Wilde's enjoyment of street guys and working class youths did far more than his ill-starred relation with the aristocratic boyfriend to bring him down. For these authors, as well as for the French writer André Gide, there is a connection between a sexuality that crosses class lines and a commitment to socialism that is quite marked. Something similar is seen in the writing of American Paul Goodman. There is, I think, an important and not often well-understood connection between male same-sex promiscuity that crosses class lines and a socialism that protests against class privilege.

In the U.S., in addition to class divisions, we must also contend with racial divisions and cultural ones as well. From James Baldwin's *Giovanni's Room* to Larry Duplechan's *Tangled Up in Blue*, we see the crossing of this boundary is itself charged with erotic value.[149]

Again, there is nothing automatic about this. After all, exploitation of class or other privilege is also possible in the development of such relationships.

---

148. E.M. Forster, *Maurice: A Novel* (New York: W. W. Norton, 2005).

149. James Baldwin, *Giovanni's Room* (New York: Delta, 2000) and Larry Duplechan, *Tangled Up in Blue* (New York: St. Martin's Griffin, 1990).

But since this is after all the "normal" role of privilege, with or without sexual crossing, I think it is fair to highlight the tendency toward the development of sympathy and so of solidarity across such lines on the basis of bodily vulnerability and reciprocity.

Obviously, when we talk of developing sympathy or solidarity, we are moving toward relations of somewhat longer duration than anonymous encounters or one-night stands. We are getting into relations that last days or weeks, long enough for there to be a solidification of friendliness into shared knowledge of one another as people.

Testimony:

> I owe the fact that I have a wonderful set of friends and acquaintances with whom I have shared sexual encounters and from whom I have gained an enlarged sense of empathy to my own innate erotic openness. In bed with Black and white, Hispanic and Asian, Muslim and Jew, Hindu and Buddhist and atheist, investment banker and homeless runaway, I have gained some understanding of what it is like to be a man of quite different social, racial, cultural, economic, and religious location than myself. Some of these have become long-term friends, others I will never see again. From each I have learned about life and love, and with each I have shared what I could of affection and understanding and respect. And because of them, I care not only what happens to them as individuals but also to the peoples they in some way represent. Promiscuity has made me a better person than I otherwise would have been.

There are of course problems. I have indicated that there is nothing automatic about the outcomes I wish to celebrate. After all, gay male promiscuity can also replicate the class and race divisions of society as a whole. That should not be surprising at all. But it should be contested as a betrayal of the potentiality for good, for what Whitman spoke of as the potential for democratic connection that is embedded within gay male promiscuity.

There are other problems as well. What I have said about gay male promiscuity may or may not apply to lesbian sexuality. Certainly promiscuity is often more inhibited here and more constrained, though whether this is more or less inherent to female sexuality or is due to social constraints I cannot judge. I have certainly known lesbian friends who have been quite hearty in their celebrations of the possibilities of a distinctive women-centered promiscuity.

155

It seems more difficult to recommend this order of promiscuity in the context of cross-sex relations. Here, the tendencies to possession and accumulation are strong, due to the long history of straight male domination, possession, and use of women. However, as feminism makes inroads into the social psyche, this danger may be abating. The empowerment of women to choose what they will and will not permit, to be active agents of their own sexuality, is the true sexual revolution of our time. (Think, for example, of the TV series *Sex and the City*).

Ethical Promiscuity

What is ethical promiscuity, then? It is simply the extension of a general ethic of human relations into the sphere of sexual activity. It means being honest, rather than deceitful and manipulative. It means being attentive to the other's well-being as well as to one's own. It means the sharing of embodied vulnerability and pleasure. It means taking care to make vulnerability a site of celebration and consolation. It means responding to one another in ways that enhance dignity and respect. It means basic decency and courtesy.

In addition, it is important to seek ways in which promiscuity can subvert the social divisions and competitiveness that shape social life under conditions of division, exclusion, and domination, while at the same time being sensitive to the ways these exclusions and power differentials may creep into the practices of sexual exploration and encounter.

Sexual promiscuity is not, however, an obligation. There is no obligation to be sexually promiscuous in order to prove a point. People have different levels of sexual need and availability. Respecting this in oneself and in others is also important. Those who do not feel a need or desire for sexual adventure of these sorts should not be denigrated for being uptight.

As in other ways of developing a sexual form of life, it is important that there be ways in which people of different styles can be open and honest with one another, can raise questions without being censorious, and can reply without defensiveness. In Romans 14, Paul provides this advice: "Welcome one another, but not for disputes about opinions … let each be fully convinced in their own minds … but without having to make others agree with one's own opinions."

As we have already discussed, Raja Halwani has considered the issues around promiscuity in *Virtuous Liaisons*. Here it is useful to recall his argument that "we can show that being promiscuous does not undermine the agent's psychic and moral health [and] that being promiscuous does not undermine something else (an activity, a practice, a value) that the agent needs for a flourishing life."[150] In arguing this case, he takes as a counterpoint an article by Kristjan Kristjansson that such a way of life "can lead its practitioner to be incapable of forming a meaningful and loving relationship with another."[151] Kristjansson shows that promiscuity can lead to forfeiting the chance at something like romantic love; but, Halwani concludes, the argument only indicates the possibility, not the necessity.[152] For Halwani, we are discussing very different things, different life aims, different values.

To be sure, a person may opt for non-monogamous sex with multiple partners as a lifestyle choice because they have determined not to seek a romantic relationship leading to monogamy. Or the person may choose promiscuity as a more or less temporary expedient: This is not the right time in my life, given other circumstances, to undertake a romantic lifelong partnership. Does this latter preclude a later turn to embrace at least the desire for and possible successful accomplishment of a committed relationship? Of course it may do so, especially if certain forms of promiscuity approaching what we have termed addiction are embraced. But to suppose that this is always the case would require proof, and this is harder to come by. Since there seem to be many folk who in one way or another have lived in ways that fit one or more definitions of promiscuity and yet have also chosen (before or after) and actualized a romantic committed relationship, the idea of incompatibility seems to not be as obvious as is sometimes claimed. Halwani concludes that promiscuity is compatible with temperance and so with a flourishing and ethical life.[153]

Reflections

Choosing to actualize one's sexuality in multiple relationships need not mean choosing to be callous or callow, nor forfeiting basic human decency and care. Virtuous promiscuity simply means living out one's sexuality in ways that seek to take the other seriously when and where the encounter takes place. It is also true that we all need friends who can help us be aware of the perils involved in any sexual lifestyle choice, whether it be marriage or open relationships or polyamory or promiscuity. A significant part of the danger inherent in any lifestyle decision is that we are perhaps too often left to our own devices without reliable friends with whom to sort out our choices and deal with the evaluation of the risks and potential rewards of any such choice.

---

150. Halwani, *Virtuous Liaisons*, 211.

151. Halwani, *Virtuous Liaisons*, 211

152. Halwani, *Virtuous Liaisons*, 213.

153. Halwani, *Virtuous Liaisons*, 224.

Indeed, promiscuity offers its own set of distinctive opportunities for ethical relationships. It offers the chance to meet and take seriously all sorts of people that we might not otherwise encounter, to escape from the nexus of sexuality and possession, and to encounter others as equals. Thus while it has certain perils, it also has certain rewards. An ethical approach maximizes these opportunities while seeking to steer as clear as possible from the moral perils involved. But of course this is true of any form of life, including, for example, marriage. Instead of promoting only monogamous fidelity in marriage and celibacy in singleness, we would do far better to speak of justice and generosity in all relationships, including sexual ones.

Chapter Thirteen

Public Sex

Anonymous or public sex occurs in contexts that permit sexual practices to take place without the structure of "dating." Thus this sort of sexual expression is to be distinguished from even "one-night-stands" common to heterosexual experience, as well as homosexuality. The contexts used for anonymous or public sex include bathhouses, public restrooms (also called tea rooms), outdoor spaces such as parks or wooded areas, cubicles in adult book stores and sometimes in gay porn theaters, "dark rooms" in gay bars, abandoned urban sites, and sex clubs. These venues provide the opportunity for persons to seek one another out for sexual encounters that occur "on the spot" rather than requiring a relocation to another space such as a home or a hotel. One of the conventional ways of dismissing gay sexuality is to characterize its relational paradigm as "anonymous" sex. It is this dimension of sexual expression that is currently re-labeled "public" sex. If we are to address the character of sexuality beyond its institutionalization in marriage and marriage-like relational structures, it is important to address this dimension of sexual expression.

The various venues for public sex provide distinctive opportunities for sexual encounters and entail specific forms of behavior for negotiated consensuality. Before looking at some of the specific forms of sexual activity, it may be helpful to identify some of the common characteristics of these venues. All of them have in common that the persons who assemble at these sites are presumed to be there for the purpose of having a sexual encounter. Such encounters are understood to be delimited in at least three dimensions: space, time, and personal disclosure. The sexual activity will occur at the site itself, within a relatively limited time frame ranging from a few minutes to a couple of hours, and requires the exchange of no more verbal interaction than is necessary to accomplish the goal of sexual gratification. It is this last characteristic that gives to these encounters the name of anonymous sex, since what is definitive is the exchange of minimal identifying information.

In some of these venues what occurs is simply the presentation of penis and receptacle (hand, mouth, anus) after screening the face and/or the rest of the body. This is "glory hole" sex, the height of anonymity. In other cases, sex may take place in a context that permits conversation and some degree of relaxed conviviality (as well as facial and bodily exposure), as in bathhouses and sex clubs or parties. Of course, in some of these encounters it is possible to launch a less restrictive communication directed at either conviviality or at prolongation of the encounter beyond the space-time containment that defines these particular encounters (in the baths, for example). But this extension is an exception to the tacit rule governing such encounters.

Public Sex and Gay Male Culture

While the contexts and content of this sexual modality is primarily available for men who have sex with men, there are such contexts that are made available to women as well. Thus some sex clubs and sex parties, as well as some bathhouses, have catered to women either apart from men or (more rarely) with men. (Some of these sex clubs will be discussed in connection with the reflections on BDSM below).

We should also note that the participation in venues for public sex by men seeking sex with men is rather unstably related to questions of gay community or identity. Many of the men availing themselves of the opportunities provided by such sites may have a public "heterosexual" identity, including participation in institutions of marriage and family. Participating in public or anonymous sex may serve to enable forms of sexual release that do not compromise other commitments that define them in the "straight" world. This may be, but is not necessarily, related to a closeted preference for or orientation toward same-sex sexual gratification. Some men find the ready availability of sex in these venues to be reason enough to avail themselves of the opportunities provided, even though they might otherwise prefer sexual encounters with the other sex. One may have a primary relational partner (either of the same or the opposite sex) but wish to have other sexual adventures that would not compromise a primary loyalty. Others may find that work or lifestyle or other factors preclude the development of relationships of longer duration. Perhaps they have no time for elaborate courtship or no talent for it, or else seek to avoid venues that permit it but also entail consumption of alcohol (bars, etc.).

That the men who make use of these venues may or may not identify themselves as "gay" has resulted in large sectors of the gay liberation and gay rights movements simply ignoring these men or even expressing open disavowal of them and their venues. With the ascendancy of an assimilationist strategy that values relational paradigms that mimic straight marriage, the tendency to "amputate" these forms of sexual expression has gathered momentum. This tendency has been fueled in the gay community by a concern about HIV infection that has scapegoated "anonymous" sex as a means of HIV transmission, even when many of the sexual practices involved are at low or minimal risk of such transmission.

The irony of this distancing of the "movement" and the "community" from these forms of sexual expression is that those upon whom the oppressive apparatus of the state in opposing same-sex activity most regularly and often falls is precisely those who are "caught" in these sites. Moreover some of these sites have played a crucial role in the development of gay community—most notably the baths. In spite of this, some of the leaders of gay community have joined forces with the state in efforts to police and even eliminate such sites and to further marginalize those who make use of them.

Public and Private

The term "public sex" requires some reflection, given the debatable border between the private and the public, especially as this bears upon sexual activity. The relation between private and public sex for same-sex sexual activity is an especially troubled and conflicted one. In the Supreme Court decision of *Bailey v. Hardwick*, the sexual activity that drew the attention of the police was consensual (oral) sex between adult males in the bedroom of the home of one of the men. Attempts to argue that this was private met with dismissal on the grounds that only cross-sex behavior enjoyed protection under a so-called right to privacy. Thus all prohibited sex was excluded from the realm of the private. Even sex in the privacy of the home was redefined as public sex, just as if the sex acts involved had taken place in a space open to the public and so to surveillance by the officers of public decency. The subsequent Supreme Court decision *Lawrence v. Texas* did overthrow the sodomy statutes that had been involved in the earlier case, but did not diminish the confusion about the private/public divide.

If the distinction between public and private disappears even in the home, it is even more true in those venues open only to those who wish to engage in sex and whose admission to the venue entails a membership in the club. Thus sex in bathhouses and sex clubs or parties takes place in spaces that may be deemed public, in that persons have a right to shared space and/or participation in the venue. Of course, where the sex acts may be viewed by other persons (as in jack-off parties or in orgy rooms), the degree of publicity is even greater.

At a further remove are sites such as tea rooms or parks where no membership is necessary and where there is no formal exclusion of the general public, since the sites are, by definition, provided for the "public." Even here, however, it is clear that participants use elaborate methods to avoid viewing by the public. These strategies include relative seclusion of the site, use of the site when it is most unlikely anyone not in the know would visit it, or the use of spotters and codes of recognition of intent and so on.

161

Another of the features of public sex is the possibility of observation by another person not engaged in the sex act, in ways that suggest that sex is not simply private. The seclusion of the sex act is a relatively recent, and perhaps still rare, phenomenon. This is true of cross-sex encounters, obviously. In the urban landscape there exists a tacit complicity between folk who have sex without closing the curtains and those who possess telescopes for watching. The burgeoning market in do-it-yourself porn is another illustration of this exhibition of the body. Being seen and admired even in the sex act is by no means an unknown pleasure.

Another feature of some of these venues is the possibility of multiparty participation in the sex acts. This is an extension of visibility into tactile availability. Approval or admiration may be expressed tactilely, not only by watching, or by verbal encouragement. Here the sexual activity is shared among many, giving and receiving with a certain abandonment of self, distance, and vision. In gay sex what may be especially important is dissolving the difference between active and passive, top and bottom. Above all what is at stake is dissolving the hiddenness of sexual desire and pleasure.

Venues for Public Sex

We may briefly describe some of these venues.

Bathhouses

This is perhaps the most important institution of public sex. Beginning from the association of men in "Turkish baths," the private all-male space of bodily exposure and pleasure opens the way for the predominance of a clientele that is interested in the exploration of sexual possibilities beyond the voyeuristic pleasures of exposed bodies and shared stimulus of steam and water.[154] In the 1960s and '70s, some of the baths restricted themselves to a clientele that sought sexual pleasure with other men. This produced a reconfiguration of the site with cubicles, intended not only for dressing but also provided with cots for "private" sexual gratification as well as sites for more public sexual acts (as in "bunkhouses" and "orgy rooms") as well as spaces for de-sexualized conviviality. Some of these developed into entertainment complexes with shows that launched the careers of entertainers such as Bette Midler.

---

154. Allan Bérubé, "The History of Gay Bathhouses" in *Policing Public Sex,* ed. Ephen Glenn Colter, Wayne Hoffman, Eva Pendleton, Alison Redick and David Serlin (Boston: South End Press, 1996), 187-220.

By the end of the '70s and beginning of the '80s, such baths appeared also in smaller cities. The need to draw upon a wider range of clientele meant that increasingly exclusionary policies of some of the big baths (excluding people on the basis of age, for example) were not adopted. At the end of this period there was experimentation with openness to women and "swinging" heterosexual couples. Thus it seems true that the bathhouse provided an opportunity for men to celebrate their sexuality in a context of cordiality that helped to create solidarity that fueled the gay rights movement. However, the recognition of the dangers of AIDS led to a demonization of bathhouse sex by people like Randy Shilts[155] and Larry Kramer,[156] and this has carried over into attempts to police bathhouse sex in the age of AIDS.

The dangers of bathhouse sex may, however, be exaggerated. To be sure, the proliferation of sexual partners that this venue facilitates makes it more likely that one will have sex with someone infected with the virus but it is also a location for the incorporation of safe sex education (and the distribution of condoms). There is also considerable absence of reason here insofar as a designation of unsafe sex goes. First, it certainly seems no more likely that people will have unsafe sex in a cubicle of the baths than they will in a hotel or at home, and secondly, the indiscriminate lumping together of anal and oral sex (and a number of other sexual practices as well) as unsafe practices actually mystifies the discussion of safe sex and assimilates it to rhetorics of opposition to same-sex sexual practices generally.

Tea Rooms

Another venue for men to have sex with men is that of the public restroom. (In England this is called "cottaging.") Care is taken so that the "general public" does not intrude on what are generally acts of oral sex. While these may occur "in the open," as it were, the acts also often take place in stalls where the actors are hidden from view of other persons gathered for the same purpose. There are often "glory holes" bored out between stalls so that men may present their penises to unknown adjacent stall users who may choose to fellate or masturbate, or, more rarely, be anally penetrated. (This is more rare because of the way in which the positioning of the body and of visible feet gives away what is going on.) The ethnographic work of Laud Humphries shows that a number

155. Randy Shilts, *And the Band Played On: Politics, People, and the Aids Epidemic* (New York: St. Martin's Griffin, 1988).

156. See the satirical take on bathhouse culture in Larry Kramer, *Faggots* (New York: Grove Press, 2000).

of the men who make use of such venues are or were otherwise committed to straight family structures.[157] In many of these venues, the risk of exposure is greatly minimized by location, time, or the use of spotters. In others, a certain risk may be a part of the pleasure.

"Bushes"

In the 1970s and '80s, there were a number of venues in public parks that became well known as places where men could encounter other men for sex in the open air. The most famous of these was Fire Island in New York.[158] In Chicago, the Belmont Rocks served for some years in this capacity, but there have long been other parks that function at night as locations for men to wander paths "cruising" one another and having sexual encounters in pairs or even in groups. Thus, for example in Atlanta, a certain area of Piedmont Park came to be known as a place where a maze of paths and arbors created an ideal site for men in search of sex. In Sacramento, a section of the river parkland that was especially overgrown provided paths and secluded spaces for nude sun bathing and for sexual encounters. In these and many similar locales there was the development of a certain degree of camaraderie among the habitués. Sex in the "woods" may have its own pleasures: a sense of going back to nature, the risk, the hunt, the fun of playing hide and seek. The eroticization of woods and streams, of chance encounter, of hiding in plain sight, of getting away with forbidden things is by no means restricted to male same-sex sexual cruising. After all, straight couples may also enjoy sex in the woods and other places that include risk of exposure and so heightened pleasure.

Arcades

In bookstores that sell porn to men or in movie houses that show porn for male audiences, there may also be provided booths where men may not only masturbate while watching porn but also share a cubicle. This is an expansion and specialization of another venue, the adult movie house where men may grope one another in the seats or even have oral sex there or in the "johns." A

---

157. Peter M. Nardi, "Reclaiming the Importance of Laud Humphreys's 'Tea Room Trade: Impersonal Sex in Public Places,'" and Laud Humphreys "Tea Room Trade: Impersonal Sex in Public Places," in *Public Sex/Gay Space*, ed. William L. Leap (New York: Columbia University Press, 1999), 23-54.

158. David Bergman, "Beauty and the Beach: Representing Fire Island," in *Public Sex/Gay Space*, ed. William L. Leap (New York: Columbia University Press, 1999), 95-114.

good example of this sort of encounter plays an important role in the iconic movie *Midnight Cowboy*.

Clubs

The closing of bathhouses and the awareness of safe sex practices generated the institutionalization of jack-off clubs and sex parties. Because club membership is required, the sexual practices here are public in the sense that bathhouse sex is, but not in the same sense as sex in the tea room or the "bushes." These venues now cater to a variety of clientele, including clubs for lesbians and for straight couples. Perhaps the best-known clubs are those that are especially geared toward BDSM (explored in another chapter). These venues seem to emphasize the visibility of the sexual within the restricted public of the attendees.

Dark Rooms

In some gay bars, rooms have been set up for groping sex without illumination. To be sure, this is a modification of what often was also a specialized part of the gay baths. These are especially popular in Europe and also exist in Mexico. Even those who have little success in cruising with the lights on may find this a congenial and effective form of gratification. Even if things go no further than groping and being groped, this may nonetheless be pleasurable: It is as if the experience serves to re-eroticize the body. Here as in other such venues, the elimination of certain forms of distinction and discrimination is important as a way of democratizing of sex. In this context, sex may most often be masturbatory or oral, although occasionally anal sex may occur, as the presence of a number of discarded and used condoms attests when the lights go on at closing time.

Warehouse Sex

The use of abandoned buildings, warehouses and docks is a feature especially of the New York scene, memorialized in a number of fictional accounts. Here the industrial urbanscape is eroticized, in contrast to the bucolic atmosphere of parks and wooded areas. Such venues tend to be popular with members of the Leather crowd.

With respect to most of the venues for public sex, risk and adventure are often part and parcel of the experience, as in things like mountain climbing, bungee jumping, car racing, and other activities in which risk is an integral part of the attraction of the activity. Thus the courting of risk and adventure that is so often gendered as masculine behavior helps to define these forms of sexual expression, which, in addition to being characterized as public or anonymous sex, could as well be called adventure sex or recreational sex.

There is obviously in some of these venues an eroticization of public space, which subverts the private/public distinction. This is less true obviously of clubs and baths, but more so of tea rooms and bushes. This may also be seen as a protest against the disembodied character of much of everyday life as we experience greater and greater rationalization, bureaucratization, and depersonalization—with the accompanying loss of affect, of pleasure, of encounter, and so of the erotic. Thus the eroticization of the everyday is a kind of opposition to the dematerialization of the body in the modern social reality achieved through the reassertion of touch and tactile connection.

The Ethics of Public Sex

We now turn to questions of the ethical status of this form of sex. Of course, for many, the "contained"—or, anonymous and fleeting—character of the sexual expression involved here is enough to disqualify it from ethical reflection. Sex is, instead, for the development of relationships and best occurs within the context of a relationship. (We omit from consideration the views of those who would oppose any same-sex activity.) In the chapter on sexual ethics, some attention was given to an essay by Martin Stringer, which illustrated the rhetoric of mutuality and intimacy whereby some who are quite open to same-sex activity nevertheless seem to preclude sexual expression where the development of marriage-like relationality is absent. This objection would apply also to prostitution as typically conceived, as well as to pornography (its production and use) and perhaps even cross-generational sexual relationships insofar as these seem to lack a generational structure of "equality." However, these perspectives apply with particular force to the anonymous, public and episodic forms of sexual expression now under consideration. Are these relationships devoid of moral content? Are they really dehumanizing"? Are they so far gone with respect to "objectification" and "alienation" that they are to be regarded as off the moral scale?

In brief, I believe the answer to be: No. In fact, I believe these encounters to be no more devoid of ethical content than any other encounters that occur between persons that are not elaborated into relational intricacy, such as encounters with strangers in public space: waiters, clerks, barbers, beggars, convention goers, fellow passengers in planes or buses—in short, the myriad encounters with our fellow human beings that make up the dense texture of everyday relationality and sociality. The same ethical content of fairness, justice, respect, courtesy and cordiality that make these relationships life-enhancing apply to the sexual practices, encounters, and sites that we are discussing.

Similarly, these sexual encounters may also "go wrong" in ways that non-sexual encounters of this sort may also go wrong, and so diminish the quality of life of those who are involved. Brief encounters, sexual or not, may exhibit the prejudices, the boorishness, the disregard that constitute everyday injustice.

This approach to ethical reflection is crucially dependent upon not making sexual expression a special case. This means contesting the erotophobia that is often at work in making sex a unique zone of ethical danger. Of course, there are also other ways in which sex may be made a special case without overtly introducing erotophobia. We may suppose that sexual expression entails a certain bodily vulnerability that requires special care, or we may contend that because sex connects people in an intense bodily experience, it should be reserved for the construction of more permanent relational glue to bind people together over time.

Without denying the importance of other forms of sexual expression or denying the limitations of so-called public or anonymous sex or avoiding the ways in which such encounters on their own terms may go wrong, I want to draw attention to four aspects of ethical care with respect to the other person that come to expression in these encounters and help to make the case that such forms of sexual expression may have positive value as compared to (or inclusive of) other forms of sexual connection.

First, ethnographic evidence supports the supposition that these encounters carefully protect their consensual character. No one is coerced or seduced into sexual activity that they have not clearly signaled a willingness and even a prior desire to participate in.

Second, the studies portray the development of strategies of solidarity, such as warding off of unwanted intrusion either by the general public or the police.

Third, there are rituals of courtesy in invitation and acceptance that largely protect the dignity of each: the "thank you" whispered in the john, the cigarette shared in the bath cubicle, the brief hug in the woods. These courtesies often stand in marked contrast to encounters in the non-sexual arena and seem to be recognition of the shared vulnerability of the participants to one another.

Fourth, acts of public sex serve to combat a mystification of sex that all too often entails one person's attempted possession of the other. Here the essential separateness of subjects is respected. This is no trivial matter, as Emmanuel Levinas's reflections on ethics as first philosophy make clear. Is subjectivity in sex necessarily only a good thing? In casual or adventure sex what is brought to the fore is that we escape the need to be subjective and thus from the need to subject the other. When sex is de-sentimentalized or de-romanticized, is that always a bad thing? The very absence of discourse makes for the diminution of chances for lying, for the manipulation of discourse that is one way of identifying the ethical problem as such.

In some of these venues, persons who are marginalized because of age or appearance from successful use of venues such as bars and discos find sexual release. This is an important and positive feature of what is sometimes called de-personalization. For what is often erased here are the masks of persona. Thus class differences are normally put aside in virtually all of these venues. Although certain signifiers of fitness or age status may be privileged, for example, in the baths, these also seem to be greatly diminished in the tea room. Even language barriers may be easily circumvented in venues where verbal communication is minimized or even tacitly discouraged. In a world in which even fleeting intimacy is circumscribed by boundaries of race, class, and culture, these are not unimportant opportunities for the crossing of these compartmentalizations of life.

Further, without disparaging what is sometimes called "solitary sex," it should be noted that in the forms of sexual expression that are spoken of as public sex, the encounters seem to underscore the importance of shared pleasure and so the essential relationality of being human.

We may also identify important reasons why persons may choose these venues over other opportunities for having sex with men. The use of such venues may make it possible to have a sexual outlet that does not jeopardize other commitments. Even in the case of persons who are living in cross-sex marriages with children, this is not to be dismissed as closeted. It may be a positive value to maintain the family structure without denying other desires and needs that do not compromise those commitments, as Laud Humphries emphasized in his study of tea room sex. In other cases, vows of celibacy may preclude relationship building. In still others, commitments to kinds of work (such as traveling salespersons) may make other relational patterns functionally impossible, at least for a time. If one is concerned about the contamination of commerce into sex (prostitution) or the unwise prodigality of expenditure of resources, then the non-commercial character of these relationships may hold attractive possibilities.

In general, it appears that both the decision to make use of such sites and the conduct within them may be reflective of values that ought to be encouraged, rather than heaped with derision and opprobrium.

When these factors are taken into account, I think the protection of such venues can be seen to be an important part of a wider sexual culture. It does not seem to be the case that such venues mitigate against the development of other kinds of sexual relationality. Of course, where the use of such venues unnecessarily crowds out other forms of sexual expression that the person might find life-enhancing, then concern may rightly be expressed—just as in the case of obsessive engagement in relatively diminished forms of human contact (such as watching too much TV, cruising the internet, playing video games, etc.). Just as most people require a mix of relational forms in order to flourish as human beings, they may also require a variety of forms of sexual expression.

The basic argument here is that the occasions for public or anonymous or recreational sex also involve the expressions of a number of values that are easily lost sight of in more restrictive practices associated with courtship and dating and marriage. Of course, there are also limitations to the kinds of values that may be instantiated here due to the variety of containment strategies we have identified. There are, here as elsewhere, many chances for encounters to go wrong; there may be violation of the dignity of another person or violations of trust and respect. But these are not specifically endemic to these sites. Moreover, one may suppose that sexuality needs other forms of expression to be "well rounded." And many may find that they have no need or desire to participate in any of these forms of public sex, but there seems to be no good reason for a moral censoriousness to obtrude here, nor any warrant for a public policing or attempted elimination of such sites. Only where sexual display or harassment is foisted upon that part of the public that wishes to be let alone should there be any occasion for policing these expressions of sexuality. But as we know, current forms of policing usually involve extravagant clandestine surveillance, deceit, and attempted exposure. It is this which is truly a violation of the ethical. Anyone with a minimal regard for the most basic ethical norms would find it necessary to strenuously protest against this routine violation of human dignity.

Chapter Fourteen

Kinky Sex and Queer Ethics

Overview

Kinky sex is not a common topic in church circles. Even those who welcome inclusion of lesbian and gay persons in the Christian community may not have had the opportunity to consider the ethical aspects of sexual practices that are considered unusual. The term "kinky" can cover a wide range of practices, but for purposes of this essay, we will focus on practices of BDSM. The acronym stands for bondage and discipline, domination and submission, and sadomasochism.[159] These practices and the persons for whom they are important have often been stigmatized as being perverse and beyond the ethical pale. At the same time, these practices hold powerful appeal and meaning to a significant minority of heterosexual as well as to many lesbian, gay, and bisexual persons. The marginalization shared by those who practice BDSM has at times resulted in solidarity across sexual orientation identities, reflected in pansexual organizations and social gatherings.

In one sense, BDSM practices are simply minoritarian practices, an example of Gayle Rubin's description of our society's penchant to categorically (and undeservedly) label certain sexual variations as sexually dangerous. Meanwhile, this particular marginalized sexuality has taken its place in advertising, fashion (leather, chains, uniforms, and the like), and entertainment (for example, songs such as Rihanna's "S&M" on her 2010 album, *Loud*), reflecting an interesting fascination with the accoutrements of BDSM.

BDSM has been examined and interpreted from multiple perspectives—psychological, sociological, theological, legal, and others. Sometimes the voices of BDSM practitioners are heard among those examinations, but often they are not. Before turning to the possibilities for BDSM as part of a queer sexual ethics, it is important to consider at least some of these perspectives.

---

159. "Sado-," from the term sadism (after the seventeenth century French writer Marquis de Sade), refers to deriving pleasure from inflicting pain. Masochism (after the eighteenth century German writer Leopold von Sacher-Masoch) refers to deriving pleasure from receiving pain.

Is BDSM "Sex"?

We may also note the way in which discussions of many BDSM practices problematize standard notions of "sex." Those who practice BDSM may or may not include genital contact and orgasm in their activities. For some, the experience is erotic and pleasurable without such contact or climax. Is that still "sex"? Or some other form of recreation? What is the sexual component of the scene? The enactment of submission, pain, and mock degradation may serve the purposes of release without these being directed toward a specifically genital climax. It is for this reason that these practices may not fall under prostitution statutes, even when payment is involved. Some persons earn their livelihoods as male "dominators" or female "dominatrices" for hire, but are generally not subject to prosecution under the anti-prostitution laws since they are selling a private entertainment service that is not specifically sexual in character (although it may certainly be erotic).

Objections

On account of what many regard as the extreme enactments of bondage and discipline with ritualized degradation and pain, objections to BDSM abound. Those who are rightly appalled at domestic violence and at the routine use of rape and torture in national and international conflicts may be outraged by the ways in which BDSM seems to mimic such violence. A vociferous debate occurred among lesbian feminists in the 1980s, with one group arguing that all (heterosexual) pornography aimed at S&M and was a particular form of violence against women, encouraging or perhaps even stimulating not only rape fantasies but also rape practices among male consumers of porn. Thus they may suppose that BDSM is simply a reflection of social violence and degradation or may even encourage such violence. Other lesbian feminists, notably the Samois collective in San Francisco,[160] strongly challenged this perspective as yet another example of one group enforcing "correct" sexual practice on another. Gayle Rubin, whose work on sex has been important to the perspective taken in this book, has done considerable research into Leather communities in San Francisco and has been a strong defender of the BDSM community and its practices.

At stake in such debate is the role of fantasy—especially when fantasy plays with the themes of domination, bondage, punishment, and so on. Does fantasy compensate for and defuse internal conflicts, or is it an incitement

---

160. See Samois Collective, *Coming to Power: Writings and Graphics on Lesbian S/M* (Boston: Alyson, 1983).

to heinous crime? Is this therapy for the masses or the training ground for unspeakable acts of horror? Fantasy has many purposes. Some of these may be therapeutic; some may by prophylactic. Fantasy may play with the past and its resolution, with the present and its relief or its critique, and with the future, its anticipation or avoidance. In the practices of BDSM, we come upon fantasy in full roar. It would be unwise for those who believe in the importance of fantasy—and of the religious imagination, in particular—to join in the disapproval of fantasy as such, even when its contents make us uncomfortable. For what is the Bible if not a series of articulations of fantasy that, at their best as well as their worst, have the capacity to make us uncomfortable? Perhaps we may be made uncomfortable in ways that help us to imagine a world that might be desired from a number of different "subject positions," including those that involve domination and submission.

Psychological Perspectives on BDSM

Next we may ask: What is going on psychologically in BDSM? It is a fascinating question to which much commentary on BDSM readily turns, often landing on the idea that surely those who participate in such activities must have some psychological disorder or other. From such a conclusion springs notions that no healthy and sane person would (or reasonably could) consent to such activities. The early history of psychiatry and sexology included efforts to understand BDSM practices in a way that moved beyond religious interpretations of such practices as evil or criminal in nature. Instead, such practices were categorized as psychological illnesses to be cured, thereby fostering a medicalized approach, and replacing the stigma of sin with that of mental illness. Even if the intent of early sexologists and subsequent psychologists was to move the social response to such behaviors out of the criminal justice system and into the medical realm, the result was often enough that psychology and psychiatry came to reflect, rather than to challenge, social stigmatizations in the name of the health of the social body.

Michel Foucault has pointed to the modern innovations of a biopolitics that intrudes ever more completely into the regulation and supervision of everyday life.[161] Thus medical or quasi-medical stigmatization of behaviors may legitimately be viewed with suspicion, since the result is the normalization (and heterosexualization) of the social body and psyche. Even if some persons who engage in these practices may seem to have "psychological problems" or to be

---

161. Michel Foucault, *Society Must be Defended: Lectures at the College de France, 1975-76*, trans. David Macey (New York: Picador, 2003).

vicious rather than virtuous, that is not true of all, or even most, persons who engage in the stigmatized practices, any more than we would be willing to accept that all gay people are sex addicts or lacking in virtue, or that all heterosexual persons are into the domination of women or the abuse of children.

Multiple psychological theories have been offered to explain BDSM practices. Perhaps they serve to replay and to dramatize scenes of childhood instinctual repression, or else link to past erotic fantasies of being punished and receiving attention from admired or feared adults. Perhaps rituals of domination and submission represent a working through of earlier conflicts, or provide the submissive with a certain freedom from responsibility for their erotic desires. More recently, some psychologists have noted the ways in which human beings (perhaps unique to us as a species) can link pleasure and pain, illustrated by the endorphin releases that comes with marathon running or eating hot peppers. Similarly, BDSM practitioners will comment on the endorphin rush they experience during these activities.[162]

The issue of consent is a key one in considering BDSM. Since many people find the practices involved rather unsettling and even alarming, it is often difficult for them to believe that any true consent is possible. One might suppose: "If I wouldn't agree to this, then nobody in their right minds would," but the same argument might also be entertained with respect to skydiving, bungee jumping, and similar activities. The consent issue has at times become a legal one. In a notorious case in the United Kingdom, persons engaged in consensual BDSM were prosecuted for and convicted of assault on the grounds that a sane person could not consent to the forms of degradation and pain that the activity entailed. This may be an exceptional case, but it does suggest something of the possible legal issues that BDSM can raise.

Noteworthy in the BDSM community is the emphasis on consent and negotiation before any actual behaviors are enacted. Equally important are the consistent recommendations for agreement on a "safe word" that would immediately stop the action if any of the participants say it. The process of preparing for BDSM interactions include establishment of trustworthiness and a surprisingly extensive review of each participant's limits, favorite activities, and plans for what will transpire. Multiple-page questionnaires are used by some BDSM practitioners as part of their planning for activities![163] Particular attention is paid to the limits and the desires of the submissive, the participant who can also be referred to as a "bottom." By definition, the "bottom" agrees

---

162. Jay Wiseman, *SM 101: A Realistic Introduction*, (Emeryville: Greenery Press, 2000).

163. Wiseman's *SM101* includes a ten-page sample questionnaire on 68-77.

to submit and obey the dominant partner, or "top," but it is also true that the negotiations prior to the start of the scene delineate carefully what the top can do to, or require of, the bottom, and the top must also attend closely to the responses of the bottom to avoid moving beyond pleasure or inflicting unwanted pain. These negotiations mean that BDSM practices may often be more consensually arrived at than is typical of a standard sexual encounter.

We may also note the apparent necessity for the "top" to change role or to get out of character in order not to be destructive of relationship. Thus many "doms" or tops who take on the training or education of less experienced tops insist that their protégés experience for themselves the roles of the submissives so as to more carefully enact the role of top. This seems to reflect an important ethical and religious point: One can appropriately enact power only if one can do so in ways that are schooled in empathic identification with those who are in the subordinate or submissive position. Whether one thinks here of the incarnation as God's assuming the submissive role in order thereby to become better able to identify with humanity, or the insistence that psychotherapists themselves undergo psychotherapy, this apparently fairly widespread practice in the BDSM community seems to be exemplary.

Sociological Perspectives

Some sociologists have interpreted BDSM practice as theater. One of the most striking things about BDSM is its ability to ritualize and focus (i.e., theatricalize) social dynamics of power, control, and compliance. Such an interpretation makes certain sense in light of the terms by which BDSM practitioners describe themselves and their activities. As noted above, activities are discussed as "scenes," while the "roles" that dominants and submissives "play" are often referred to as "top" and "bottom," respectively. The theatrical nature of scenes is also reflected in the way the event is understood to be separate from day-to-day reality, not unlike the suspension of disbelief expected of theatergoers and film viewers.

Another important sociological facet of BDSM practice is its ability to deal not only with an interior drama but with a social one as well: the drama of, as Foucault might say, "discipline and punish." BDSM literature often mentions the apparent difficulty of finding enough tops to fill the need (see Kipnis). Most want to be the bottom—the one who is disciplined and/ or dominated. Moreover, there appears to be an especially strong market for dominatrices: women who will play the dominant role, especially for male clients. It is interesting to speculate about men's desire to overcome the daily effects of having to be in control by seeking a compensatory fantasy to balance that power. In fact, notions of conscious and deliberate power exchange are often seen by BDSM practitioners as a key dimension of these practices. The awareness of power dynamics in scenes and the willingness to engage them stands in contrast to our society's usual patterns of wielding power in hidden, unspoken, and politically expedient ways.

Religious Perspectives

Next, we should ask how certain biblical images and narratives play into this fantasy world and the eroticism of submission. The staging of submission, of endurance of pain, and of acceptance of punishment is deeply embedded in the religious imagination. It is even possible that this may serve some beneficial purpose; that is, it may incite non-violence or it may de-valorize the role of the torturer relative to the tortured. Surrender to the ferocious love of YHWH is, or may be, an invitation to a kind of masochism. And is this an entirely bad thing? Might it actually serve to reduce our penchant for violence?

Images of Abraham's sacrifice of Isaac seem perfectly suited to the genre: Submission to the violence of the father, which, because it is "perfect submission, perfect delight," is also rewarded by not only survival but also flourishing. The prophets also figure the relationship between God and Israel as one in which there is both apparently violent discipline and tender reconciliation. While these scenes have sometimes been heterosexualized, it is important to keep in mind that both characters are male, even if one of them (Israel) is transgender. And think of Job's credo: "Though he slay me yet will I trust him" (Job 13:15). And what of the cross and the believer's identification with the obedience of the son and with the suffering there? The victim who through suffering and obedience serves not only as a model but as redeemer (who is raised) provides a model for Christian life that has often emphasized endurance of pain and suffering for the sake of identification with the Christ.

Numerous mystics and spiritual writers throughout Christian history have emphasized submissive obedience, endurance of suffering, and often physical penitential practices as essential to progress in the spiritual life toward the ecstasy and joy of divine encounter. It is easy to imagine that such treatises create or reflect an erotics of submission in the western cultural imagination. Stories of the various passions of the martyrs and their re-enactments may function similarly. Perhaps for this reason St. Sebastian with his arrow-pierced body has served as the prototypical gay martyr.

What is especially striking from the standpoint of religion in BDSM scenes are reports by submissives of near religious or actually religious experiences of transcendence.

Testimony:

A friend of mine, a rabbi, once told me that our sole purpose in life was to be true expression of our soul. As a MtF transsexual woman, I am now embodying that true expression. However I first endured twenty-five years of a depression-producing denial of that true expression before beginning my transition. My transition from male to female was just the beginning of my decision to live more authentically to myself. There was more in the shadows of my life that I would choose to embrace rather than suppress. What I had also chosen to suppress was my submissive nature—a deeply felt need to find personal fulfillment in the service of another. But rather than seeing submissiveness as a potentially healthy form of sexual expression, I had feared that it would be seen as being weak and constitutionally incapable of assertiveness. But I would come to see that this was far from the truth.

BDSM is seen by many to be out on the lunatic fringe of sexual expression. To the moral majority, sadomasochism is morally reprehensible and bears no resemblance to acceptable forms of normal sexual expression. Many members of the BDSM community are forced underground for fear of losing their jobs, children, and reputation should their involvement in the S&M lifestyle be discovered. Many like me choose to join clubs where they become part of a close knit community of like-minded kinksters.

What is not generally recognized are the high ethical standards that govern the S&M lifestyle. All true S&M relationships and activities are completely consensual, and practiced with the well-being and sexual gratification of each partner as the goal. The idea of Master/slave is distasteful for many. Particularly if the slave/submissive is a woman, the practice, like prostitution, is seen as perpetuating a patriarchal system of oppression against women. For me however, I find the thought of serving and pleasing my lover to be incredibly erotic and personally fulfilling. We are recreating a "power over" relationship for the purpose of mutual sexual gratification: both of us knowing exactly what we want and claiming it. In truth, we are equals.

This type of relationship requires a level of honesty and trust that is seldom seen in the "vanilla" world of sexual relationships and practices.

As a seminarian, I developed an interest in sacred pain— the Christian desire for suffering. This led me to explore the possibility of achieving states of ecstasy through pain. I had never before thought of pain as being desirable, but as a member of the local BDSM scene, I am now able to freely and safely experience the electrifying ecstasy that is to be found in the lash of a whip. My choosing to live more authentically to myself has made this possible. I write these words with no sense of guilt or condemnation. This is who I am.

This student's testimony may refer to exceeding the threshold of pleasure and pain, to the loss of subjectivity or of the Western construction of subjectivity (which, from the Eastern traditions, might be regarded as an unnecessary and indeed inhumane burden to bear). Perhaps for these reasons, Julia Kristeva has signaled that an especially salutary feature of the Christian symbol system is that it has a sado-masochistic structure, permitting the working through of these issues on a public and social scale.[164]

We note also the way in which the top in this relationship takes extraordinary care of the bottom and her body, providing pleasure, nurture, and even ecstasy. What we have here, then, is one who is able to play the role of "master" without losing track of solicitude for the other. That this care is masked by apparent heedlessness is what induces the need for trust, for submission. But it also means that the top will not have a willing bottom if he or she is not scrupulously trustworthy. In the ecstasy of self-abandonment and in the care for the well-being of the submissive, we have important clues to not only an ethical but also a religious and even a theological understanding of S&M.

In approaching BDSM from the standpoint of a religiously informed ethic, it seems to be important to recognize that however alien certain sexual practices may seem, those practices may have very different meanings and effects for others than one first imagines or recognizes.

---

164. Julia Kristeva, *This Incredible Need to Believe* (New York: Columbia University Press, 2009).

Lessons for Queer Sexual Ethics

It is clear that various S&M practices are important to a significant minority of persons as a part of their sexual repertoire. This in general seems far less problematic than the real-world enactments of domination, oppression, and the infliction of pain on those who do not derive pleasure from it. When this is combined with the many ways in which BDSM echoes certain aspects of religious traditions and spiritual practices, it would seem quite wrong to stigmatize either the practices or the practitioners.

It is at least possible that if the understanding of the BDSM community was more widely available to society generally, it might provide a more salutary outlet for the needs to dominate or to be submissive than the way this is often worked out unconsciously in the workplace, the family, or even the institutional church. It is possible that the world would be a safer place if one's impulses to dominate or to submit were acknowledged and ritualized within BDSM scenes.

Moreover, attempts to limit the dissemination of literature and depictions of these practices means only that people are likely to be less safe when they are forced to make this stuff up without mentoring and the controls built into group formation and referral. In this sense, the BDSM community may even be a model that other apparently less-fraught situations or scenes might do well to imitate. The "safe, sane, and consensual" guidelines for BDSM practice require self-awareness and the ability to give voice to one's sexual desires, fantasies, and limits in preparation for a BDSM scene. The various BDSM and Leather communities do a fairly good—and sometimes even exemplary—job of emphasizing an ethical approach to BDSM. Attention to safe sex and the prior negotiation of erotic practices, care for the most vulnerable, insistence that those who wield power know what it feels like to be on the bottom—all of these are very important aspects of ethical reflection and practice.

Chapter Fifteen

Pederasty

The question of cross-generational relationships has become something like the third rail of queer-affirmative studies. One of the principle ways of discrediting same-sex behavior and identity has been through raising the specter of the homosexual predator seeking to corrupt boys (almost always it is male "homosexuals" who are spoken of). The argument has been that because gays don't reproduce, they must recruit—and that the way this is done is by capturing impressionable boys, molesting them, and so somehow appropriating them into the gay lifestyle. While this stereotype has a long history, it has been mobilized with particular force over the last forty-plus years; thus the Anita Bryant campaign against gay rights during the late 1970s in Florida was called the "Save our Children" campaign. A similar movement was organized thereafter in California with the hope of excluding gay (and lesbian) persons from the ranks of public school teachers, a proposition ultimately beaten back by groups led by Harvey Milk. The association of queer sexuality with "child molestation" in the general public makes it imperative that we address this set of questions, in spite of the palpable discomfort that the topic provokes. Nothing like an adequate treatment of these issues is possible here given the amount of emotional baggage brought to this discussion (either because of personal history or media sensationalism), on the one hand, and the virtual absence of calm discussion in the available literature, on the other. Instead I will simply seek to raise a number of issues and questions for consideration in the hope of engendering reasoned and questioning discourse on this topic and the issues it raises.

I will first deal with some of the things that make this discussion so difficult: the panics around the sexuality of young people, along with the concern about cross-generational relationships that are erotically or sexually expressed. I then discuss the question of ensuring the sexual rights and agency of the young person as the most critical aspect of a positive approach to this topic. I then turn to two issues that are related to one another and that might be involved in progressive reform: age of consent and statutory rape. Finally, I will turn to a discussion of possible ethical (rather than legal) questions that need to be addressed. The goal here is simply to indicate some of the range of issues to be discussed, as well as to foster a more reasoned approach to some of them.[165]

Sex Panics about "Children"

The designation of "children" as a special category of human beings radically distinct from adults is a relatively recent invention in Western thought.[166] This is why laws about child labor were enacted as late as the nineteenth century. A separate juvenile court system was created at about the same time so that young criminals could be treated differently from adults. These all are positive developments.

Alongside these nineteenth and twentieth century developments, there have also been growing attempts to police the behavior of the young: legislation concerning smoking age and drinking age, for example. In this context we also see the emergence of a concern bordering on panic concerning the sexuality of the young. In the nineteenth and early twentieth centuries, there was a fixation on the "dangers" of masturbation. This resulted in campaigns in church literature as well as in schools to attempt to stamp out this pernicious practice. Indeed, in some jurisdictions in the United States masturbation may still be illegal. (In his dissent to the Supreme Court case, *Lawrence v Texas,* that decriminalized same-sex sexual relations, Justice Scalia warned that this decision might result in decriminalizing … masturbation!) In addition to the surveillance of youthful temptation to self-pleasuring, laws concerning age of consent and statutory rape were also introduced. These laws have the aim of "protecting" young people not only from other people's sexuality but also from their own.

With all this policing of youthful sexuality, the insights of Freud and the psychoanalytic tradition about childhood sexuality can serve as a destabilizing force. They point to what the policing attempts seek to deny: that all human beings, including the young, are sexual beings. At the same, time they may reinforce the attempts to suppress this sexuality.

For our purposes, what all this means is that sexuality is thought of as an outside influence that must be held at bay as long as possible to prevent, at all

---

165. For those who may wish to pursue some of the biblical resources for a discussion of some of these issues, I have dealt with the story in Matthew about "the Centurion and his 'lad'" in *The Man Jesus Loved,* 131-145. I also discuss cross-generational relationships in *Jacob's Wound,* 3-12 and 99-114.

166. Philippe Aries, *Centuries of Childhood: A Social History of Family Life,* trans. Robert Baldick (New York: Random House, 1962), and Hugh Cunningham, *The Invention of Childhood* (London: BBC Books, 2006).

costs, the awakening of sexuality among the young. In the U.S., a number of such panics arise: For example, the scandal concerning the McMartin preschool in California produced lurid headlines throughout the 1980s about Satanic worshippers using very young children as sexual objects. In spite of a decade of investigation and trials, no evidence was ever found to substantiate these fears, but it did produce a number of changes to the law to address what had never been shown to be a danger.

Further, while there may be some actual use of images to produce what is called "kiddie porn," the degree of panic about this in the 1980s and '90s seems in retrospect to be extreme. Indeed, under the Clinton administration, rather draconian laws were passed with a view to protecting children from the lewd gaze of others—at the same time, children are displayed for advertising and entertainment purposes in ways that encourage their sexualization.

The history of sex panics involving children and youth—from panic over masturbation to preschoolers in California and the barely existent kiddie porn industry—are the context within which we may understand the panics about young people, especially young males, being stalked by older adult males, from Anita Bryant's "Save Our Children" crusade to the present.

The panic feeds off the conflation of two or three groups that are lumped together in journalistic accounts and now in the law as "children." There are children from the cradle to ten or eleven years of age. There are children who are pubescent (eleven through thirteen or fourteen), and there are children who are post-pubescent but legally minors (fourteen through eighteen). Much of the sensationalism derives from supposing that seven-year-old children, rather than seventeen-year-old youths, are the ones at greatest risk of harm.

Indeed, it seems that what is going on here is something like a mass psychosis that has roots in the refusal to confront a truly horrendous problem. That problem is the widespread sexual violation of pre-pubescent children within the context of the nuclear family, or to put it bluntly: incestuous sexual abuse. Most studies have shown the sexual violation of prepubescent and pubescent children occurs within the home. More than 90 percent of all such cases are located within the household (non-related persons were guilty in only 6 percent of the cases).[167] Moreover the incidence of childhood domestic sexual abuse is truly staggering. Six percent of all males report such abuse. And two to five times as many females report this experience (i.e., 15 to 20 percent, depending on the study). Califia reports a study in California where 40 percent of the female and 20 percent of the male students reported being

---

167. Califia, *Public Sex*, 60.

sexually abused as children.[168] Some caution is required in interpreting these statistics, since it is likely that varying definitions of sexual abuse are employed in different studies.

Whichever statistic one chooses, however, this is clearly a staggering problem. For many of the victims (or survivors), sexual abuse at the hands of trusted male figures (usually fathers) means that their experience of sexuality is forever traumatized. For many of these people, the abuse at the hands of the father is a life sentence to a troubled relationship with their own body and especially their own sexuality.

It seems clear that the various child sex panics in their multiple forms are a sort of denial, displacement, and projection. They serve to focus attention away from the place of true danger and damage and toward largely invented or greatly exaggerated external threats. They cause people to believe that these external threats can never be too harshly dealt with, because nothing done to them will assuage the real source of pain and distress.

What is worse, these panics not only divert attention from the real problem, but they also make them worse by further tightening the noose of the inviolability of the family about the necks of the victims. Extolling the family as the place of safety when it is in fact the place of greatest danger only makes the situation of those caught in this trap all the more hopeless.

When this rhetoric is deployed by the religious right, it is often accompanied by resistance to questions concerning the protection of women from abusive domestic relations and even opposition to laws protecting women from spousal rape. This may even take the form of insisting that procreation gives parents something like ownership rights over their children, even in cases where abuse is documented. Our laws and courts consistently return children to the place of gravest danger on no other grounds than those of the rights of ownership conferred through biological conception.

However, the panic regarding the sexuality of young people is also at work in liberal discourse, especially in campaigns about so-called kiddie porn and the exploitation of teenage sexuality. Even liberals seem to be in an uproar about what kids might find on the Internet or in advertising and movies. MSNBC, the television network most often associated with liberal news, also runs programming that sets up sting operations against would-be internet solicitors of encounters with "underage" teenagers. As a consequence, there appears to be a disproportionate amount of federal law enforcement personnel not only policing the internet but also engaged in sting operations searching out possible "pedophiles." One result is that I must warn students in my sexual

---

168. Califia, *Public Sex*, 60.

ethics seminars researching this topic to exercise extreme caution in exploring internet and even public library research projects on this topic.

The fact that there are panics does not mean that there are no dangers, even if it is sometimes difficult to find a balanced approach to the issues that arise. The issue of clergy sexual abuse is a case in point. The combination of sensationalist journalism on the one hand and stone-walling on the part of ecclesiastical institutions on the other makes balanced judgment very difficult to come by. If incestuous abuse is severely damaging because of the violation of the parent-child bond of trust, abuse by a member of the clergy is, perhaps, similarly harmful on account of the symbolic authority invested in the priest or pastor. When the roles of parental guardian and priestly power are combined, as in cases of church orphanages in Ireland, Italy and elsewhere, the betrayal is deep indeed. When emotional proximity of this sort is combined with threats to ensure compliance, then what is involved is rape (or sexual harassment, in the least lurid cases) and punishable by law. Just as parents should not be sexually involved with children because of the ways in which the child's capacity for autonomy is compromised in such relationships, so also in the case of religious authorities. We will return to these questions later.

The Rights of Youth

What is generally lost sight of when the most lurid examples of the sexual abuse of children are made to stand in as representative of all cases, is the question of the rights of youth to develop their own sexuality. On the one hand, young people should not have an adult's sexual desires imposed upon them (this is true for other people as well). On the other hand, it is crucial that our fantasies about the sexual "innocence" of children up to the age of 18 not be used as a pretext for imposing a straitjacket on the development of sexual autonomy. Not all adolescents desire sexually expressed relationships with adults. Many seek out their peers for the development of erotic attachments and sexual exploration. But some welcome and seek out possibilities of such exploration with persons who have passed through the tumults of adolescence and come out the other side with some measure of equanimity.

It is appropriate, then, to ask whether young people ought to be able to explore sexuality beyond their own age cohort. Is exploration of sexuality always best carried out with persons who are equally inexperienced or no more formed as ethical subjects? And whatever an adult may think of this in terms of better or worse, what of the right of the youth to eroticize adult status? How is it helpful to the youth to be told that the older youth or adult that he has eroticized will, for that very reason, be regarded by society as a heinous criminal unless the eroticized adult utterly repulses every sexual advance? How is this conducive to healthy exploration of sexuality? How is this conducive to developing an appreciation for one's own sexuality?

In some cases, what is sought is not so much sexual experience as something like mentorship. The difficulty for youths is that honest and affirming methods of learning about and exploring sexuality is largely unavailable to them in home, church, or school. Many—probably most—parents are in denial about the sexuality of their "children." They are horrified by masturbation, let alone sexual exploration with others. Schools are regularly under assault if they admit that sexuality exists or if they stray beyond the rote repetition of a "just say no" mantra that passes for sex education. Churches have scarcely been places of calm and sex-affirming mentorship.

Fortunately, there are some very promising exceptions. The Our Whole Lives curriculum, created by the United Church of Christ and the Unitarian Universalist Association, is a very welcome and positive development, even if the diversity of sexual expression affirmed in that curriculum is severely restricted from the standpoint of this exploration of new horizons in queer sexual ethics. One would find there, for example, no guidance about how to evaluate possible adult partners for sexual exploration if one chose that path. Indeed, one finds there nothing for adults or youth that would deal with open relationships, let alone promiscuity (still less anything that encourages attitude changes with respect to prostitution). Despite its limitations, however, it goes further than most other resources in affirming the naturalness of sexual desire among youth. That is a very positive step in the right direction, even if much more is necessary.

Any consideration of pederasty as the erotic and sexually expressed relationship between adolescents and adults must begin with a consideration of the rights of the adolescent. Only within that context is it possible to offer meaningful ethical advice to the adolescent about such relationships. It will also then be possible to address and eliminate the demonization of those adults who are open to, or even desire, mutually agreeable erotic relationships with adolescents.

Cross-Generational Relationships

In dealing with this set of issues, it is best to begin with some of our views or prejudices about what may be termed cross-generational relationships. I have often been approached by 40-something or 50-something men who felt stigmatized in the gay community because their lovers were a decade or two younger than themselves. Similar feelings were expressed by the younger members of the pair who were regarded with disdain by (some of) their peers. Perhaps as a reaction to the suspicions directed against gay males as sexual predators, an ideology emerges that pretends that all gay relationships must be between members of the same age cohort.

This is surely an example of cultural amnesia, if not bad faith. The term "pederasty" itself was the standard Greek term for relationships between males, and in the case of Sparta, between females as well. It was assumed that sexual attraction was generally found between an adult male and a younger (perhaps adolescent or somewhat older) partner. In Greek grammar, there was no way of saying that both partners were lovers. One was the lover, the other the beloved. (This was true of male-female relationships as well.)

When, beginning in the nineteenth century, there was an attempt to validate contemporary "homosexual" experience by reference to earlier and even classical models, the evidence that was adduced was always of a pederastic and so cross-generational nature. The same was generally true of the marshaling of evidence across cultures to demonstrate the "normalcy" of same-sex relationships. Again, virtually all the evidence was cross-generational in structure. Moreover, many of the more modern western heroes of same-sex love (such as Walt Whitman, Oscar Wilde, Christopher Isherwood, and Tennessee Williams) were engaged in relationships that were pederastic in the sense of being cross-generational. There is even some evidence to suggest that cross-generational relationships between males may make for a longer-term relationship. This may be because a difference in generation may help to reduce the competitiveness that often gets in the way of males relating well with one another.

This is not to suggest that cross-generational relationships are "better" than same-generational relationships. It is only to say that the prejudice against this structure is as irrational as the prejudice an ancient Greek or Roman may have expressed against relationships between persons of the same generation (homo-generational, we might say).

Pederasty or Pedophilia?

Earlier I noted that a significant contributor to panics about sexuality among the young is the lumping together of pre-pubescent, pubescent, and adolescent youth into the category of the child. Thus while we may be rightly horrified by the sexual abuse of six- or eight-year-old children, this ought not to be confused with the sexual explorations or initiations of adolescents who are fourteen to eighteen years of age.

Although the terms in their Greek derivation may have much the same reference, it may be helpful to distinguish pedophilia, sexual desire for children of approximately elementary school age, from pederasty, sexual relations between adults and adolescents.

187

Even in antiquity, something of this distinction is clearly evident in the sources. It was shameful for a man to have a sexual relationship with a boy under twelve years of age in Greece. Great care was taken to protect younger youths from the approach of unwelcome suitors (as in sexual harassment laws of today), but relationships between adolescents and their older male suitors were either encouraged or taken with a shrug. Whereas in Greece a line was drawn before twelve, in Rome the age when a youth was considered able to relate intimately with a man was fourteen. The latter number remains the basis of the standard "age of consent" (for males, at least) in Europe.

Age of Consent

The question of the age of consent is a complicated one, especially when cultural and gender differences are taken into account. In the United States, the age of consent has been largely standardized at eighteen. In Europe, a number of countries that had followed this move to raise the age of consent have subsequently lowered it. England and the Netherlands, for example, have lowered their age of consent to sixteen—and there are strong movements in the Netherlands to lower this to twelve! At the same time, the United States has often insisted that countries that receive development aid from us increase their age of consent to eighteen as a condition of that aid. Given remaining disparities in the law, it is against U.S. law for a man to visit his younger lover in another country if that lover is of the age of consent in his country but not of the age of consent in the U.S., or to have a sexual relationship with that youth if the latter should come to the U.S. for a visit.[169] It is remarkable that we suppose that people under the age of eighteen cannot be allowed to express themselves sexually with persons of a different age cohort, while at the same time encouraging them to join ROTC programs that prepare them for military service while in high school. Do we seriously suppose that the choice to kill or be killed is less morally fraught than the choice to explore one's sexuality?

In the church, the situation is even more ironic. For church purposes we assume that people come of age somewhere between twelve and fourteen. This is the age at which those who practice infant baptism encourage youth to make an adult profession of faith. This is similarly the age at which "adult baptism" is practiced (as well as bar and bat mitzvahs in Jewish communities of faith). Do we suppose that this is a step of minor consequence compared to that of

---

169. This is another example of the U.S. supposing itself to be the sole repository of legal and ethical wisdom on a planet that is condemned to being under our tutelage (while we give the moral example of pre-emptive war, savage neo-liberal capitalism, and self-exemption from laws against abuse of human rights, including torture).

whether to explore one's sexuality? That is, we seem to suppose that a person of twelve is able to make a free and responsible decision to dedicate their lives body and soul to the church, but a sixteen-year-old is incapable of deciding whether to have sex?

Beyond this, we have to admit that the interpretations of faith to which we invite people to commit themselves (with added coercive pressure from their families) are often not conducive to ethical formation. Indeed, many religious traditions and communities are positively toxic in their effects upon people, especially in relation to their sexuality. It is not plausible that the damage done by religious traditions and by thoughtless adherence to them is less significant than the possible damage done by thoughtless or unwise precocity in erotic exploration. On the contrary, I believe that more damage is done in the world by religious extremism than by sexual exploration. Indeed, much of the damage done by religion is sexual in character: from licensing the abuse of women and children to introducing a fear and loathing of one's own and other people's sexuality. In fact, according to a poll released in October of 2010, most Americans seem to agree that the churches bear significant responsibility for the incidence of teen suicide, especially the suicides of those who are, or think they may be, gay or lesbian.

Statutory Rape

Forcing a person to have sex against their will is rape. Having sex with a willing sixteen-year-old is "statutory rape." That is, the current law presumes that no one under the age of eighteen can meaningfully consent to a sexual relationship. We should be clear that statutory rape laws mean that for a man or woman to accede to the sexual advances of a seventeen-year-old, however importunate, is to be guilty of rape and to incur not only jail terms of astonishing severity but to be permanently branded as guilty of a sex-crime. This is true even if the teenager never complains, or if the complaint is produced under duress by parents or police. Nor does there appear to be any meaningful statute of limitations. Further, it is the case that this is as true for males as well as females, for cross-sex as well as same-sex relationships. Indeed, some of the most notorious cases have involved the prosecution of women with teenage boy lovers, even where neither the youth involved—nor even his parents—brought a complaint.

I have already maintained that the greatest damage done by adult-initiated sexual involvement with children, especially prepubescent children, is in the home. Where adult desire overrides childhood resistance, the greatest damage is when statutory rape is perpetrated by parents (usually fathers, step-fathers, and other male relatives). This suggests that the severity of so-called statutory rape is greatest where the adult initiator has psychological and physical control over the child. Presumably the damage is less great where this control is diminished, and thus secondary (reduced damage) with adult teachers and only tertiary with relative strangers (such as neighbors).

On a scale of this kind, we should note that the least damage possible would stem from relationship that are initiated at a distance, for example by internet: the very place where the bulk of hysteria, police surveillance, and federal taskforce dollars is currently directed. Sting operations conducted by U.S. law enforcement agencies are nothing less than witch-hunts contrary to even the most minimal notions of the rule of law or civilized society. Persons trapped by these sting operations are subject to laws concerning attempted rape of a minor, and may be permanently branded as a sex offender, which involves publication of their name and address whereever they may choose to live after incarceration—if they ever get out, since many will be subject to permanent incarceration under some laws that permit the state to hold sex offenders long after they serve their sentences.

Is statutory rape the appropriate way to handle infractions of age of consent laws? In order to test that supposition, let us return to what has been identified as the site of gravest danger for young people with respect to the violation of their sexual integrity: the home. What about the imposition of sexual demands upon pre-pubescent children by those who are their adult guardians? We know that these impositions are the ones that are not only the most numerous, but also the most damaging, to the young person. They often impose a life sentence of alienated or damaged sexuality and incalculable suffering. They are, therefore, far more grave in consequence than a neighbor responding to the sexual advances of a twelve-year-old boy or using friendly persuasion with a fifteen-year-old boy.

Should we therefore incarcerate a father or step-father when he seduces his own prepubescent child into sexual experience? (I leave aside cases of actual rape, which should be governed by appropriate laws.) Should they be incarcerated for decades, and permanently branded as sex offenders? Should the penalties for them be doubled relative to the somewhat less traumatic advances of priest and pastors, the still less damaging advances of teachers or scout leaders or coaches, or the still less damaging relationships with neighbors or (at furthest remove) those caught on the internet? Notice that society's reversed priorities here confirm Gayle Rubin's concern about scale.

Any response at this point must take seriously the potential for grave damage done to families. But I think it unlikely that we would favor a policy that would result in the permanent incarceration of between 10 and 30 percent of parents (again, mostly fathers). Would we not rather want to take steps first to protect the children from being pressured in this way, either by separating the offending parent from access to the child or by removing the child from the situation of danger? And should we not be engaging in educational efforts directed toward families regarding the dangers here? Would we not want to correct love gone wrong rather than issue draconian punishments?

Certainly as Christians, I think we would have reason to want to turn toward mediation and education (but not forgetting protective intervention), rather than the imposition of criminal penalties. For as Christians, we are likely to be suspicious of the efficacy of criminal law as opposed to community formation. We do tend, at least some of the time, to favor confession and repentance rather than legal remedies because we believe in Gospel rather than the law. If we would be inclined in this direction with respect to what are the worst cases of the violation of children, on what grounds do we suppose that criminal law is the best remedy for what are arguably less damaging and far rarer impositions of adult sexual interest upon the young? Would we suppose that a far fairer and better remedy would be the use of civil rather than criminal law, family law rather than felony rape law? Here again we would be talking about protection of children from undue pressure through court-mandated injunctions and so on, just as we are able to do with various kinds of stalking or harassment cases.

The result of these considerations might lead us then to abolish all statutory rape laws and put in their place meaningful civil remedies that protect the child from unwanted sexual advances by family members or anybody else. Note that this is exactly the position taken by so-called "pedophile" political organizations in the U.S., Britain and the Netherlands: This is the supposedly "radical" position. This position is, however, consistent with the use of criminal law to protect the vulnerable from violence and violation: Laws against forcible rape, abduction, sex slavery, and similar crimes should obviously be vigorously enforced.

Ethics

Where might this leave us in terms of ethical reflection—apart from the law, as Paul might say? Parental guardians of pre-pubescent children should be educated from long before they become parents concerning the dangers of violating the integrity of children. At the same time, parent-child bonding at an intimate level must not be discouraged and cultural differences about what constitutes appropriate parenting practice must also be taken seriously.

Even where pre-pubescent children have a strong inclination to initiate sexual exploration with older youths or adults—and there is plenty of evidence that such cases are by no means rare and by no means necessarily pathological—

191

the children should be advised to wait. Pubescent children should be strongly encouraged to understand what they really want and to understand the consequences without unduly problematizing sexuality. The older person approached by such a youth (say of fourteen years of age) should proceed carefully and slowly, making sure that the youth retains the initiative and has the requisite understanding and judgment. This will most likely preclude relationships with a younger person over whom one has real or symbolic power.

What cannot be doubted, however, is that many gay (and possibly lesbian) youth have a strong desire to initiate relationships with older persons in order to safely explore their own sexuality. Many report this at an age of even ten or so. Moreover, studies of persons who have had such relationships early in life show that it has no impact upon their eventual sexual orientation and that where coercion or underhanded pressure has not been deployed, the effects are regarded as having been, on the whole, positive.[170]

Reflections

Again, I make no claim that I have dealt adequately with all the issues that arise in connection with erotic attachments between youths and adults. I have only attempted to raise a number of issues and to offer tentative suggestions for discussion for those who are genuinely concerned about developing a more ethically informed view of what is called pederasty. Given the societal panic around these issues, I do not suppose that such a discussion will be easy, nor do I suppose that all people of good faith will reach the same conclusion. I would hope, however, that if we do enter into discussion of these issues that we agree not to demonize one another but to seek to discern the truth, even if through a glass darkly, and then to speak that truth in love. This would go quite a long way toward overcoming the climate of sexual hysteria that leads young people to regard their own sexuality as toxic poison and that labels well-meaning adults as sexual predators. That would be itself considerable gain.

---

170. See Theo Sandfort, E. Brongersma, and A. van Naerssen, eds., *Male Intergenerational Intimacy: Historical, Socio-Psychological, and Legal Perspectives* (New York: Haworth Press, 1990); Theo Sandfort, *Boys on Their Contacts With Men: A Study of Sexually Expressed Friendships* (Binghamton, NY: Global Academic Publishers, 1984); Tom O'Carrol, *Paedophilia: The Radical Case* (Boston: Alyson Publications 1982); and Daniel Tsang, ed., *The Age Taboo: Gay Male Sexuality, Power, and Consent* (Boston: Alyson, 1981).

A Concluding Excursus
in Ethical Method

This study of new horizons in queer sexual ethics has sought to widen the range of issues that may be helpfully discussed, beyond the conventional discourse concerning marriage, whether "straight" or "gay." Today most of the energy in public discussions of sexuality has to do with marriage and whether lesbian and gay people should be included in the ecclesial rites and civil institutions associated with marriage. Fortunately, there has also been some discussion of the rights of transgender people with respect to the passage of hate crimes legislation and especially with respect to non-discrimination in housing and employment (ENDA). These are certainly important issues of justice that rightly concern persons whether in or out of the church.

However, the overwhelming amount of attention given to issues of marriage rights (and rites) threatens to create a movement toward what I have termed assimilation by amputation: a normalization of certain forms of sexual relationships that seem only to mimic the deeply troubled institution of heterosexual marriage. As a consequence, the current debates do little to address the deep-seated erotophobia that is regularly mobilized to distract us from issues of justice and mercy, which Jesus called "the weightier matters of the law." Even discussions of marriage seem to suppose that sexuality is some sort of toxic waste that must be buried deep within the lead containers of exclusive monogamous relationships, thereafter not to be interrogated too closely. While sex outside of marriage is regarded with great suspicion and even horror, sex within the containers of marriage and family is seldom interrogated with respect either to spousal abuse and spousal rape or the incidence of childhood incest. Thus sexual ethics remains locked within an erotophobia that renders victims of abuse mute while marginalizing behaviors that have no victims.

In order to contest the root causes of antipathy toward queer sexual practice and to prevent progress in these matters from simply re-inscribing the sorts of injustice to which gay and lesbian people have been subjected (and displacing this injustice onto presumably more marginal sexualities), it has been necessary to widen the conversation to include sexual practices that do not easily conform to the presumed normative lifestyles of celibacy or monogamous marriage.

The approach taken has been one that seeks to grant a certain privilege to the experience and perspectives of gay men and other queer folk and so may be termed a queer sexual ethic. However, many of the issues discussed have an undoubted relevance for "straight" persons as well. It is not only gay persons who may consider open relationships, for example, or engage in sex with multiple partners, or seek the services of prostitutes, or even become members of BDSM clubs. But emphasizing a queer perspective on these matters helps to redress the imbalance in discussions of sexuality that result when heterosexual perspectives predominate.

In opening up discussion of these various sexual practices, it has been important first of all to emphasize an open and affirmative stance with respect to what has been too often not only marginalized but treated with disdain and contempt. Throughout the book, I have insisted that only in rare cases should the sexual be treated as a special case in terms of ethical reflections on human relationality but instead that in every situation the values of justice and mercy—or, the love of neighbor—should be determinative. This does not mean that anything goes! On the contrary, careful consideration of what it means to be generous and affirming of the dignity of the other may be far more stringent an ethical claim than one that simply reduces judgment to the application of a rule book. Nevertheless, I have sought, above all, to give the benefit of the doubt to sexual practices and choices that are too often simply dismissed or disrespected. An important part of any discourse that desires to be ethical (and not just about ethics) is that it seeks to give the benefit of the doubt to that which has been silenced or marginalized. But this is not all there is to ethical discourse. There is also the matter of seeking to examine ourselves with respect to how well we are doing in exemplifying or embodying justice and mercy when we act "outside the law." Here there can be no hard and fast rules, but only conscientious improvisation.

In order to make clear how this may work as ethical discourse, I will first review some of the themes or issues that have been discussed and show what it means to embrace an ethic that seeks to embody justice, generosity, and other virtues, rather than requiring a special sexual ethic. I will also indicate how it is possible to engage in an ethical reflection that does not simply give blanket affirmation of any and all sexual practices, but rather is open to ongoing reflection and examination.

Before proceeding, I should express a word of caution. I have said earlier that just because I am arguing that a certain practice should be legal does not mean that I suppose that it should be recommended. Neither should it be supposed that I am recommending that persons launch out into embracing for themselves all of the various practices discussed in the book. First, I think that people have very different ways of being involved with their own sexuality, and such differences should always be respected. There are people who have no discernible desire to engage in sexual practices. They seem to be quite happy without "having sex" at all. There are others who seem to be virtually insatiable in their desire for sexual expression and adventure. There are those who value above all the benefits of a lifelong monogamous relationship, and others for whom this seems a life-destroying straitjacket. Any discussion of sexual ethics must make room for the possibility of diverse ways of human flourishing. Just as I hope we will not stigmatize those who engage in sexual practices to which we do not feel at all attracted, I also hope that we will not disregard as "repressed" or "moralistic" those who choose not to engage in sexual practices that we appreciate and enjoy.

Here the advice of St. Paul about the diversity of the Body of Christ seems to me to be especially helpful. Not all are hands, not all are ears, not all have this gift or that one. And that is something not to regret, but for which to give thanks. Of course, it is possible that St. Paul would be appalled at my extension of this insight to sexual lifestyles, but he did admit that all of us, presumably himself included, see through a glass darkly in this age before the final apocalypse of love.

Ethical Reflections

Let us look at some of the issues we have discussed and see how ethical reflection might work:

Open Marriage

In the discussion of this theme, I emphasized the possibilities of open relationships in helping to overcome some of the built-in pitfalls of a more conventional married relationship. Open marriage provides the possibility of overcoming the ways in which such relationships veer toward regarding one or both spouses as property rather than as partners. It may helpfully set limits to the idea that erotic partners should be the "be-all and end-all" for another person, sexually and otherwise. A choice to be in such a relationship is by no means a violation of justice and mercy, provided that there is openness and transparency in communication with one another. Indeed, it is this very openness and transparency that provides important opportunities for the actualization of justice between the partners, and between them and those others to whom they come to be related.

But there are also very real dangers to such a relationship. It is all too easy to use openness as a way of avoiding the work of building trust and trustworthiness over the long term. A relationship that aims at long-term or lifelong companionship is about more than sex and getting what one needs. It is also about all the things that go into living together and making a life together. And for many it is about caring for children and parents and so on. In all of this, sexuality, whether restricted or open, plays a significant but not all-determining role. Can opening the relationship to other sexual exploration risk making sex too important? Perhaps.

In general, I think I would be no more likely to recommend a more conventional marriage than an open relationship. Both are fraught with opportunities and risks. But I would recommend to people that they do all that is possible to deal with both the opportunities and the risks that are attendant upon these choices. Marriage, whether "open" or not, is a public display of a certain way of being together. Thus it is also important that persons take care that the way they choose to display this relationship (in marriage ceremonies, for example) not inadvertently marginalize or otherwise demean other styles of sexual relationships.

Promiscuity

What about the choice of promiscuity or of multiple partners where the aim is not lasting commitment but mutual enjoyment? I have argued that there is nothing in such a choice that intrinsically makes it incompatible with justice and mercy, with appropriate care and respect for other persons with whom one is related sexually. As such, there need be no prohibition or even undue suspicion of this life choice. This does not, however, mean that it is simply to be celebrated or encouraged as such.

There are real risks—and here I mean ethical risks—that are present in such a style of (sexual) life. As in any sort of relationship, there is the danger that one will reduce the other to a means of one's own gratification. This need not be merely at the level of sexual gratification as narrowly conceived. We can use sex to enhance our sense of power or prowess, of worth or attractiveness. Indeed this is probably unavoidable. But if it comes to predominate, then the other person and her or his needs, desires, or pleasures simply disappear from view. One then is no longer dealing with a person (a neighbor), but with a means to a self-centered end. The result is likely to be damaging to all those who are involved.

There are some good reasons for choosing this style of life. One may have already had enough experience with broken marriages to believe that that style of life is not one that is likely to enable flourishing. Or one may recognize that a lifelong commitment to another person is simply not realistic, given other choices of work or lifestyle. In either case, one may also be clear that foregoing sexual pleasure is just not viable or desirable. One may even be clear that for oneself celibacy would entail a self-destructive choice, truncating one's life in a way that could only be damaging. Thus one may be rightly persuaded that this is the best option. But this will also mean taking into account the dangers to oneself and others that are attendant upon this choice. It means being vigilant with respect to the ways in which other people are respected or not, cared for or not. That is, it means being vigilant about the love of neighbor or the requirements of justice and mercy.

Prostitution

The first ethical question here is entailed in the choice of becoming a sex worker—that is, providing sexual services to others for a fee. I have argued that sex workers should not be the object of scorn or disdain, still less of criminalization. Does this mean that I would encourage people to become sex workers? Not at all. Certainly sex work in the current situation is a dangerous enterprise, especially for women, and most especially for women who are otherwise subject to exploitation (for example, due to race or class). But I also realize that for many people, sex work is an important option for financial support for themselves and sometimes for their families or loved ones.

For some, sex work takes the form of what is called survival sex. Typically, this involves runaway youth who offer sexual services in order to have a warm, dry place to sleep, or a decent meal. I believe that the best model of ethical reflection in this and similar circumstances is that of "harm reduction," where these young people are encouraged to think about ways to reduce the dangers they are subjected to through these practices. It is not a question of saying no to survival sex, but of increasing the odds of survival: sharing knowledge hard-won on the streets, building self-esteem to make it possible to choose more wisely with whom to go home and what to do, and so on.

At a quite different level, a college student may think about sex work as a way to pay for books or tuition. They may advertise their availability for "massage" through magazines or online. Is this a good choice? I am neither going to dismiss it out of hand nor give it blanket approbation. Rather, the way of ethical reflection *with* such a person (rather than *about* such a person) is to help the person reflect upon what they are choosing. This will, of course, entail issues of safety. But it should also involve reflection on what providing sex for money may be doing to one's sense of self. There are young men who report that they find this both exciting and an occasion for meeting people that they actually like and enjoy being with. Others may find that this is damaging to their sense of self-worth and decency, and that the work is intrinsically disagreeable or disgusting. These things can be honestly talked about, faced, and dealt with.

Moving to a different level of analysis, another issue that is pertinent for those engaged in sex work is whether they themselves are finding opportunities to practice justice and mercy in their work. If they hope to be treated with respect and generosity, are they also acting in ways that express these same values? This goes a long way, here as elsewhere, toward developing the sort of practices that conduce to self-respect and a sense of human flourishing.

Similarly, one may ask about relations with fellow sex workers. Are these relationships of the sort that can build solidarity and mutual support? This is important for survival, but also for a sense of moral worth. In the best of cases, this may take institutional form in the development of cooperatives of sex workers and even labor unions, as has happened in many parts of the world.

What I am suggesting, again, is that in order to engage in ethical reflection with people, it is not appropriate either to issue blunt condemnation or blanket affirmation, but rather to engage with the people whose lives are actually involved in the exploration of the concrete ethical opportunities and risks involved in their choices.

What about those who avail themselves of the services of sex workers? Certainly it would be incoherent to side with prostitutes against the discrimination that falls upon them and then deflect that opposition against the "clients" who make their lives possible. But those who make use of the services provided by sex workers can certainly ask themselves about the ethical content of their relationship with these persons. To what extent are they relating to sex workers as neighbors, as persons of sacred worth whose dignity is to be affirmed, and whose vulnerabilities are to be protected?

Further, it would seem to be incumbent on those who use these services to be advocates for the dignity and rights of sex workers. Justice is more than simply how you treat the person with whom you happen to deal, although it certainly involves that. It also involves forms of solidarity and advocacy. It will also involve exercising care not to support those forms of sex work where fraud and force are in play. For the sake of the dignity of sex workers, it is important for clients to choose wisely and ethically which forms of sex work they patronize. It is also crucially important to be mindful of ways in which questions of race, culture, and class may complicate issues of agency and consent.

BDSM

I have argued that there are ways in which practitioners of BDSM may actually practice better arrangements for securing consent than is typically the case in most sexual relationships. Certainly given the bodily and emotional vulnerabilities at stake, this is essential to the practice of BDSM.

There are also the questions of the fantasies of power, and the way these are scripted in relation to some of the most terrible forms of human degradation: Master/slave arrangements, police or even Gestapo costuming, and other similar forms of practice. Since I have no actual experience with any of these things and find the idea of them at least initially repugnant, for that very reason I will bite my tongue and not offer gratuitous accusation or condemnation. But I would certainly hope that those who find these fantasy practices attractive would be asking themselves some hard questions about them and about how they relate to social forces that are deeply destructive—and about what needs and desires are being cultivated here. I don't believe that I know the answer to these questions. I realize that fantasy is not the same as reality and may even be an antidote to the reality it mirrors or subverts. But I also don't imagine that role playing of such relationships is automatically innocent either. There are no hard and fast rules here, but rather it is a domain for ongoing reflection on the part of participants.

Pederasty

In the current climate, this is certainly the most ethically fraught form of sexual relationship with which we have dealt. Where there are significant differences of age and status, it is essential that the dignity of the younger partner be zealously protected. This means both permitting sexual agency on their part (their right to explore their sexuality with partners they trust), but also guarding their ability to refuse sexual advances or opportunities. Older partners must beware of consciously or unconsciously using their symbolic power to induce young people to explore sexuality beyond their readiness. Obviously those with authority over the youth must never use this authority to impose sexual relationships upon them. The most egregious form of this comes in what is sadly the most frequent form: the imposition of parental authority to gain erotic satisfaction for the parent. However, religious authorities also have particular reason to avoid even the appearance, let alone the reality, of using that authority to extract favors. Sexual harassment is never an ethical relation.

Where a youth who is not under one's supervisory power initiates a relationship, then the elder must simply ask themselves and the youth whether the proposed relationship is one that can really promote human flourishing for both parties. The younger parties to such relationships, especially if under the legal age of consent, should also ask seriously whether their desire for this relationship may endanger the object of their affections. They too should take into account the vulnerabilities of their chosen partner to public scorn and to legal reprisal. On both sides, then, a commitment to the well-being of the other person is essential to the ethical content of the relationship. Both parties also should commit to foster forms of solidarity and advocacy: solidarity through groups that support gay and lesbian and transgender young people against school bullying, for example, or in finding peer groups where youth can talk freely and frankly about their perplexities, their joys and difficulties, or advocacy in the revision of age of consent laws or in combating forms of police harassment and entrapment.

Ethical Themes

In conclusion, I want to mention some of the basic themes that seem to me to be important in developing ethical consciousness around new horizons in a sexual ethic that is both Christian and queer.

Justice and Mercy as Meaning of Love of Neighbor

In thinking about Christian ethical reflection, it is important to try to coordinate at least two ways of thinking about the ethical. On the one hand, we may speak of the love of neighbor. But by itself, this may allow a lapse into sentimentality. Thus, on the other hand, it is also important to add a consideration of justice and mercy in order to flesh out what it means to love the neighbor.

The basic meaning of love of neighbor in New Testament ethics is a commitment to the welfare and the dignity of another person. It is not so much a sentiment, still less an emotion, as a pattern of action that engages the other person in ways that concretely benefit the other. This is why it is possible to speak also of the love of the enemy, whether in the sayings of Jesus or the words of Paul. Because it is not a feeling but a pattern of action, Paul can speak of feeding the enemy. Paul maintains that the entire law is fulfilled in the love of the neighbor, and his immediately preceding reflections make clear that this includes the enemy and the persecutor. Paul makes this case in his letter to the Romans, a document that is supremely concerned with justice as that which God calls for in all human beings and societies. Love and justice are thus basically identical concepts. Similarly, in the Gospel of Matthew where Jesus speaks of the love both of neighbor and of enemy, he also invokes as a correlative ethical guide the prophetic call for justice and mercy as the meaning of adherence to the claim of God. Justice and mercy here entail the solicitude for the well-being of the other—especially the vulnerable other.

In Christian ethical reflection, therefore, we are concerned not with a set of prohibitions or legal formulas, but with what conduces to the welfare of those with whom we are in relationship. In the case of sexual ethics, this will mean being attentive to the vulnerabilities of others in relationship. And it will mean being especially attentive to the ways in which others may, by reason of differences of age, race, class, culture, or other factors, be even more vulnerable than oneself.

Improvisation Rather Than Rules

The contrast between a rule- or law-based ethic and one that is oriented toward love of the neighbor, justice and mercy reminds us that ethics is not about looking for rules, either old ones or new ones. The ethical life, therefore, is one of continual improvisation around the themes of love of neighbor and justice and mercy. It is more like a dance than a march, more like jazz than repeating the scales.

Of course, the reason that people sometimes prefer rule books is that they suppose that if they follow the rules they can avoid guilt, or they won't have to make decisions, or they won't mess up. But ethics requires responsible freedom. Thus decisions are never pre-programmed by a set of rules. If they were, there would be no responsible decision. And rules don't save us from the unintended consequences of our actions, nor do they prevent us from doing real harm to ourselves and others, including the harm done by judging or condemning others whose ways are different from our own.

But embarking upon a life of responsible freedom, and so one in which there is even a question of ethics, means constant improvisation, constant invention of ways to be responsive to the others we encounter in the contexts in which we encounter them.

To be sure, we will make mistakes. We will involve ourselves with others in ways that we may later come to regret, but that happens if we follow some or other set of rules as well. We will have to rely on other people being able to welcome us in spite of our mistakes, and so not hide from them or ourselves that we have not yet achieved moral perfection. In life we are learning as we go—learning how to live, how to love. We will always be struggling against our own fears and ignorance. We will always struggle against the default tendency, as Paul described it, "to think more highly of ourselves than we ought to think," to be preoccupied with our own satisfaction at the expense of others. In sexual ethics, a dose of fear and trembling is always helpful, as is prayer and humility.

The Ethical and the Political

One of the pitfalls of some ways of reflecting on sexual ethics is the tendency to focus too narrowly on the specificities of particular relationships and encounters, rather than seeing them in the broader public frame in which they occur. Relations with persons of the opposite sex are always set within a context predetermined by the masculine domination of women. The other people we meet, as well as we ourselves, are always already set within contexts of sexism, racism, classism, ageism and other oppressive structures. When we involve ourselves in the exploration of new horizons in sexual ethics, we also incur certain political obligations: to be in solidarity with, and an advocate for, those who are excluded, marginalized, or demeaned.

The very opposite of this is exposed in the press with dismaying frequency: politicians, priest, and pastors who are publicly homophobic, yet who secretly have relations with male prostitutes or with youth under their charge, or get caught in public places seeking sexual adventure. This is a radical division between what is sometimes called one's private and one's public life. The cases I have mentioned are clearly unethical. But we may all get caught up in a false division between the personal and the political, focusing only on the quality of a particular relationship in abstraction from contesting the wider social forces and institutions of marginalization.

Communities and Companions

One of the best ways to seek balance appropriate to ethical reflection on sexual practices and relationships is to have friends and companions with whom one can be open and frank in discussion of sexual practices. Such a friend would be neither censorious, seeking to find fault or to condemn, nor simply a cheerleader who is unaware of the pitfalls of ethical existence. Friends, Aristotle suggested, are those who seek one another's excellence. In a different framework, John Wesley suggested that members of his bands of believers should help one another toward "perfection." In this case, the perfection involved is that of growing in the capacity to love one's neighbor as oneself, whether that neighbor is a spouse, a person who is encountered in a bar or a bathhouse, or a sex worker (or a client). Is one being fair in one's dealings with others or not? Kind and respectful? Generous and merciful?

Having communities and companions of ethical reflection helps to get us out of the self-preoccupation that can be so damaging to ethical consciousness. To the extent to which we try to go it alone in ethics, we become trapped. As Levinas reminds us, ethics is about relation to the other. It is not about the cultivation of a good (or bad) conscience. Ethical reflection therefore requires dialogue, including conversation with "interested parties" as well as with others who are less directly involved.

Unfortunately, it is very difficult to imagine Christian churches or congregations being the sort of contexts in which it would be possible to engage in non-judgmental, open exploration of sexual lifestyles. But perhaps this project and others like it can open the way to the development of groups of persons who are willing to undertake this work together, whether inside an existing congregation or not.

Again, this is not something that is good only for relationships that involve sexual practices. As a professor with a lot of teaching experience, I nevertheless am glad to have the advice of colleagues and also of students about how I might do better as a teacher. In doubtful cases, I will also seek out the advice of someone I trust about an evaluation of a student's work. I routinely seek out the advice of others about things I have written or am thinking about writing. Sexuality is not radically different from other aspects of life in this regard. I, and perhaps you too, may benefit from seeking advice from others about what we do sexually and why.

Conclusion

In the work of reflection and self examination, it is important to be neither overly scrupulous nor overly cavalier. If we are overly scrupulous, we may become paralyzed and thus make it impossible to rightly enjoy the good gifts of sexuality. If we are overly cavalier, we may lapse into a default state of self-centeredness that is ultimately destructive of ourselves and others. Perhaps the best way might be indicated by the author of Ecclesiastes who, much to the consternation of the uptight among us, celebrated the joys of food and wine and sex. But that ancient writer also noted that there is a certain rhythm that is healthy. For our purposes we could paraphrase this: a time to enjoy, a time to refrain; a time to play and a time to reflect; a time to repent and a time to be adventurous.

Works Cited

Adler, Rachel, *Engendering Judaism: An Inclusive Theology and Ethics* (Boston: Beacon, 1998).

Aelred of Rievaulx, *Mirror of Charity* III.39.110 (Kalamazoo: Cistercian Publications, 1990).

Aggleton, Peter, ed., *Men who Sell Sex: International Perspectives on Male Prostitution and HIV/AIDS* (New York: Routledge, 1998).

Agustin, Laura Maria, *Sex and the Margins: Migration, Labour Markets and the Rescue Industry* (London: Zed Books, 2007).

Aries, Philippe, *Centuries of Childhood: A Social History of Family Life*, trans. Robert Baldick (New York: Random House, 1962).

Alexander, Priscilla, "Bathhouses and Brothels: Symbolic Sites in Discourse and Practice," in *Policing Public Sex*, ed. Dangerous Bedfellows (Brooklyn: South End Press, 2008).

Alleuder, Dan B., *The Wounded Heart: Hope for Victims of Childhood Sexual Abuse*, new ed. (Colorado Springs: NavPress, 2008).

Althaus-Reid, Marcella, *Indecent Theology: Theological Perversions in Sex, Gender, and Politics* (New York: Routledge, 2000).

Angelides, Steven, *A History of Bisexuality* (Chicago: University of Chicago Press, 2001).

Baldwin, James, *Giovanni's Room* (New York: Delta, 2000).

Barry, Kathleen, *Female Sexual Slavery* (New York: New York University Press, 1984).

Bérubé, Allan, "The History of Gay Bathhouses" in *Policing Public Sex*, ed. Dangerous Bedfellows (Brooklyn: South End Press, 2008).

Boswell, John, *Christianity, Social Tolerance, and Homosexuality: Gay People in Western Europe from the Beginning of the Christian Era to the Fourteenth Century* (Chicago: University of Chicago Press, 1981).

Boswell, John, *Same-Sex Unions in Premodern Europe* (New York: Villard Books, 1994).

Bourdieu, Pierre, *Masculine Domination* (Stanford: Stanford University Press, 2001).

Bronski, Michael, *The Pleasure Principle* (New York: St. Martin's Press, 1998).

Brown, Peter, *Body and Society: Men, Women, and Sexual Renunciation in Early Christianity* (New York: Columbia University Press, 1988).

Bury, Robert Gregg, trans., *Plato's Laws* (Cambridge: Harvard University Press, 1984).

Califia, Pat, *Public Sex: The Culture of Radical Sex* (San Francisco: Cleis Press, 1994).

Card, Carol, "Against Marriage and Motherhood," *Hypatia* 11.3 (Summer 1996).

Carter, Vednita, and Evelina Giobbe, "Duet: Prostitution, Racism and Feminist Discourse," in *Prostitution and Pornography: Philosophical Debate About the Sex Industry*, ed. Jessica Spector (Stanford: Stanford University Press, 2006).

Cassius Dio, *Roman History*, I-IX (London: Loeb Classical Library, 1914-1927).

Cecco, John P., and Michael G. Shively, *Bisexual and Homosexual Identities: Critical Theoretical Issues* (New York: Routledge, 1984).

Corbin, Alain, *Women for Hire: Prostitution and Sexuality in France after 1850*, trans. Alan Sheridan (Cambridge, MA: Harvard University Press, 1996).

Countryman, William, *Dirt, Greed, and Sex: Sexual Ethics in the New Testament and Their Implications for Today*, revised ed. (Minneapolis: Fortress Press, 2007).

Courtois, Christine, *Healing the Incest Wound: Adult Survivors in Therapy* (New York: W.W. Norton & Co., 1996).

Cunningham, Hugh, *The Invention of Childhood* (London: BBC Books, 2006).

D'Emilio, John, *Sexual Politics, Sexual Communities: The Making of a Homosexual Minority in the U.S. 1940-1970* (Chicago: University of Chicago Press, 1983).

Derrida, Jacques, *Learning to Live Finally: The Last Interview*, trans. Pascale-Anne Brault and Michael Naas (Hoboken: Melville House, 2007).

Derrida, Jacques, *On Cosmopolitanism and Forgiveness* (New York: Routledge, 2001).

Derrida, Jacques, and Anne Dufourmantelle, *Of Hospitality: Anne Dufourmantelle Invites Jacques Derrida to Respond*, trans. Rachel Bowlby (Stanford: Stanford University Press, 2000).

Dover, K.J., *Greek Homosexuality*, rev. ed. (New York: MJF Books, 1997).

Duplechan, Larry, *Tangled Up in Blue* (New York: St. Martin's Griffin, 1990).

Easton, Dossie, and Catherine A. Liszt, *The Ethical Slut: A Guide to Infinite Sexual Possibilities* (Eugene, Ore.: Greenery Press, 1997).

Forster, E.M., *Maurice: A Novel* (New York: W. W. Norton, 2005).

Foucault, Michel, *Society Must be Defended: Lectures at the College de France, 1975-76*, trans. David Macey (New York: Picador, 2003).

Garber, Marjorie, *Bisexuality and the Eroticism of Everyday Life* (New York: Routledge, 2000).

Gilligan, Carol, *In a Different Voice* (Cambridge: Harvard, 1982).

Gilfoyle, Timothy, "From Soubrette to Show World: The Contested Sexualities of Times Square: 1880-1995," in *Policing Public Sex*, ed. Dangerous Bedfellows (Brooklyn: South End Press, 2008).

Goodman, Paul, "The Politics of Being Queer," in *Nature Heals: the Psychological Essays of Paul Goodman* (New York: Free Life Editions, 1977).

Halperin, David, *One Hundred Years of Homosexuality: And Other Essays on Greek Love* (New York: Routledge, 1989).

Halwani, Raja, *Virtuous Liaisons: Care, Love, Sex, and Virtue Ethics* (Chicago: Open Court, 2003).

Itiel, Joseph, *Sex Workers as Virtual Boyfriends* (New York: Haworth, 2002).

Ipsen, Avaren, *Sex Working and the Bible* (London: Equinox Publishing, 2009).

Irenaeus of Lyons, *Against Heresies* (Whitefish: Kessinger Publishing, 2004).

Jennings, Theodore, "Homosexuality and Christian Faith: A Theological Reflection" in *The Christian Century* 94.5 (February 16, 1977); republished in *Homosexuality and the Christian Faith: A Symposium*, ed. Harold L. Twiss (Valley Forge: Judson Press, 1978).

Jennings, Theodore, *Jacob's Wound: Homoerotic Narratives in the Literature of Ancient Israel* (New York: Continuum, 2006).

Jennings, Theodore, *The Man Jesus Loved: Homoerotic Narratives from the New Testament* (Cleveland: Pilgrim Press, 2003).

Jennings, Theodore, *Plato or Paul?: The Origins of Western Homophobia* (Cleveland: Pilgrim Press, 2009).

Jennings, Theodore, "Reconstructing the Doctrine of Sin," in *The Other Side of Sin*, ed. Andrew Sung Park and Susan Nelson (Albany: State University of New York Press, 2001), 109-122.

Jennings, Theodore, "Theological Perspectives on Sexuality," *Journal of Pastoral Care* 33, no. 1 (March, 1979): 3-16.

Jennings, Theodore, and Tat-Siong Benny Liew, "Mistaken Identities but Model Faith: Rereading the Centurion, the Chap, and the Christ in Matthew 8:5-13," *Journal of Biblical Literature* 123.3 (2004)

Jordan, Mark D., *Blessing Same-Sex Unions* (Chicago: The University of Chicago Press, 2005).

Kara, Siddhartha, *Sex Trafficking: Inside the Business of Modern Slavery* (New York: Columbia University Press, 2010).

Kipnis, Laura, *Against Love* (New York: Pantheon Books, 2003).

Kramer, Larry, *Faggots* (New York: Grove Press, 2000).

Kulic, Don, *Travesti: Sex, Gender, and Culture among Brazilian Transgendered Prostitutes* (Chicago, University of Chicago, 1998).

Kuo, Lenore, *Prostitution Policy: Revolutionizing Practice through a Gendered Perspective* (New York: New York University Press, 2002).

Lacan, Jacques, *The Ethics of Psychoanalysis* (New York: W.W. Norton & Company, 1997).

Laeuchli, Samuel, *Power and Sexuality: The Emergence of Canon Law at the Synod of Elvira* (Philadelphia: Temple University Press, 1972).

Leap, William L., ed., *Public Sex/Gay Space* (New York: Columbia University Press, 1999).

Leite, Gabriella, "Women of the Life, We Must Speak," in *A Vindication of the Rights of Whores*, ed. Gail McPheterson (Seattle: Seal Press, 1989).

Levi-Strauss, Claude, *Elementary Structures of Kinship*, trans. J.H. Bell and J.R. von Sturmer (New York: Beacon Press, 1971).

Levinas, Emmanuel, *Totality and Infinity: An Essay on Exteriority*, trans. Alphonso Linguis (Pittsburgh: Dusquesne University Press, 1969).

Marlowe, Julian, "Thinking Outside the Box: Men in the Sex Industry," in *Prostitution and Pornography: Philosophical Debate About the Sex Industry*, ed. Jessica Spector (Stanford: Stanford University Press, 2006).

McWhirter, David P., and Andrew Mattison, *The Male Couple: How Relationships Develop* (Englewood Cliffs: Prentice Hall, 1984).

Mill, John Stuart, *On the Subjection of Women* (London: Hesperus, 2008).

Mohr, Richard D., *Gay Ideas* (Boston: Beacon Press, 1992).

Noddings, Nel, *Caring: A Feminine Approach to Ethics and Moral Education* (Berkeley: University of California Press, 1984).

Nussbaum, Martha, *Sex and Social Justice* (New York: Oxford, 2000).

O'Carrol, Tom, *Paedophilia: The Radical Case* (Boston: Alyson Publications 1982).

O'Connell Davidson, Julia, *Prostitution, Power and Freedom* (Ann Arbor, MI: University of Michigan Press, 1999).

Persky, Stan, *Boyopolis: Sex and Politics in Gay Eastern Europe* (New York: Overlook Press, 1996).

Policing Public Sex: Queer Politics and the Future of AIDS Activism, ed. Dangerous Bedfellows (Boston: South End Press, 2008).

Prieur, Annick, *Mema's House, Mexico City: On Transvestites, Queens, and Machos* (Chicago: University of Chicago Press, 1998).

Quan, Tracy, "The Name of the Pose," in *Prostitution and Pornography: Philosophical Debate About the Sex Industry*, ed. Jessica Spector (Stanford: Stanford University Press, 2006).

Rouselle, Aline, *Porneia* (New York: Barnes & Noble, 1996).

Rubin, Gayle, "The Male Traffic in Women" in Rayna Reiter, ed., *Toward An Anthropology of Women* (New York: Monthly Review Press, 1975).

Rubin, Gayle, "Thinking Sex: Notes for a Radical Theory of the Politics of Sexuality," in *Pleasure and Danger: Exploring Female Sexuality*, ed. Carole S. Vance (Boston: Routledge & K. Paul, 1984).

Ryan, Chris, and C. Michael Hall, *Sex Tourism: Marginal People and Liminalities* (New York: Routledge, 2001).

Samois Collective, *Coming to Power: Writings and Graphics on Lesbian S/M* (Boston: Alyson, 1983).

Sandfort, Theo, *Boys on Their Contacts With Men: A Study of Sexually Expressed Friendships* (Binghamton, NY: Global Academic Publishers, 1984).

Sandfort, Theo, E. Brongersma, and A. van Naerssen, eds., *Male Intergenerational Intimacy: Historical, Socio-Psychological, and Legal Perspectives* (New York: Haworth Press, 1990).

Sassen, Saskia, *The Global City: New York, London, Tokyo* (Princeton: Princeton University Press, 2001).

Schmidgall, Gary, *Walt Whitman: A Gay Life* (New York: Plume, 1997).

Scroggs, Robin, *The New Testament and Homosexuality* (Minneapolis: Fortress Press, 1983).

Shilts, Randy, *And the Band Played On: Politics, People, and the Aids Epidemic* (New York: St. Martin's Griffin, 1988).

Smith, Morton, *Clement of Alexandria and a Secret Gospel of Mark* (Cambridge: Harvard University Press, 1973).

Spong, John Shelby, *Living in Sin?: A Bishop Rethinks Human Sexuality*, reprint edition (New York: HarperOne, 1990).

Steinbock, Bonnie, "Adultery" in *The Philosophy of Sex: Contemporary Readings* 2nd edition, ed. A. Soble (Lanham: Rowman and Littlefield, 1991).

Stringer, Martin, "Expanding the Boundaries of Sex," *Theology and Sexuality* 7 (1997).

Sullivan, Andrew, *Virtually Normal* (New York: Vintage Books, 1996).

Tacitus, *The Annals: The Reigns of Tiberius, Claudius, and Nero*, trans. Anthony A. Barrett and J. C. Yardley (New York: Oxford University Press, 2008).

Thistlethwaite, Susan Brooks, and Rita Nakashima Brock, *Casting Stones: Prostitution And Liberation In Asia And The United States* (Minneapolis: Augsburg Fortress, 1996).

Tsang, Daniel, ed., *The Age Taboo: Gay Male Sexuality, Power, and Consent* (Boston: Alyson, 1981).

Vogell, Heather, "Neighbors Join Forces to Keep Out Prostitutes," *Chicago Tribune*, 15 Oct 2000.

Warner, Michael, *The Trouble with Normal: Sex, Politics, and the Ethics of Queer Life* (Harvard: Harvard University Press, 1999).

Wesley, John, "The Uses of Money." Edited by Jennette Descalzo, student at Northwest Nazarene College (Nampa, ID), with corrections by George Lyons for the Wesley Center for Applied Theology. < http://wesley.nnu.edu/>.

Wesley, John, and Samuel Auguste David Tissot, *Thoughts on the Sin of Onan* (London: Author, 1767).

West, Donald J., *Male Prostitution* (New York: The Haworth Press, 1993).

Whitman, Walt, *Leaves of Grass* (New York: Mentor Books, 1958).

Wilson, Nancy L., *Our Tribe: Queer Folks, God, Jesus and the Bible* (San Francisco: Harper San Francisco, 1995).

Wiseman, Jay, *SM 101: A Realistic Introduction* (Emeryville: Greenery Press, 2000).

Žižek, Slavoj, *The Ticklish Subject: The Absent Centre of Political Ontology* (London: Verso, 2000).

Made in the USA
Lexington, KY
01 July 2014